Harrington on Hold 'em

Expert Strategy for No-Limit Tournaments Volume I: Strategic Play

By
DAN HARRINGTON
1995 World Champion

BILL ROBERTIE

A product of
Two Plus Two Publishing LLC

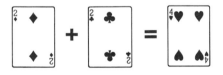

FIRST EDITION

THIRD PRINTING
December 2005

Printing and Binding
Creel Printers, Inc.
Las Vegas, Nevada

Printed in the United States of America

Harrington on Hold 'em: Expert Strategy for No-Limit Tournaments; Volume I: Strategic Play COPYRIGHT © 2004 Two Plus Two Publishing LLC

For information contact: **Two Plus Two Publishing LLC**
32 Commerce Center Drive
Suite H-89
Henderson, NV 89014

ISBN: 1-880685-33-7

Dedication

For my mother, Alice Harrington

Ladyfingers: You raised tens on a lousy three-flush?

The Man: That's what it's all about, isn't it?
Making the wrong move at the right time.

From *The Cincinnati Kid* (1965)

Table of Contents

About Dan Harrington

Dan Harrington began playing poker professionally in 1982. On the circuit he is known as "Action Dan," an ironic reference to his solid, but effective style. He has won several major no-limit hold 'em tournaments, including the European Poker Championships (1995), the $2,500 No-Limit Hold'em event at the 1995 World Series of Poker, and the Four Queens No-Limit Hold 'em Championship (1996).

Dan began his serious games-playing with chess, where he quickly became a master and one of the strongest players in the New England area. In 1972 he won the Massachusetts Chess Championship, ahead of most of the top players in the area. In 1976 he started playing backgammon, a game which he also quickly mastered. He was soon one of the top money players in the Boston area, and in 1981 he won the World Cup of Backgammon in Washington D.C., ahead of a field that included most of the world's top players.

He first played in the $10,000 No-Limit Hold 'em Championship Event of the World Series of Poker in 1987. He has played in the championship a total of thirteen times and reached the final table in four of those tournaments, an amazing record. Besides winning the World Championship in 1995, he finished sixth in 1987, third in 2003, and fourth in 2004. He is widely recognized as one of the greatest and most respected no-limit hold 'em players, as well as a feared opponent in limit hold 'em side games. He lives in Santa Monica where he is a partner in Anchor Loans, a real estate business.

About Bill Robertie

Bill Robertie has spent his life playing and writing about chess, backgammon, and now poker. He began playing chess as a boy, inspired by Bobby Fischer's feats on the international chess scene. While attending Harvard as an undergraduate, he became a chess master and helped the Harvard chess team win a number of intercollegiate titles. After graduation he won a number of chess tournaments, including the United States Championship at speed chess in 1970. He also established a reputation at blindfold chess, giving exhibitions on as many as eight boards simultaneously.

In 1976 he switched from chess to backgammon, becoming one of the top players in the world. His major titles include the World Championship in Monte Carlo in 1983 and 1987, the Black & White Championship in Boston in 1979, the Las Vegas tournaments in 1980 and 2001, the Bahamas Pro-Am in 1993, and the Istanbul World Open in 1994.

He has written several well-regarded backgammon books, the most noted of which are *Advanced Backgammon* (1991), a two-volume collection of 400 problems, and *Modern Backgammon* (2002), a new look at the underlying theory of the game. He has also written a set of three books for the beginning player: *Backgammon for Winners* (1994), *Backgammon for Serious Players* (1995), and *501 Essential Backgammon Problems* (1997).

From 1991 to 1998 he edited the magazine *Inside Backgammon* with Kent Goulding. He owns a publishing company, the Gammon Press (www.thegammonpress.com), and lives in Arlington, Massachusetts with his wife Patrice.

Introduction

Poker is a fascinating game with a long and colorful history. It originated early in the nineteenth century as a game called *poque*, centered in New Orleans and on the Mississippi riverboats. *Poque* used only 20 cards and permitted only one round of betting. Gradually, the game spread across the country, always evolving new forms as old variations became well-understood. Five-card draw, five and seven-card stud, lowball, hi-low, and, more recently, Texas hold 'em and Omaha were a few of the variations that expanded the map of poker. As time passed, the game continued to grow in popularity, from home games, to private gambling dens, to public casinos, to tournaments, to online play, and finally to televised tournaments.

In the last couple of years poker has exploded in popularity with the advent of minicams that enable television viewers to watch major events and follow the hands as they are played. As a result, tournaments that were once dull as dishwater can now be followed on the screen with some real understanding of what the players are trying to do. A game once mysterious has become, improbably, the latest spectator sport.

Television tournaments have focused on one variation of poker in particular — no-limit Texas hold 'em. The no-limit variation has been used to determine poker's World Champion since the very first tournament back in 1970. Nowadays there are about as many no-limit hold 'em tournaments as all other kinds combined, and every major tournament has a high-stake no-limit event as its culminating contest. On television, you can watch no-limit hold 'em tournaments at least three days a week (not counting reruns). Online, there are thousands and thousands of no-limit hold 'em tournaments *every day*, ranging from single table events with a $1 buy-in to multi-table events with buy-ins of hundreds of dollars and prize funds of over $100,000.

A gap, however, exists in the world of poker. In the bookstores, there are many, many poker books, all teaching you how to play — *limit* hold 'em. There are hardly any books on the new rage these days — *no-limit* hold 'em tournaments. This is understandable if you consider the history of hold 'em. For many years there were just a few high-stakes no-limit hold 'em tournaments every year. Almost all the hold 'em action was in casino card rooms, where they spread limit hold 'em games at varying limits. If you were a newcomer to the game, small-stakes limit hold 'em was where you started.

But now that's all changed, and many newcomers are starting with various kinds of small-stake no-limit hold 'em games and tournaments. So the need for a book dealing directly with this very exciting and very complex form of poker is pretty clear. *Harrington on Hold 'em: Expert Strategy for No-Limit Tournaments, Volume I: Strategic Play* is that book.

Organization

No-limit hold 'em is such a big and complicated game that I couldn't squeeze all the information into just one book, so *Harrington on Hold 'em* is a two-volume set. In this first book, Volume I, I'll show you how to play in the beginning and middle stages of a no-limit hold 'em tournament.

Part One serves as an introduction to the game as a whole. I'll show you why no-limit hold 'em is considered the "Cadillac of Poker," and what you need to consider when you try to evaluate a hand. I'll also take you inside a very interesting and complex hand from the final table of the 2003 World Series of Poker. You might have seen this hand on television; I'll show you what the players were really thinking.

Part Two covers playing styles. If you watched some poker on television, you've heard players described as "conservative," "aggressive," "super-aggressive," and "willing to play any two cards!" In Part Two I'll show what these terms really mean and how to play in each style. Most important, I'll explain why you need to switch from style to style as the situation demands.

Part Three, "Reading the Table," explains how to observe the action and keep track of both physical tells and betting patterns. It also explains how to *observe yourself*, and why that's so important.

Part Four, "Pot Odds and Hand Analysis," explains all the math you'll need to know to play no-limit hold 'em. (There is some, but fortunately there isn't a lot.) The chapter covers pot odds, expressed and implied odds, and analyzing hands in relation to the odds being offered.

Part Five covers the whole topic of "Betting Before the Flop." I'll introduce a complete strategy for betting for value in pots that haven't been opened yet, and I'll also show you what hands you need to call or raise for value when the pot has been opened in front of you.

Part Six, "Betting After the Flop," shows you how to think about your hand when the flop arrives. I'll show you a number of sample hands and compare them to various flops, explaining which flops are good, which are bad, and which are deceptively dangerous.

Part Seven covers fourth and fifth street action, including getting extra money in the pot, playing against drawing hands, and betting (or not betting) on the end.

In Volume II I'll talk about the tough issues involved in negotiating the later stages of a tournament. There you'll find discussions of moves and bluffs, zones and inflection points, the stack ratio and what it means for your play, changing your style, playing short tables, and handling heads-up play. Master the material in these two books, and you'll know how to win a no-limit hold 'em tournament. The rest is up to you.

The Hands

Much of the real value of these books lie in the sample hands, which are collected at the end of each chapter. You should treat these hands as small quizzes, and try to answer the questions before moving on to the explanations. It would be easy to read through the text and convince yourself that, of course, you would have made exactly that play at the table, but you'll find the explanations much more informative if you wrestle with the questions on your own first.

The hands have been compiled over the years from a variety of sources, including my own play, hands I've seen in major tournaments, satellites, and online events. In each hand I've laid out the table position and chip counts, as well as information about some of the players at the table, if known and pertinent to the hand. Study the hands, answer the questions, read what happens next, answer the next question, and in that way work yourself through the hand. Some of the hands hinge on the single crucial decision of whether or not to enter the pot. Others involve a series of difficult moves as the hand evolves. Take the hands seriously, study them carefully, and you'll be well rewarded.

Poker on television needs to appeal to a wide audience of mostly casual players. As a result, the hands selected for inclusion tend to be dramatic all-in showdowns and major clashes. I don't have any quarrel with that; if I were a television producer I'd probably do exactly the same thing. But that's not real poker. Tournaments are won and lost in the trenches, where average-plus hands butt heads with average-minus hands. That's the workaday world of no-limit hold 'em, and most of the hands you'll find in this book are of that sort. My goal is to teach you how to think like a poker player. Anyone can win a pot when he flops a monster. It's how you play when you don't flop one that will decide whether you're a winner or a loser.

With the help of this book, I hope you become one of those winners.

♣ ♦ ♥ ♠

This is not a beginner's book. I'm assuming that the reader already knows how to play no-limit hold 'em, either from actual play, online play, or just watching on television. However, this is not a complicated book either. I've tried to present the game the way I play it — with simple, common-sense rules and a minimum of mathematical calculation. A little math facility is a good thing, and there are some simple percentages that you'd do well to commit to memory. But you don't need to be a math whiz to play good poker. Keeping your head at the table and thinking clearly is far more important.

♣ ♦ ♥ ♠

In many cases good arguments can be advanced for an alternate play to the one I recommend in this book. No-limit hold 'em is not an exact science. My recommendations are always reasonable but under certain conditions a different play could be slightly or even clearly better. Obviously, Bill Robertie and I can't enumerate every possible change in condition that would make this so without having a 2,000 page book. But with experience you should be able to recognize most of them when they come up.

Brief Glossary

If you've watched some television tournaments, you've probably picked up most of the terminology you need to read this book. But in case you've been out of touch the last couple of years, here's an explanation of some key terms, and it's also how I talk poker.

All-in: A bet or raise of all the chips you have in front of you.

Antes: Money placed in the pot by all players at the beginning of a hand. In a typical tournament, players don't ante up until five or six betting rounds have passed.

Big blind: A forced bet made by the player to the left of the small blind, to generate even more action.

Big stack: The player with the most chips at the table. If he uses his chips to push the other players around, he may be known as the table captain or table bully.

Blinded away: If the player with the short stack doesn't play many pots, he may eventually lose all his chips when it comes his turn to play the blinds.

Button: The player to the right of the small blind, who acts last on each betting round after the flop. The button is marked by a white disk which moves around the table clockwise.

Covered bet: Your all-in is covered if your opponent has more chips than you. In that case, you will be eliminated if you lose the hand, but he will not.

Cut-off seat: The player to the right of the button.

Domination: When two hands share a common hole card, the player with the lower other card is said to be dominated. When two players hold ace-king and ace-queen, the player with the queen is dominated.

Flop: Three cards turned face up simultaneously in the center of the table. These cards are common to all hands. The flop is followed by a betting round

Fifth street (also known as the "river"): The fifth and last card turned up in the center of the table, also common to all hands. Fifth street is followed by a final betting round.

Fourth street (also known as the "turn"): The fourth card turned faced up in the center of the table, also common to all hands. Fourth street is followed by a betting round.

Hole cards: The two down cards dealt to each player at the beginning of the hand. No other player can see these cards.

Initial pot: The sum of the blinds and antes (if any) before the betting starts.

Nuts: A player with the best possible hand has the nuts.

Out: A card which will give you a winning hand if it arrives.

Short stack: The player with the fewest chips at the table.

Side pot: When several players go all-in, a side pot will include those chips than cannot be covered by the smallest stack. In a few cases, there may be multiple side pots.

Small blind: A forced bet made by the player to the left of the dealer to initiate action.

Stack: The pile of chips in front of each player.

Stack ratio: The ratio of the number of chips in your stack divided by the initial pot. This number determines how aggressively you want to play.

♣ ♦ ♥ ♠

Finally, I want to thank David Sklansky and Mason Malmuth for their comments throughout this manuscript; Dr. Alan Schoonmaker for his help with the English, and Ed Miller for his help in creating the index.

Special thanks goes to Patrick Nguyen of the Two Plus Two forums at www.twoplustwo.com for his front cover design. In addition, I want to thank Gary Alstatt of Creel Printing for his back cover design and art work throughout this book, and Christy Creel, Brandon Smeltzer, and Tom Lesher, all of Creel Printing, for their help in putting this project together.

Dan Harrington

Bill Robertie

October, 2004

Part One

The Game of
No-Limit Hold 'em

The Game of No-Limit Hold 'em

Introduction

Like all variations of poker, no-limit hold 'em looks like a card game. But it's not, really.

No-limit hold 'em is actually a game of wagering based on imperfect information that uses cards to construct the situations for wagering. Players make bets and call bets based on their estimate that their hand (which they see) will, in the end, be better than their opponent's hand (which they can't see). To make an informed estimate, they have to take four factors into account:

1. The likelihood that their hand will improve as more cards are dealt, which is pretty much a straight mathematical exercise.

2. An estimate of the hand their opponent may hold, which is an exercise in inductive reasoning, based on hands he has held in the past, his general style of play, and the bets he has made thus far.

3. The likelihood their opponent's hand will improve, another mathematical exercise, but complicated by the fact that their opponent's hand is not known for sure.

4. The money odds being offered by the pot.

When a good no-limit hold 'em player plays a hand, he looks at his cards, looks at his opponents, considers the betting, and makes an educated guess whether to check, bet or call, raise or fold. In many hold 'em hands, one factor becomes so important that the other factors don't require much thought. For example:

1. A player holds a hand so strong that he doesn't really care what his opponents have.

2. A player holds a hand so weak that he thinks he's sure to lose a showdown.

3. The pot odds are so large that he can play the hand with almost any holding.

Don't make the mistake, however, of assuming that even these hands are easy to play. *In no-limit hold 'em, there are no trivial hands.* Since you don't have to show your cards down to win, under the right circumstances any hand can be a winner.

The Cadillac of Poker

If you've watched televised poker at all, you've no doubt heard no-limit hold 'em described as the "Cadillac of Poker."[1] It's a true statement, but few players understand why the game deserves that reputation.

Professionals rank the different forms of poker by how much they consider their entry fees in a tournament to be worth. Top seven-card stud players, for instance, think that the true value of an entry into a seven-stud tournament is about twice the entry fee. (Paying $1,000 to enter a seven-stud tournament should yield, over a long run of tournaments, about $2,000 in prizes.) An entry to a razz or Omaha tournament yields about the same value. But the best no-limit hold 'em players think that a $1,000 entry fee is worth $4,000 to $5,000, and in huge events like the World Series of Poker, with many beginners in the field, perhaps as much as $7,000 to $8,000.

What makes no-limit hold 'em poker so much more skillful for good players, and so profitable for the best players? Many think it has something to do with making big all-in bets, or orchestrating outrageous bluffs. But actually it hinges on two technical factors: the amount of information available to the players, and the ability to control the pot odds offered to your opponent. Let's look at each factor in turn.

Information Availability

Poker is a game of incomplete information, but not all games of incomplete information are created equal. From game to game,

---

[1] The term "Cadillac of Poker" was first used in Doyle Brunson's book *Super/System*.

there are degrees of information availability. How much information is hidden and how much is available greatly affects the interest and playability of a game.

In classic five-card draw poker, all your opponent's cards are hidden. Aside from the betting patterns, the only source of information you have is the number of cards your opponent chooses to discard. With so little information to weigh, your strategic options are limited, and the game plays very mechanically. Nowadays, classic five-card draw is only played in home games.

At the other extreme of poker variations lies another classic game, five-card stud. Here players have only one hidden hole card, while all other cards are dealt face-up. Once again basic strategy becomes mechanically simple ("Don't play unless you can beat the board."), this time because too much information about each hand is available.

The best poker variations strike the right balance between hidden and exposed cards. Texas hold 'em lies right in the center of that sweet spot. Two hidden cards allow plenty of room for deceptive maneuvering, while five exposed cards allow a good player to make plenty of deductions about the opposing hands.

Controlling Pot Odds

The goal of all forms of poker is to avoid making mistakes while inducing as many mistakes as possible from your opponents. Every time you make a mistake, you lose, and your opponents gain. Every time you induce a mistake from your opponents you gain, and they lose.

These gains and losses don't occur immediately. You may make a bad mistake and still win a hand and pull more chips into your stack. But in the very long run, your results at the poker table will approach the sum of all your opponents' mistakes, less the sum of your mistakes. This principle governs all games which are mixtures of skill and chance.

There are a variety of mistakes one can make in poker, but one of the most serious is to make a bet or call which is not correct given the pot odds available to you, either because you haven't made the right deductions about your opponent's cards, or because you have a generally correct idea about his cards, but you've ignored the pot odds entirely.

The no-limit form of hold 'em poker is very advantageous to good players for a simple reason. By making superior deductions about the hands their opponents hold, *they can make bets that offer their opponents more chances to make errors.* Whenever their opponent misreads the situation and makes such an error, the good player gains, and his opponent loses.

Example No. 1. Suppose you are playing *limit* hold 'em (bets are limited to a specified amount each round) and you believe, from the previous betting, that your opponent has four cards to a spade flush with just one card to come. The flush, if he hits it, will beat whatever hand you have, but he will lose otherwise. The pot now contains $100, and the betting limit is $10, and you bet that amount.

It's now your opponent's turn. He has seen six cards so far, the two in his hand and the four common cards in the center. If he's drawing to a flush, four of these cards are spades. Of the remaining 46 cards in the deck that he hasn't seen, your opponent needs one of the nine remaining spades. The other 37 cards will lose for him. The odds against hitting his flush are 37-to-9 against, or just a little over 4-to-1. The pot now contains $110 and it costs him $10 to call, so he's being offered 11-to-1 pot odds. Since the pot odds are bigger than his odds of making the winning hand, it's correct for him to call. Your bet was perfectly correct as well since you're a 4-to-1 favorite to win the hand. But with the betting limit of $10, there was no way for you to prevent your opponent from drawing at the winning hand.

Now suppose we have the exact same hands and pot, but the game is *no-limit* hold 'em. You can bet any amount you want, not just $10. This time you bet $100. Your opponent can still call the bet, but now there is $200 in the pot and he has to call for $100. The pot is only offering him 2-to-1 odds, but his chances of hitting his flush are still 4-to-1. Since the pot odds are smaller than the chance of making his hand, he's supposed to fold. Because you had an unlimited choice in what to bet, you were able to pick an amount that enabled your opponent to blunder if he wanted to contest the pot. By controlling the pot odds, you allow your opponents to make errors that they couldn't make in a limit hold 'em game. Those errors end up as money in your pocket.

What is a Hand?

If you go to a poker tournament, you'll notice that the top players are always sought out for their advice. A typical hand discussion between a beginner and a top player might go something like this:

Beginner: Can I ask you a question about a hand?

Pro: Sure, go ahead.

Beginner: OK, thanks. So I'm holding king-queen suited, see, and there's one call in front of me ...

Pro: What position are you in?

Beginner: Oh I don't know — I guess maybe I was fifth to act ...

Pro: What position was the first caller in?

Beginner: I guess he was second ... no wait, he was right under the gun ... yeah, that's right... no, maybe he was second... well, it was something like that.

Pro: How many chips did you have?

Beginner: Gee, a lot, maybe $4,000, $5,000 — right in there.

Pro: And what were the blinds?

Beginner: Oh, not that much, maybe $50/$100, $100/$200, something like that. But anyway, I called, see, and then this guy *behind me raised! And everyone else folded around to me, and I didn't know what to do…*

Pro: How many chips did he have?

Beginner: You mean the guy who raised me? I don't know, who can remember all this stuff? Hey, I want to talk about the hand!

To the beginner, his hand was the cards he held, and what the players immediately before and after him did. To the pro, a "hand" was a lot more than that. It's an entire situation, full of different elements, which has to be seen as a whole before good plays can be made.

Elements of a Hand

A hand in no-limit hold 'em has many facets, only one of which is the cards you hold. A good player considers all elements of the hand before making a play. Here are the basic elements:

1. What's the status of the tournament?

2. How many players are at your table?

3. Who are the players at your table?

4. How does your stack compare to the blinds and antes?

5. How big are the other stacks at your table?

6. Where do you sit in relation to the aggressive and passive players?

7. What bets have been made in front of you?

8. How many active players are left after you act?

9. What are the pot odds?

10. What is your position at the table after the flop?

11. What are your cards?

This might seem like a lot of things to consider before making a play. Actually, it is a lot! That's why playing no-limit hold 'em well is difficult but rewarding. If this were a short list, the game would be much easier, more people would do it well, and fewer players would make any real money. So if your goal is to become a top no-limit hold 'em player, be glad that it's a tough, rather than an easy thing to do. That just means your hard work will be well rewarded.

Now let's take a look at the elements one by one, and see how each affects your decision-making:

1. **What's the status of the tournament?** Most tournaments pay prizes to about 5-10 percent of the field, although a few pay much less. (One notable tournament in 2003 paid nine places out of 197 entries, which is about as tough a payout structure as I've ever seen.) As long as the cut-off point for prize payouts is distant, play proceeds normally. As the number of players shrinks and gets close to the prize cutoff, play changes dramatically. Most players turn conservative and try to preserve their chips. Good players become more aggressive and see this period as the best chance to make some easy money by stealing chips.

2. **How many players are at your table?** A full table (9-10 players) requires generally tighter play. The more people there are to act behind you, the greater the danger in moving at the pot with a weak hand. At a short table (6 players or less), hand requirements shrink and there's much more opportunity to pilfer pots. At the end of a tournament, when the table has shrunk to just two, three, or four players, you'll need to be involved in many more pots than usual just to have a chance to stay alive.

3. **Who are the players at your table?** Are they aggressive players, conservative players, or a mix of the two? Are there name players with known styles, or are the players all unknowns? The most profitable style to play at any moment is usually the *opposite* of the style of the other players at the table. If the table is aggressive, be conservative. Enter pots

only with solid hands that you can play with confidence. If the table is tight, move out and try to steal a few pots. You'll get away with it often enough to make money.

The character of the players at your table also determines how *slow* or *fast* you want to play. A table with a lot of passive players is a comfortable table. You want to stick around, steal pots, and accumulate money slowly, but surely. It's a good situation, and you don't want to risk it with a lot of all-in bets. But if the table has a lot of aggressive players, your strategy has to change. Aggressive players are harder to read, and you'll find that your raises are getting reraised frequently. Now you'll often want to make money in one fell swoop, since otherwise you'll be whittled down, and it's hard to make any money with a small stack at an aggressive table. Pick a good hand and be prepared to go all the way with it.

4. **How does your stack compare to the blinds and antes?** You don't actually care about the absolute size of the blinds and antes. What's important is their size relative to your stack of chips. If they're tiny compared to your stack, then you can survive many rounds without playing, so you're under no pressure to enter pots. If, however, your stack is just a few times larger than the blinds and antes, then you have to move quickly or the blinds will gobble you up. In no-limit hold 'em tournaments, the blinds and antes increase on a regular basis. Unless you can accumulate chips steadily, your stack size will shrink in relative terms, and your play has to become more aggressive to compensate.

5. **How big are the other stacks at your table?** If you have a large stack compared to the other players, then you can probably bully them around. You have the power to eliminate them completely from the tournament, so they have to give you respect. If your stack is in the middle of the pack, you can still bully the smallest stacks, but you have to be careful

about tangling with the bigger stacks. If you have the smallest stack, your ability to steal pots is limited. You'll have to pick a spot and try to double or triple up.

6. **Where do you sit in relation to the aggressive and passive players?** Since action proceeds clockwise around the table, your ideal situation is to have the aggressive players on your right,[2] the conservative players on your left. That way, you act with knowledge of what the aggressive players have done, and your pot-stealing chances are enhanced when you have tight players reacting to you. With aggressive players sitting behind you, the right strategy is to play fewer hands, but play them more decisively.

7. **What bets have been made in front of you?** The only absolutely strong hand before the flop is a pair of aces. All other hands have to be evaluated in terms of the betting that has already occurred. A pair of jacks is a good hand when several players in front of you have folded, but if you're facing bet-raise-reraise, it's likely to be second- or third-best.

8. **How many active players are left after you act?** If your action potentially ends the betting on the hand, you're in a more secure position than if active players will remain behind you no matter what you do. If for instance, you are last to act and the betting in front of you has been bet and call, then you can shut down the action by calling. If however, the action has been bet and raise, then you can't end the action no matter what you do. Either a call or a raise can be answered by a reraise from the first player. You have to play much

---

[2] The exception is *very* aggressive players. Reason? You can check your strongest hands to them with the intention of check-raising both that player and those who call him.

more cautiously when you can't be sure of the action behind you. The more potential action, the more cautiously you play.

9.   **What are the pot odds?** When making a bet, you are always comparing the odds offered by the pot to the odds of making your hand. You always want the pot to offer you better odds than the odds of filling the hand you're drawing to.[3] You're also watching the odds you are giving to your opponent as he tries to make his hand, to see if you can deny him the odds he needs to call. Top players calculate pot odds routinely when deciding whether to play or fold.

10.   **What is your position at the table after the flop?** It's bad to act first in a hand, because you have to act with no new information about your opponents. It's good to act last, because you get to see what your opponents have done, hence gaining information, before you have to make a decision. Your position at the table, relative to the other players, is a hugely important feature of every hand, one that good players understand instinctively and poor players overlook.

Position is so important that players will make moves just to secure favorable position on subsequent betting rounds. Before the flop, you might reraise instead of merely calling, just to chase players sitting behind you out of the hand. Marginal hands might be played if you know you will have position on other players, but folded if you won't.

Here's an example of just how important position can be. If a world-class player were to play a heads-up session against a player of mediocre skills, but the lesser player could act last every hand, *the world-class player would have the worst of it.*

---

[3] Of course it is often worth drawing to a hand without the proper odds if you believe your *implied* odds (the present pot plus possible future bets you can win) are there.

11. **What are your cards?** Yes, you do actually have cards, and they do matter. But so do all these other aspects of a hand, and in many hands they matter more than your cards. You will sometimes find yourself in situations where you'll make a play regardless of the cards in your hand.

Playing good poker is a matter of *balance*. You look over the situation, weigh all the factors, and find the move that strikes just the right note. As in many competitive occupations, you can play very well for awhile, believe that you have mastered the game, and then get subtly out of synch, and find that your results have deteriorated, even though you feel you're playing as well as ever. When that happens there's no recourse but to be ruthlessly determined and objective until you put the puzzle back together again.

A Sample Hand

To see no-limit hold 'em thinking in action, let's take a look at a sample hand of some complexity. It's from the final table of the 2003 World Series of Poker, when the tournament was down to its last seven players. (Those of you who have seen the ESPN broadcasts of the tournament might recognize the hand, as it occurred during the early part of the final table coverage.)

At the start of the hand, the blinds were $10,000 /$20,000, and the antes were $2,000 each. With seven players left, there was $44,000 in the pot to begin the hand. Here were the players, their chip counts, and the starting hands of those who played:

Small Blind	Amir Vahedi	$865,000	T♦8♣
Big Blind	Tomer Benvenisti	$645,000	
1	Sam Farha	$1,530,000	9♦9♣
2	Yong Pak	$215,000	
3	Jason Lester	$1,161,000	
4	Dan Harrington	$1,080,000	A♥K♠
5	Chris Moneymaker	$2,894,000	T♠9♥

Sam Farha. Sam was first to act after the blinds. A pair of nines is a good hand at a seven-handed table, and Sam made a raise of $60,000, three times the big blind. Professionals have a convention for describing the size of raises. Before the flop raises are usually described as multiples of the big blind. After the flop raises are described as fractions of the existing pot. The range for initial bets is usually about two to five times the big blind.

Yong Pak and Jason Lester. Folded their hands.

Dan Harrington. My A♥K♠ gave me a choice of plays. I could certainly put in a good-sized raise, say $150,000 to $200,000. I could also just call and see how the hand develops. I like to alternate between these two plays in similar situations (with hands like ace-king or ace-queen), so my opponents can't get a read on me. But I don't make my choices completely at random. In this case two factors pushed me towards calling instead of raising:

1. I was just one off the button, so I was likely to have position on subsequent rounds. When I have position, I don't need to play the hand as strongly before the flop, since my good position will let me win some hands after the flop with less overall risk. In other words, I can let position, rather than bet size, do the work for me.

2. I thought I was one of the better players remaining at the table, so I wanted to reduce, rather than increase, my volatility on the hand. (Volatility is a mathematician's word for the size of the money swing on the hand.) A weaker player in the same situation should be looking to increase volatility; hence he would definitely want to throw in a bet.

After weighing the various considerations, I decided just to call.

Chris Moneymaker. Chris elected to call with his T♠9♥. It's not a strong hand, but there were two other factors besides his cards that argued for a call, pot odds and position. The pot odds were quite favorable: there is $164,000 in the pot, and it cost Chris just $60,000 to call. In addition, Chris would act last for all subsequent betting rounds.

Another factor might have entered into his decision. Chris had been playing conservatively at the start of the final day, and he'd gone through a relatively long stretch with unplayable cards. He may have just wanted to mix things up a bit, and perhaps also thought that his recent inactivity would buy him a little credibility if he decided to bluff later. He couldn't know, of course, that three of his cards were already out in other hands.

Amir Vahedi. Amir had T♦8♣, and he was out of position, and there were three other players in the pot ahead of him. Nonetheless, Vahedi called. According to traditional hand evaluations, this was a clear fold. But Amir enjoys making plays like this, and since he has one of the best records on tour, he has to be taken very seriously. Notice that part of his motivation for calling was the excellent pot odds. It contained $224,000, and since Vahedi was the small blind, he had already put $10,000 into the pot, so it cost him only an additional $50,000 to call. His pot odds were 224-to-50, or about 4.5-to-1. I'll have much more to say about the subject of pot odds and hand analysis in Part Four, but for here I'll just say that big pot odds are always a tempting reason to stick around, and Vahedi saw it that way as well.

Vahedi's play was a little riskier than it looked, however. He had the additional problem that Tomer Benvenisti, in the big blind, had yet to act. If Benvenisti folded or just called, the action is capped, and we go on to the flop. But if Benvenisti had a hand and elected to raise, then we go around the table one more time, and anyone who was slowplaying before will now get a chance to make a move. So Vahedi can't be sure that his $50,000 call would actually buy him a peek at the flop, and if the betting got heavier, he would certainly let this hand go.

The strength of Vahedi's style is that it's almost impossible to know what he's holding at any time, and it's also nearly impossible to look at a flop and know if it helped or hurt him. Vahedi wins huge pots when a flop perfectly matches one of his mysterious holdings, and he can pick up other pots with shrewd bluffs after the flop. Balanced against that is a series of small losses when unpromising hands like this one don't pan out. Vahedi's style works for him, but "beginners" should be warned that it's a very difficult style, and requires enormous skill to play properly. I'll have more to say about playing styles in Part Two.

Tomer Benvenisti. Folded in the big blind.

The pot was $274,000 before the flop, and there were four players.

The flop came

Analyzing the texture of the flop. The arrival of the flop is a key moment in a hold 'em hand. Each player has to evaluate the flop for what we call its "texture," meaning the characteristics of the flop and the likelihood that it helped each of the different players at the table. I view the flop in the light of three questions:

1. Did the flop help me?

2. Given how I'm perceived at the table, will the other players think the flop helped me?

3. Given what I know about the other players, is the flop likely to have helped someone else?

At this point, I was thinking as follows. With my A♥K♠ holding, the flop certainly didn't help me. Furthermore, since I'm seen as a conservative player, the other players will think it didn't help me (since I mostly play high cards). So my bluffing chances are pretty much gone. Since Moneymaker has been playing conservatively, the flop probably didn't help him. The flop might have helped either Vahedi or Farha, since they play a wider mix of hands. Finally, barring some unusual event, I'm done with the hand. I'll discuss playing after the flop in more detail in Part Six.

Amir Vahedi. Vahedi knew the flop didn't help him much. He did have a gutshot straight draw (a straight draw missing an inside card, a seven). The probability of hitting that straight was about 8 percent if he got to see only one card, and about 16 percent if he could see the hand to the end, which wasn't likely. If he did hit that straight however, he might win a huge amount of money, as it would be very hard for the other players to put him on that hand. He also knew the other players have to be worried the flop might have helped him, given his history of playing odd cards. And he knew that the flop probably didn't help either Moneymaker or me, but it might have helped Farha.

If Vahedi were up against just a single opponent, I'm pretty sure he would have made a bet of about half the pot here. A half-pot bet would have given his best chance to win the pot since it carried a great risk-reward ratio. (If he thought the bet would win the pot just one time in three, it's at least a break-even bet.[4] Imagine the pot is $200 and you make a bet of $100. If this situation occurs three times and you win one of them, you win $200 once and lose $100 twice, for a net break-even result. If you win more than one-third of the time, the bet will earn you a profit.)

Against two or three opponents, that bet gets riskier, just because the chance that Vahedi is up against a hand somewhere keeps increasing with the number of players. I can't fault him for checking here, but leading out with a bet was his best chance, in a theoretical sense, to win the hand. (He couldn't know, of course,

---

[4] It's better than break even as long as there is some chance your bet will be merely called, since you will also win some of these times.

that Farha was sitting behind him with three nines.) In any event, Vahedi checked.

Sam Farha. Sam has hit the jackpot, flopping top set, three nines. With no flush or straight draws on board, his hand was so strong that his only concern was figuring out how to make the most money possible.

An inexperienced player in Sam's position would probably check, with the idea that he could lure other players to bet and then swoop in with a raise. To understand why Sam took a different approach, let's list a few facts which at this moment were clear to everyone at the table:

1.   Amir Vahedi checked in first position.

2.   Sam Farha is a very aggressive player who opened for a raise preflop.

3.   The flop probably missed Harrington and Moneymaker.

Given these facts, it should be clear that Sam *ought* to be betting in this spot, even with a mediocre hand. With his aggressive reputation and a favorable situation at the table, only a non-bet from Sam will arouse suspicion; a bet will just be seen as a routine attempt to take a pot that's available.

So Sam correctly decided to bet. With a pot of $274,000, he picked a nice amount to bet: just $80,000. That's what we call a *probe bet*. It's a small bet, between one-fourth and one-third of the pot, and it's usually an attempt to get some information cheaply, while holding out the possibility of winning the pot right there if no one wants to fight. It also reveals absolutely no information about Sam's real hand, since it's exactly what he would be expected to do with almost anything. A very smart play.

Dan Harrington. I have two overcards, but right now my hand is just ace-high. I don't know what the other sharks have, but these waters have become too dangerous for swimming. Even the generous pot odds aren't tempting me to call. I'm out of there.

Chris Moneymaker. There was now $354,000 in the pot and it cost Chris just $80,000 to call. He can't lay down top pair yet, but it's a low top pair, and with Farha and Vahedi still in the pot, he was right to be cautious.

Chris elected to call here, which was reasonable. I would have probably raised with his hand, but it would be a defensive raise. If my raise didn't win the pot on the spot, I'd be done with the hand. I like to play in a way that defines my situation with a single bet. With the murky action around the table, a raise would clarify the situation and prevent me from losing more money on later rounds.

Amir Vahedi. Vahedi had nothing, but the other players haven't shown any strength, and they might both be on drawing hands. Sam's bet seems to be asking "Am I strong or weak here?" I'm sure at this point that Vahedi was contemplating a move to win the pot. But should he make it right now, or on fourth street?

Vahedi elected to wait, which was a good idea. (Good in a relative sense, of course; we know Vahedi is actually up against trip nines.) With any luck, the fourth street card will not help either Farha or Moneymaker, and a bet from Vahedi will give the appearance that the card filled his hand in some way. So Vahedi simply calls Farha's bet and prepares to move next round. The pot now contains $514,000.

The fourth street card is the 6♥, putting a pair of sixes on board and, unknown to the other players, giving Sam Farha a full house, nines over sixes.

Amir Vahedi. To Vahedi, the 6♥ represented a mixed blessing. An ideal card, aside from a perfect seven, would be something larger than the 9♠ on board (but not an ace), so that a bet would represent an overpair to the board. An ace would be bad since, with two other players at the table, it's possible that one or both of them has been playing with an ace. Still, the six is a harmless card, not likely to have helped either of the other players. It serves his purposes, allowing him to represent a six in his hand and hence a holding of trip sixes.

Vahedi now made a move at the pot, betting $300,000. On camera, this bluff looked foolish, since we know he had nothing and was facing a full house. But it was actually quite a good move. Based on what Vahedi had seen so far, a tentative probing bet from Farha, a call from Moneymaker, and a harmless card on the turn, it's reasonable for him to think that this bet will win the pot at least 50 percent of the time, perhaps more. In the long run, similar bets in similar situations will be quite profitable. In the short run, namely this hand, his bet can't win, but only we know that.

Sam Farha. Sam was delighted to see Vahedi's bet, of course, since he knew he held the winning hand. Could he extract any more money from Moneymaker? Probably not, but a raise will certainly chase him away, so Sam does what he can and just calls.

Chris Moneymaker. Vahedi says he has a big hand, and Farha calls him, so a pair of nines doesn't look like much anymore. Chris commented "You boys have fun" and threw his hand away.

On fifth street, a 3♣ came, which didn't affect any of the hands.

Amir Vahedi. Sam's call last turn showed Amir that he was beaten, so he checked.

Sam Farha. With Amir's check, Sam realized that he probably can't win any more money this hand, but he dutifully put in another $300,000, and Amir folded.

The Hidden Luck
Factor in No-Limit Hold 'Em

Everyone knows that there's a lot of luck in poker. But not everyone appreciates exactly how much luck is involved, or the various forms that luck can take. When we see someone stay alive by hitting a 45-to-1 shot on the river, we all say "What luck!" In this hand, we might think that Sam Farha was very lucky to hit trips on the flop (and indeed he was) but we might not notice some of the other big lucky swings in the hand.

For instance, let's go back and look again at my decision to just call, rather than raise, with my A♥K♠ before the flop. I thought at the time it was a very close play, and a couple of factors pushed me towards a call. But suppose I had been just a little impatient, or had let my concentration flag for a bit, and decided to raise instead? Here's what would have happened:

1. I raise $150,000.

2. Moneymaker now sees a raise and a reraise in front of him and folds his T♠9♥, saving $140,000.

3. Vahedi sees the same thing and folds his T♦8♣, saving $440,000.

4. Sam calls with his 9♦9♣.

5. After the flop Sam checks his trips.

6. I make a move for the pot and bet $250,000 or so.

7. Sam comes over the top with his trip nines.

8.   I realize I'm beaten and fold, losing $400,000.

9.   Sam wins $400,000 on the hand, about $160,000 less than he won in the actual hand.

10. I'm crippled, having lost almost half my chips, while Vahedi is still in the hunt.

Going the other way with my close decision would have radically affected the situation at the table — a hugely lucky (but invisible) swing for everyone concerned.

Part Two

Playing Styles and Starting Requirements

Playing Styles and Starting Requirements

Introduction

Imagine you're watching a major-league pitcher known for his blazing fastball. Up to the plate walks an opposing batter. Wham! Strike one is a high fastball on the inside corner. Wham! Strike two is a another fastball, waist-high on the outside part of the plate. The batter hunkers down and wonders where the next fastball is going. Oops. The next pitch is a sharply breaking curve. The batter lunges, but his timing is off. Strike three.

Now imagine you're watching a tennis match at Wimbledon. The server blasts a ball to the backhand side of the court. His opponent returns the ball with difficulty. The server blasts another shot to the same area. The opponent again returns the ball, moving even closer to the service line. Now the server flips a drop shot to the opposite side of the court. His opponent runs across the court but can't quite reach the ball. Game, set, match.

Like these two examples, poker is a game of misdirection. There are several styles in which no-limit hold 'em can be played. In this chapter, we'll describe the styles and show you how to play each way. Depending on your personality, one of these styles will appeal to you more than the others, and you'll adopt it as your basic approach to the game. However, no matter which style you adopt, you'll discover that *you will make your easiest money when you make plays that are the opposite of your normal style.* As in baseball and tennis, it's the plays in your normal style that will set up big wins when you switch to a different style. Keep that in mind as we work our way through the different approaches to no-limit hold 'em.

Style 1: The Conservative Approach

For a conservative investor in the equity markets, the most important consideration is capital preservation, utilizing low-risk instruments like bonds and dividend-paying stocks. A conservative approach to no-limit hold 'em works the same way. The emphasis is on preserving your stack by using a set of defensive strategies:

1. Playing fewer, but higher-quality hands than the average player.

2. Playing the hands in a way that makes your subsequent decision-making easier and clearer.

3. Avoiding all-in moves unless your hand is *highly* likely to prevail in a showdown.

In the early days of no-limit Texas hold 'em, the game was almost entirely played as a money game (also known as a *ring game*), starting in Texas and Louisiana and only gradually moving to the casinos in Las Vegas. (Tournament play evolved later, and very slowly. For many years the World Series of Poker was the only no-limit hold 'em tournament in the world.) Money game no-limit hold 'em rules differ from the tournament version in only one respect: the level of the blinds, once established, never increases. Since players almost always buy in for an amount equal to several hundred times the blinds, there is no need to play a lot of hands or to make any great effort to steal the blinds (except to set up future situations). Optimal money strategy is to simply lay back and wait to score on your occasional big hands.

When experienced money players made the occasional move into tournaments, they naturally brought their conservative strategies with them, and what I'm calling the conservative style became the accepted "correct" way of playing in the 1970s and the early 1980s.

Opening Requirements in Conservative Play

These suggested opening hands apply to a full table of nine or ten players, where you are the first player to act.

Early (first or second) Position: Raise with a high pair (aces, kings, or queens). Raise also with a medium pair like jacks or tens in an effort to reduce the field. Raise with ace-king (suited or unsuited) or ace-queen (suited).

Middle (third through sixth) Position: Raise with all the above hands. Also raise with nines or eights, as well as ace-queen, ace-jack, or king-queen (suited or unsuited).

Late (seventh or eighth) Position: Raise with all the above hands. Also raise with sevens, ace-x, or high suited connectors like queen-jack or jack-ten.

Remember there is a difference between opening a pot and entering a pot that has already been opened. If you decide to enter a pot that someone else has already opened, you want a better hand than you would require to open yourself from his position. If someone before you opens from middle position, you want one of your early position opening hands to make a raise. David Sklansky, in his excellent book *Tournament Poker for Advanced Players,* called this the "Gap Concept," and we'll discuss the reasons for it in a later chapter.

When you play conservatively, a number of things will happen:

1. You'll enter comparatively few pots. Good, solid hands don't arrive all that often.

2. When you do enter a pot, you'll usually be the favorite in the hand. Players will have to draw out to catch you.

3. You'll have relatively easy decisions to make after the flop. If you start with good hands and the flop hits you at all, your hand will be very strong. When the flop misses you, you may still have the best hand, even if someone else has improved.

4. You'll win a lot of small pots, but not many big ones. Unless the players at your table are asleep at the switch, they'll soon peg you as a "rock," and adjust their play accordingly.

Most books recommend that beginners adopt conservative play as their style, at least until they acquire some experience. I agree. Playing conservatively has the great merit of keeping you out of a lot of trouble, and that's very important. *Every pot you enter has the potential of consuming all your chips.* That grim reality necessitates a certain degree of caution when starting out. In the 2003 World Series of Poker, one player had seized the chip lead by the middle of Day Four by virtue of many, many hours of solid, patient play. In the space of just two hands and five minutes of play, he was out of the tournament. Always remember that no-limit hold 'em is a very dangerous game.

If you try conservative play and you like it, that's fine. It may be your natural style. But if it leaves you feeling a little cramped, perhaps you're just a bit too flamboyant for conservatism. In that case you may want to look at the merits of the aggressive style.

Style 2: The Aggressive Approach

Someone using the aggressive style would open with all of the hands used by conservative players, plus many more. The following hands are all possible opening hands for an aggressive player:

1. All pairs

2. Any two face cards.

3. Ace-anything

4. Suited connectors, even as low as five-four suited.

Aggressive players aren't terribly concerned with positional requirements, so all of these hands are suitable for opening even in early position.

Compared to conservative play, aggressive play has several advantages.

1. An aggressive player plays a lot more pots.

2. An aggressive player steals a lot more pots.

3. An aggressive player is much harder to read.

4. It's much harder to tell if the flop helped an aggressive player or not.

5.   An aggressive player is more likely to win big on his monster hands.

That's the good news. Balancing it is some bad news.

1.   By playing lower-quality starting hands, an aggressive player will face more difficult decisions after the flop.

2.   By playing and betting more hands, an aggressive player will more often run into well-concealed monster hands.

3.   An aggressive player will face much bigger swings in stack sizes.

The aggressive style is not inferior to the conservative style in theory, but it requires much more skill to play well. That's why beginners are well-advised to begin with conservative play, and only later experiment with aggressive moves. Aggressive play requires a well-developed feel for the table. Playing aggressively, you'll often find yourself after the flop holding medium pair or low pair, and needing to figure out if your opponent has a better hand or is just making a move on you. Beginners tend to lose all their chips in these situations, but an experienced player with a good read on his opponents can stay out of a lot of trouble.

If even aggressive play seems too tame for you, then perhaps you're ready for the very highest-octane mix. Let's look now at the super-aggressive style.

Style 3: The Super-Aggressive Approach

"Starting requirements? We don't need no stinkin' starting requirements!"

We don't need to spend a lot of time on opening hands for this style, since there are none. A super-aggressive player is quite capable of opening with any two cards, in any position, at any time. That's what makes this style so exciting to watch, albeit dangerous to play.

The idea of the super-aggressive style is to play a lot of pots and see a lot of flops, cheaply. Because a super-aggressive player can play a lot of hands from a lot of different positions, his opponents can't easily look at the flop and tell if it is dangerous for them or not. When facing a conservative player, a flop of

is almost certainly harmless. Against a super-aggressive player, you could be facing a straight, two pair, or a set.

Super-aggressive players decide whether or not to enter a pot in two ways. Of course, they'll come in with two cards that represent solid value. But even if their hand doesn't have solid value, they might still enter the pot if the other elements of their position are favorable. Have a lot of players already folded? Will they have position after the flop? Are the players behind them weak or intimidated? Do the players behind them have smallish stacks? Are the players behind them playing conservatively?

If the answers to these questions are mostly yes, then a super-aggressive player might take any two cards and make a move, figuring he could win in three ways:

1. No one calls and he takes the blinds right now.

2. Someone calls, but he hits the flop and wins with the better hand.

3. Someone calls, and he misses the flop, but bluffs his opponent out anyway.

To succeed with this approach, you must be observant and imaginative. It's a highly demanding style, but its most successful practitioners, players like Gus Hansen, Daniel Negreanu, and Phil Ivey, have enjoyed great success recently.

The main advantage of the super-aggressive style is that you play, and have a chance to win, a lot of pots. At a table of weak players, whether active or passive, simply getting in the pot is advantageous, and the super-aggressive style is probably optimal for that situation. The disadvantages of the style are the energy required and the danger courted. You're always dancing on the edge, always facing tough decisions, and mostly you're holding weak cards. All the delicate maneuvering required is tiring, and a tired player is more likely to blunder at some point.

Origins of the
Aggressive Styles

When I first started playing tournament poker in the 1980s, most players assumed that the same conservative style that was correct for money play must be correct for tournament play as well. But as I started to get some experience in tournaments, I began to get suspicious. Many of the great no-limit money players didn't have especially good tournament results. At the same time, I saw players doing very well in tournaments who weren't feared in money play.

Before I played poker full-time, I had spent some years playing competitive backgammon, where I had seen the same dichotomy. Strong money players were not doing as well as they should in tournaments, and successful tournament players weren't respected in money games. In backgammon some of my friends and I had reasoned out that a more aggressive doubling strategy paid off in tournament play, because players were unwilling to put an entire match on the line at a crucial point when they were an underdog; they'd rather pass a double and start a new game where they were even money. But the points they surrendered without a fight were just too costly. They were getting offered the odds they needed to take a bad position, but they were passing anyway. The equity they surrendered couldn't be recouped with skillful checker play.

I began to watch the players who were doing very well in the tournaments of the 1980s. The best players of that period were Stu Ungar, Jack Keller, and Bobby Turner. I could see that their approach to the game was very similar. Although they would start a tournament in a conservative mode, much like the other players, after a while they became very active, playing a lot of hands and moving in on a lot of pots. As the blinds grew large and the tournament wound down, they became even more active, stealing pots while other players were hunkering down, just trying to get in the money. Ironically, it was their very willingness to pick fights just before players were in the money that brought them into the money so often. (A fact immortalized in Amir Vahedi's great quote — "In order to live, you must be willing to die.")

Eventually, I realized that in order to be successful in tournaments, I had to incorporate their insights into my own style. Conservative play was fine, perhaps even optimal, for the early stages of a tournament, but some variation of super-aggressive play was necessary for the end of tournaments. My own approach was to use elements of the super-aggressive style in a way that worked for me. Many of the early super-aggressive players just shoved their chips in the pot without proper regard for the situation at the table. Even that approach was good enough to work, but I tried to pick my spots a little more carefully. Since I had already established a tight reputation, it wasn't hard to play off that and maneuver just below everyone's radar screen.

The Art of Defense

If you know an opponent's basic style, how do you defend?

Against a player with a conservative style, there's surprisingly little you *can* do. Conservative players are playing mostly good cards. If they bet, and you don't have much, you just get out of their way. When they move in, you need a real hand to play with them. Of course, this advice illustrates the power of the conservative style which, as long as the blinds are small relative to the chip stacks, is close to an optimal style in a game-theoretic sense. Even the most conservative player will be bluffing from time to time, and their bluffs will tend to be very successful because of the image they've established.

Against a super-aggressive player, there are a number of things that you can and *must* do. The two main defensive strategies are the Hammer and the Rope-a-Dope.

The Hammer

When you see a super-aggressive player move into a pot, and you have some kind of reasonable hand, don't just call; come over the top with a big raise. This takes courage, but if you've assessed your opponent correctly, you'll win the pot immediately a substantial amount of the time. Remember that, paradoxically, *super-aggressive players aren't looking for expensive confrontations.* They just want to keep stealing blinds and pots, investing as few of their chips in the process as possible. Once in a while, of course, they'll actually have a real hand, and you'll be in big trouble. But you don't really have a choice; if you and the other players don't stand up, eventually the super-aggressive player will scoop all the chips at the table. (When you see one of the well-known aggressive players at a final table on television, notice how often they have either the biggest or the second-biggest stack at the table. That's because weaker players backed down throughout the tournament.)

Example No. 1. You're in fourth position with

The player first to act folds. A super-aggressive player in second position opens for triple the big blind. The player in third position folds. *What do you do?*

> **Answer:** You come over the top with a big raise, say pot-sized or even larger. A conservative player would need a real hand to open in second position, and against such a player you could lay down your K♣Q♥. But against a player who's willing to open with any piece of trash, king-queen is a fine hand, so play it aggressively.

The Rope-a-Dope

With genuine strength, you can just call a super-aggressive player, rather than making what would be normal raises against another player. By indicating an indifferent hand or perhaps a drawing hand, you encourage him to keep trying to push you out of the pot. When employing this strategy, you make only one raise, at the very end of the hand.

Example No. 2. You pick up A♦K♠ in late middle position and make a modest bet. A super-aggressive player on the button raises you. You just call. The flop comes K♥8♣3♠. *What do you do?*

Answer: Just check, and when he bets at you, call again. Repeat on fourth street. On the river either check or make one bet of about half the pot and see if it gets called. Remember that *against a super-aggressive player, all your hands are stronger than they appear*, because he is playing weaker hands than most other players.

Showing Hands

Managing the hands you choose to show or not to show is a crucial skill for players of different styles. The most general advice, which is always sound, is not to show your cards unless you have a very good reason. The more hands you show, the more information about your style you're revealing to a shrewd and observant opponent. It's a good rule, and one that I personally never violate.

But if you're playing a different style, there may be some tactical advantage to occasional showing a hand voluntarily. I once watched one of the most successful super-aggressive players as he played in the early stage of a major no-limit hold 'em tournament. Although I couldn't see his cards, I noticed that he was playing about one-third of the hands in the first couple of hours. He was the only name player at his table, and the other players were according him plenty of respect. He was grabbing lots of small pots with well-timed raises either before or after the flop. During the time I was watching, he never actually had to show a hand down. However, he would periodically turn over his cards when he bet and his opponent folded — an ace-king here, an ace-queen there, a few pairs mixed in. What he was doing was controlling the table by showing the hands where he wasn't bluffing, as if to say "Look, I'm playing a lot of pots, but see, I really am holding great cards." Of course, he wasn't showing most of his hands, where he was no doubt holding utter trash. But since people remember what they see, and not what they don't see, he was leaving an impression of a player that could not be faced unless you were holding great cards.

Since the super-aggressive style is built around stealing pots, it's very important for practitioners of this style to keep their bluffing frequency well-concealed. One tactic that works for this purpose is to make a bet on the end of a hand *solely to avoid showing the hand down.* It's an unusual move, but when it works you win the pot and keep your opponents from seeing what you're playing.

Managing the Tournament

When you play in a certain style, you should have a game plan for the tournament. Let's look at the conservative game plan and the super-aggressive game plan, and see how they differ.

Conservative Game Plan. The conservative plan is pretty simple. Play tight, pick off some small pots on a regular basis, and try to stay even or a little ahead of the increasing blinds and antes. Don't jeopardize your whole stack on a tossup situation. Just keep accumulating chips and wait for the occasional opportunity to double up with a monster hand. One or two double-ups a day will keep you afloat.

Super-Aggressive Game Plan. The super-aggressive style requires a big stack of chips to work properly, so your first job is to acquire that big stack. You should be very active right from the start. If the table is passive, then build a stack by just scooping pots. If the table is active or the players fight back, retreat a bit and start limping into cheap pots, hoping to flop monster hands where you can double up. Once you acquire a big stack, you'll become very dangerous, as you'll able to muscle the table with relatively little risk.

Varying Your Style

No matter what style you like, you can't stick exclusively to that style. Your opponents are always observing you, trying to figure out what you're doing. Once they have you pegged, you might as well be playing with your cards face-up. They'll know what you're doing and what your bets mean, and from that point you'll be winning small pots and losing big ones.

Once you begin modulating your style, however, you'll discover one of the amusing paradoxes of poker: *You'll make the easiest money when you're playing in a style opposite to your natural one.* The conservative player will have great success stealing pots and bluffing, because players will give him credit for having real hands. The super-aggressive player will find that his great hands are getting called, because no one knows that he's stopped playing trash.

When should you switch? There's no clear-cut answer to this question. It just depends on how quickly players react to your natural style. If you're playing solid hands, and people keep calling you down, there's no need to switch. The same holds if you're stealing pots and players won't fight you. Keep playing your natural style until you get a sense some number of the players have picked up a line on you. Then switch. Wait to switch back until you've had to show down a couple of hands that reveal your new approach. Over the course of a long event, be prepared to move and keep moving.

Pursuing a Balanced Strategy

No matter what style you finally adopt as your own, you'll have to learn to play what I call a balanced strategy. Simply put, this means that you have to learn to vary both your raises and calls, as well as the actual size of your bets, to avoid giving your opponents a read on your style. You'll have to do this even when you believe that a certain bet is clearly correct. What you sacrifice in terms of making a slightly incorrect bet on a given occasion will be recovered later, when your opponents have to guess at what you're really doing, and they guess wrong.

Here's a simple example. Suppose you believe that when you hold aces in first or second position, the "right" play is to open with a raise of about three times the big blind. (A very reasonable thing to believe, by the way.) If you always make this play with aces, what will happen is not that your opponents will know that a raise indicates aces (because you are probably raising with some other hands as well) but they'll know that *when you call, you don't have aces.* This is dangerous information to be giving away, so you need to take some countermeasures.

The simplest countermeasure is to vary your play at random, giving a higher probability to the play you think is correct, but mixing in other plays frequently enough so that your opponents can't put you on a hand easily. In Part Five, when we discuss betting before the flop, I'll advocate a mix of 80 percent raises and 20 percent calls in this exact situation. I'll also advocate varying the bet size, mostly raising three and four times the big blind, but occasionally raising only twice the big blind, and sometimes raising as much as five times the big blind.

How do you implement a balanced strategy? It's hard to remember exactly what you did the last four or five times a given situation appeared, but fortunately you don't have to. Just use the little random number generator that you carry around with you all day. What's that? You didn't know you had one? It's the second hand on your watch. If you know that you want to raise 80 percent of the time with a premium pair in early position and call the rest, just glance down at your watch and note the position of the second hand. Since 80 percent of 60 is 48, if the second hand is between 0 and 48, you raise, and if it's between 48 and 60 you just call. The nice thing about this method is that even if someone knew exactly what you were doing, they still couldn't read you!

Tournament Types: A Quick Overview

No-limit hold 'em tournaments come in many varieties and formats. Live tournaments may involve substantial entry fees and attract hundreds of participants. Online tournaments typically have smaller entry fees, but may involve thousands of players. At live events there are single-table satellite tournaments, where ten players ante up some money to try to win a seat at a bigger event. There are also satellite tournaments online, as well as "Sit-and-Go" tournaments, where ten players put up a small entry fee and play down to a single winner, with cash prizes going to the top three places.

Although these are all no-limit hold 'em tournaments, the exact conditions of play can dictate some very substantial changes in strategy, no matter what your basic playing style may be. Let's look at some different tournament formats and consider just how you should adjust your play to suit the circumstances.

Major Live Tournaments

Major tournaments are held around the world, usually in casinos. The entry fees are typically $2,000 to $10,000, although the final of the World Poker Tour at The Bellagio sports an entry fee of $25,000, hefty even by poker standards. Traditionally these tournaments featured super-strong fields with a scattering of talented and wealthy amateurs. In the last couple of years online sites have begun running massive numbers of qualifying tournaments, so you can get into these events now with a very modest investment and lots of luck. This development has changed the composition of the fields dramatically, and altered the strategy somewhat. Here are the main features of live major tournaments and a brief note on how each feature affects your play.

1. **Entry Fee.** When everyone pays a big entry fee, players feel they have a real investment in the tournament, one they want to protect. This makes for conservative play, and the best strategy to apply is judiciously aggressive play, probing for the stealing situations which will be available. When players are tight, aggressive play becomes even more successful. An obvious show of strength will be respected until proven otherwise, so raises and check-raises will win lots of pots.

2. **Round Length.** In tournament terminology, a "round" is the length of time that the blinds stay at a given level before increasing. In a live tournament, this time is typically an hour to an hour and a half, although at a few tournaments (like the World Series of Poker) it's two hours. Although it takes awhile to deal the cards, a round will still consist of 40-50 hands. Long rounds favor good players, because there is more time for their skill to tell and less pressure to accumulate chips quickly. The long rounds in major live tournaments make conservative play more optimal in the early stages.

3. **Players per Hand.** In major tournaments there are fewer players involved in each hand. The vast majority of hands will involve only two or three players, while a few hands will just be folded around to the big blind. Under these circumstances, high card hands become more powerful and drawing hands less so, since the pot will rarely supply the implied odds needed to make the drawing hands playable.

4. **Experience.** With long rounds, there is more chance for players to observe the other players at the table and put those observations to use. The better and more experienced a player is, the better his chances for making use of this information.

Less experienced players should play more aggressively than usual, to accumulate chips before the experienced players at the table have had a chance to accumulate information about them.

5.   **Bluffing**. Except from the experienced super-aggressive players, there will be somewhat less bluffing than you might expect. The newcomers in the field will be nervous, and afraid that the experienced players will be able to read their bluffs easily. As a result, they'll be looking to play only rock-solid hands. You can generally assume that unknown players will tend to have the hands they are representing in the early stages of the tournament. There's a corollary of course: An unknown player who is willing to bluff at the beginning will be able to take down some easy pots. Meanwhile, the superstar super-aggressive players will be bluffing furiously, taking advantage of both their reputations and the newcomer's reluctance to play less than premium hands.

6.   **Trapping**. The relatively slow pace of the tournament allows time for observing opponents and setting complex traps, the success of which hinges on play in preceding hands. A faster-paced tournament doesn't necessarily allow this, because players are eliminated too quickly and the tables break up and are reshuffled.

Small-Stakes
Multi-Table Online Tournaments

Every major online site runs some of these tournaments each day. In the case of the major sites, there may be dozens of such events every day. Entry fees range from $1 to $30. (Larger entry fees than this go in a separate category, as they will start to attract the pros.) The number of players could be as high as several thousand. Your buy-in will get you $1,000 to $1,500 in tournament chips, and the blinds will start in the $5/$10 or $10/$20 area. The blinds will increase rapidly, however, as the rounds will typically be very short: perhaps 5, 10, or 12 minutes each, allowing only 8-to-12 hands per round.

These tournaments obviously involve much more luck than the slower live events. The combination of the large number of inexperienced players, short rounds, and rapidly-increasing blind structure means that you're compelled to play quickly and aggressively just to stay ahead of the blinds. However, there's still plenty of scope for strategy, and a skilled player can do much better than average. Here are a few tips.

1. **Don't plan on being able to use your powers of observation very much.** Players will constantly be moving all their chips in and getting knocked out, so tables don't stay together long enough to get solid information on the other players. Most of your hands will need to be evaluated in a vacuum.

2. **Don't plan on running any bluffs.** Players are extremely aggressive; they're looking to double up quickly, and they don't need much to call. You'll see plenty of all-in showdowns where a pair of fours butts up against an ace-six offsuit. The bottom line: Your shrewd, well-considered bluff to steal the pot will probably be answered by a big reraise followed by an all-in! Don't bother. Just make sure you have a hand when you get a lot of chips in the pot. (Interestingly, although bluffs don't work in these games, you'll still see plenty of bluffs tried.)

3. **Betting patterns are very different from normal poker.** At least in the early stages of these tournaments, there's very little actual value betting. Slow-playing, trapping, and all-in

bets predominate. A solid value bet, for instance, is almost always paid off, sometimes with a big reraise.

4. **Crowded pots.** Before the flop, the pot may be crowded with five to seven limpers. A significant raise after several players have limped in won't thin the field; it will only function as a pot-sweetner.

5. **Optimal strategy.** With so many players playing so aggressively, a conservative strategy ought to pay big dividends, since strong hands rate to get paid very well. If the blinds were increasing slowly, and the rounds were longer, this would certainly be true. But with short rounds and sharp blind increases, a strictly conservative approach won't yield results fast enough to keep your stack from shrinking as the blinds come charging. While you should be generally conservative, you have to mix in two other ideas:

   A. In late position, try to see some cheap flops with suited-connectors or small pairs, in the hope of flopping a monster that could let you double up. The large number of players in each pot makes your implied odds huge when you hit a set, straight, or a flush.

   B. Push your good hands (top pairs, trips) to the maximum, again with the hope of doubling up. You're much more likely to be called all-in than in a normal tournament. Remember that even your weaker top pair hands, like nines and eights, go up in value while high unpaired cards go down in value.

High-Stakes
Multi-Table Online Tournaments

In addition to the small-stakes online tournaments, there are also events with relatively high entry fees of $100 and up. In these tournaments, the fields are typically smaller and the caliber of play is much higher. Many of the Vegas pros pass their time between live tournaments by playing in one or two of these events every day.

Also falling in this category are tournaments with smaller initial entry fees, but with rebuys and add-ons. While the exact conditions vary from tournament to tournament, in general a *rebuy* allows you to pay an additional entry fee and receive an initial set of chips. Depending on the tournament, you can do this if you either lose all your chips or fall below your starting count. Rebuys happen only during a *rebuy period* at the start of the tournament.

An *add-on* is an additional purchase made at the end of the rebuy period, and is open to all players regardless of their chip count. In some tournaments, a *bonus add-on* allows you to pay another entry fee and buy even more chips than you started with. If you're a better-than-average player and your chip stack is not too large, rebuys and add-ons are generally a good deal, but they have the effect of making the actual entry as much as three to six times higher than the posted entry fee.

In most respects these tournaments are similar to the live multi-table events. The rounds are long compared to most online events, perhaps 15 minutes or so, which combined with the rapid play of the hands means that you see far more hands per round than in the small-stakes events, although still not as many as in the live tournaments. Fewer hands per round means that you are under more pressure to accumulate chips, so your play has to be more aggressive, and you need to push your good hands a little harder. But the overall play of the hands more closely resembles a serious tournament. Players bet their good hands, they fold their bad hands, and slow-playing and all-in moves are the exception rather than the rule.

Single-Table
Sit-and-Go Online Tournaments

Another popular format on most online sites is the sit-and-go tournament. They run 24 hours a day and most of them start as soon as a table of ten is filled. Entry fees range from $1 to $100, which usually buys you $1,000 in tournament chips. Blinds start low but rise rapidly, about every ten hands or so, and the tournament pays the last three places.

The proper strategy for these tournaments is a little different from the other online events. In the early rounds, the blinds are very small compared to the chip stacks around the table, so conservative play is a good idea. At the same time, you can observe the other players at the table and see what kind of cards they're playing. Some of the players will be rocks, while others will play any two suited or connected cards. In the first two or three rounds, most pots will be fiercely contested, so make sure you have a real hand when you get involved.

By the time you reach the fourth or fifth round of play, several things have happened.

1. Two, three, or four players have been knocked out.

2. The blinds have increased to levels that represent 10 to 20 percent of the original stacks.

3. The remaining players who still have substantial chips don't want to jeopardize their chances of finishing in the money.

You're now in prime stealing territory. Most pots won't be contested at this stage, so if the hand is checked to you, go for it.

Just move in for the minimum raise with any two reasonable cards. Unless you have a real hand, fold on the few occasions when you are raised (which *will* represent a strong hand, not a bluff). You'll win far more hands than you lose.

By the time the field is reduced to three or four players, the blinds will be so large that the game becomes a crap shoot. If you've done enough stealing on the previous few rounds, your big stack will make you the favorite. Otherwise, try to take the lead in the betting and hope for the best.

Live Single-Table Satellites

Satellite tournaments occur in conjunction with most major tournaments. A casino running a $10,000 buy-in major event might hold satellites with $1,000 entry fees, with the winner getting a seat to the main event. There will also be satellites for satellites — put up $100 to try to win your seat at the $1,000 satellite, and so on.

These tournaments are very similar to the single-table online tournaments discussed above, with two exceptions:

1.   The tournaments are live, so your powers of observation can come into play.

2.   Only one winner is paid, so finishing second or third doesn't mean anything.

The strategy tips for the single-table online tournaments apply here as well. In addition, be aware that deals are commonplace once the field gets reduced to two or three players.

For example, the satellite plays down to just two players, both of whom have $5,000. One player says to the other, "Let's split. I'll take the entry prize, and I'll pay you $5,000." It's a fair offer. Both players receive $5,000 in value for their efforts so far. If one player is clearly the better of the two, the deal might get structured a little differently. The better player might offer to take the entry fee and pay out only $4,600 in return, for instance. Now the fairness of the deal depends on the perceived difference between the two players.

Another way of structuring the deal might be for the player receiving cash to get a percentage of the other player's winnings in addition to some cash. Players are creative and deals can get quite ingenious. If you're offered a deal and you don't like it or can't figure it out, just say no. (Deals will be discussed extensively in Volume II.)

The Problems

Each chapter in this book (with the exception of Chapter 1) is followed by a set of problems illustrating some of the ideas in the chapter. Each problem puts you at a table and follows the action of a hand through from beginning to end. You'll be asked what you would do each time a decision is required, until the player in your position is finally out of the hand. Since these hands are taken from real life, in some cases the player in your position will take an action that's not best, or at least not what you would do. Take the hands seriously and try to respond with the actions you would take at a real table. You'll get the most out of each hand when you actively involve yourself in the decision-making process.

In Problems 2-1 and 2-2, you're seated behind a player and are trying to play aggressively with weak hands. See if you would choose to just fold these hands, or try to make something of them.

Problem 2-3 shows an example of adjusting your calling requirements when facing a known super-aggressive player.

Problem 2-4 shows how to play against a super-aggressive style when faced with a standard post-flop decision.

Problems 2-5 through 2-7 show some of the difficulties and traps when playing against a super-aggressive player.

Problem 2-8 illustrates a good defense against super-aggression by using the Hammer.

Hand 2-1

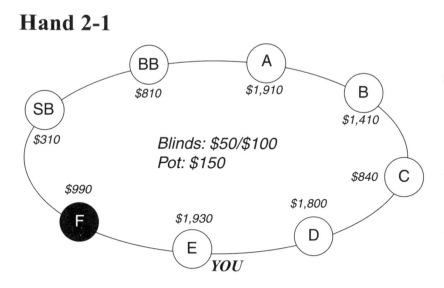

Situation: Online single-table tournament. You are the chip leader with eight players left. The players are generally aggressive and most pots are contested.

Your hand: 8♣6♣

Action to you: Players A and B fold. Player C calls $100. Player D folds. Pot is now $250.

Question: *What's your play?*

   Answer: Suited connectors are playable as a way to vary your choice of starting hands, and keep your opponents off-balance. When you play them, your main goal is to see a flop cheaply. You're hoping to flop a monster and bust a player or two, while tossing your hand away when the flop is not favorable (which, by the way, is most of the time).

   Here, however, you have to fold. First, your hand is not a true suited connector. There's much less chance of making a straight with an eight-six holding than with two consecutive cards like eight-seven or seven-six. In addition, these are low cards rather than high ones. If you play jack-ten suited, there's some chance that the flop may come under your cards, giving you an additional way to win.

But there's still another problem with the hand. The three players yet to act have $990, $310, and $810 respectively, while the one player already in the pot has $840. With the blinds at $50 and $100, all of these players are under pressure to make a move soon. That's not what you want to see when holding suited connectors. If one of them decides it's time to take a marginal hand and shove all his chips in, you're going to have to throw your hand away.

However, let's say the player in your position decides to play.

Action: You call $100. The button raises to $200. The blinds fold. Player C calls for another $100. The pot is now $650, and it costs you $100 to call. What do you do?

Answer: The pot is offering you 6.5-to-1 on your money, and your flush and straight possibilities make this an easy call. Notice what's happened here, though, because this is very important. Your hand started out as a somewhat silly, speculative move. Now in just a second it's morphed into a straight value play. You won't see that kind of move in the stock market very often, but in poker it happens all the time. Not only shouldn't you fall in love with a hand, you shouldn't fall in love with your *evaluation* of a hand. They change all the time, and you have to be ready to change as well.

Action: You call for another $100. The pot is now $750. The flop comes 9♠3♣2♣. Player C checks. What do you do?

Answer: That's a very good flop for you. Two clubs, and only one overcard to your 8♣6♣. You should make a move to win this hand right here, but cheaply if you can. Players C and F have $640 and $790 respectively. A bet of $100 is too little (too easily called) but $200 to $300 looks about right to shake out any weak holders. This way his pot odds won't be too good in case he has a call.

Action: You bet $200. Player F calls. Pot now $1,150.

Fourth Street: 7♣

Question: *What's the play?*

Answer: Now the only hand that beats you is a higher flush, which is always a danger when you're in the habit of playing low suited cards. But in an online tournament, with the blinds going up every ten hands or so, you have so little time to make money that you just have to forget about those possibilities and push your good hands to the limit. You should assume you have a lock hand, and try to figure out the best way to get Player F's remaining $590. I'd bet $200 to $250 here, figuring that the pot odds would force him to call, then go for the rest on fifth street. (This play is not correct if you feel your opponent will only call with a set or a high club. If so, you may need to bet more to give him lesser odds.)

Action: You actually go all-in, and Player F calls. He shows down Q♣T♣, and takes the pot with a better flush.

Hand 2-2

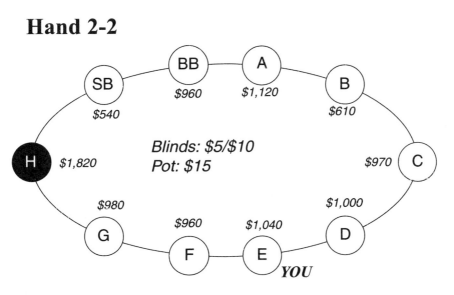

Situation: Very early in a one-table satellite.

Your hand: 8♦6♥

Action to you: Players A, B, C, and D all fold.

Question: *Should you try to steal the pot? If you think so, how big a bet should you make?*

    Answer: You shouldn't try to steal here, even if you're consciously trying to play an aggressive or super-aggressive game. True, you've had four folds in front of you, which is a nice sign. The table is effectively only six players. The trouble is that you're early in the tournament, there aren't many chips in the center of the table for you to win, and there are still five players to act behind you. That adds up to a poor risk-reward ratio in my book. If you make a smallish bet (say three to four times the big blind) you may just get a few callers behind you, because the amount isn't large enough to chase anyone out. If you make a large bet, you'll chase out everyone who doesn't have a good hand, but you've put a lot of money in play to win the pathetic little pot out there, and the strong hands will still look you up.

When the blinds are very small relative to your own, and the chip counts of the other players, conservative play should be your default strategy except in unusual circumstances. Here you have eight-six offsuit, and there's nothing unusual about your circumstances at all. Just fold.

Action: You bet $30, in an attempt to steal the pot. Player F folds. Player G calls. Player H calls. The small blind puts in another $25 to call. The big blind folds. The pot is now $130.

Disaster. You got three callers, you'll be second to act out of four players, and in all likelihood your hand is fourth-best right now.

Flop: 9♥8♠7♠

Action: The small blind checks. *What do you do?*
> **Answer:** Not a bad result for you. You've got middle pair, plus the idiot end of a straight draw. (The low end is called the idiot end — only an idiot would have been playing the cards to hit that end!)
>
> You should bet here. You have a hand now, and the texture of the flop is good. It will have missed the players calling with face cards. I'd bet about half the pot, say $70 or so.

Action: You actually check, and Player G bets $10. Player H raises to $80. The small blind folds.

Question: *What now?*
> **Answer:** Fold. The button says he has a hand, and Player G may have one also. While you have something, you're sandwiched in between two players, either one of whom might have made their hand already. Time to let this go.

Action: You fold. You were actually up against a pair of nines and a pair of tens, and a third ten came on fourth street. Player H wins with his three tens, although you would have made a straight had you stayed.

By not betting after the flop, the player in your position made two mistakes in the same hand, combining a silly aggressive play before the flop with a scared play after the flop. You'll see a lot of this in online play, where a player makes a move hoping to steal a pot without resistance, then runs as soon as someone puts up a fight. It's a sure recipe for losing a lot of chips.

Hand 2-3

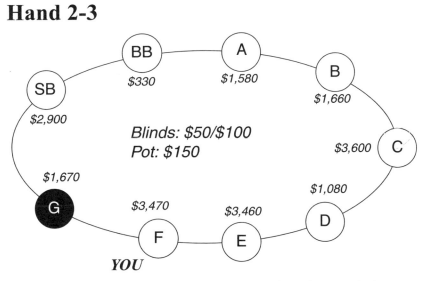

Situation: Major tournament, a few hours in. Player E is loose and aggressive, playing a lot of pots. He's shown down a couple of less-than-marginal hands, but has drawn well. Players G is super-tight, the small blind and big blind seem like solid players.

Your hand: A♠J♠

Action to you: Players A, B, C, and D all fold. Player E raises to $300. Pot now $450.

Question: *What's your play?*
    Answer: According to Sklansky's Gap Concept, you need a stronger hand to call a raise than you need to raise in the first place. You should certainly raise to open the pot in late position with ace-jack suited, but now you're coming in behind a raiser who has put in three times the big blind. Against a tight player, you should fold here. But we know Player E is loose and aggressive, so you can downgrade your standards a bit, especially since the players behind you are known to be tight. You should call. (In a limit game this is an easy reraise. It might also be a reraise in a tournament if you and your opponent's chips weren't so deep.)

Action: You call. The button and small blind fold, but the big blind goes all-in for his remaining $230 chips. Player E calls the extra $30. The pot is now $1,010.

Question: *Do you call?*
    Answer: Yes, it is a trivially easy call.

Action: You call, making the main pot $1,040.

Flop: K♣T♣3♠

Action: Player E checks.

Question: *Do you check, or bet $600 with the idea of chasing E out?*
    Answer: Check. A bet would make sense if E was the only player left. But here the big blind can't be driven out of the main pot, and there is as yet no side pot to win. The risk-reward ratio for a bet is very bad, and checking this hand

down to the end would be a good result if you don't hit your hand.

Action: You check. Fourth and fifth street are the 5♣ and 5♦. The hand is in fact checked down to the end, and the pot is won by the big blind, holding a pair of eights.

Hand 2-4

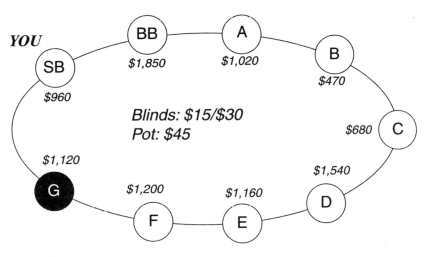

Situation: Early in a single-table satellite. The big blind is a very aggressive player who fights for most pots and has won several in the early going.

Your hand: K♦Q♦

Action to you: Players A through G all fold.

Question: *Do you call or raise?*

> **Answer:** Your hand is obviously good enough to raise. The fact that the big blind is an aggressive player just makes it more likely that you'll get a call that you welcome. About three times the big blind is a good amount.

Action: You put in $100. The big blind calls you for an additional $85. The pot is now $230.

Flop: 5♦3♣2♣

Question: *What do you do now?*

Answer: This was a reasonable flop for you, with three low cards that missed your hand but probably missed his as well.

There are two ways to play the hand now: The merely aggressive way, and the hyper-aggressive way.

The merely aggressive play is to just make a standard continuation bet of half the pot. You probably have the best hand right now, and you have several outs if you are just called (three kings, three queens, and two running diamonds). This gives you a good shot at winning the pot at a reasonable price. It's the play I would probably make here.

The hyper-aggressive play is to check here, figuring that your aggressive opponent will himself make a move for the pot, and you can then come over the top and take his raise away from him. It's definitely a play, and many of the top players like to play this way. It's especially good if you've established an image, or shown down some big hands already.

Action: You check, he bets $240, and you reraise all-in. He throws his hand away, and you take the pot.

Was the all-in raise necessary? If both players had more chips, the answer would be no. A raise of $400-$500 chips would suffice. But here, if you bet $500 and then somehow lose the hand, your chip count is down to $350 and you're effectively crippled. So an all-in move gives you the best chance of winning the hand.

A conservative critic would say this kind of all-in move works every time but one, when it eliminates you from the tournament. But that's a short-sighted argument. Single-table tournaments are so quick, and the blinds increase so fast, that you have to make moves like this from time to time to give yourself any chance at all of winning.

Hand 2-5

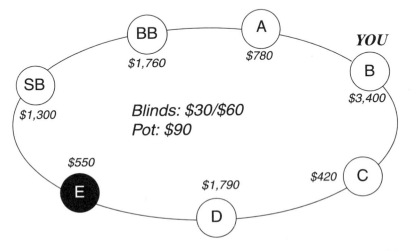

Situation: Middle of a single-table online tournament. The big blind and Player D are very aggressive. Both have check-raised on several occasions.

Your hand: Q♣J♦

Action to you: Player A folds.

Question: *Do you fold, call, or raise?*

> **Answer:** Even at a short table, Q♣J♦ is not a powerhouse hand in early position. You might consider calling or even raising with it if the table has been unusually passive. Here you know that there are two aggressive players yet to act, and of course one of the other players may have picked up a real hand. You should just fold here.

Action: Actually you decide to call. Player C folds and Player D calls. Player E and the small blind fold, and the big blind checks. The pot is now $210. You will act second after the flop, between the two aggressive players.

Flop: K♠J♥3♠

Action: The big blind checks. *What do you do?*
> **Answer:** Many players tighten their game when they find themselves in a pot with players who are known to push people around. It's a natural tendency, but you have to resist it and try to play good, percentage poker. Your real goal against players like that is to play fewer pots, but to play them more aggressively than usual.
>
> Here you've flopped middle pair, and there's no reason yet to think you're beaten. There is a flush draw on board, and you can't give anyone a free draw at a flush. Just bet half the pot and see what happens.

Action: You in fact check, and Player D checks. The pot remains at $210.

Fourth Street: 4♦

Action: The big blind checks again. *What should you do?*
> **Answer:** The four was a great card for you. There are no flushes or straights yet, and the four shouldn't have improved anyone's hand. Correct your mistake of last turn, and bet between one-half and three-fourths of the pot. The fact that no one bet after the flop indicates that neither player has a king. They might be on drawing hands, or holding ace-small. One of the worst mistakes you can make in poker is to give someone on a draw a free card to beat you. Make them draw against the odds.

Action: You check, and Player D checks. The pot is still $210.

Fifth Street: 6♠

Action: The big blind checks. *Should you bet on the end?*
Answer: The flush card came, so now there's no reason to bet. If Player D has nothing he'll throw his hand away, and if he hit a flush he'll raise you. Just check and see if you have the best hand.

Resolution: You bet $100, and Player D raised to $200. The big blind folded and you called. Player D had Q♠2♠ for a flush.

This hand shows one of the hidden strengths of very aggressive play. Because of the active players at the table, the player in your position was afraid to make his normal moves. As a result, he committed the cardinal sin of giving free cards to an opponent drawing at a flush, then compounded the error by betting on the end. Aggressive play puts a level of pressure on your opponents that conservative play does not, and that pressure can translate directly into chips won.

Hand 2-6

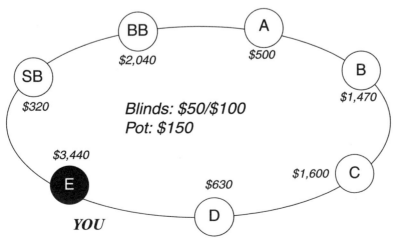

Situation: Middle of a single-table online tournament. The big blind and Player C are very aggressive. Player D has been conservative.

Your hand: A♠Q♣

Action to you: Players A and B fold. Player C calls. Player D calls. The pot is now $350.

Question: *Do you fold, call, or raise?*

Answer: You probably have the best hand right now. The calls from the players in front of you, particularly from Player C, don't indicate any particular strength. You should raise, and raise strongly, to around $400. You'd like to win this pot right here, since it's already a sizeable amount, but at the very least you want to reduce the field to just you and one other caller at most.

Action: You raise, but only to $200. The small blind goes all-in for his last $270. Player C and Player D both call for another $220. The pot is now $1,260. It costs you $120 to call. *What should you do?*

Answer: The small blind is now in the main pot with whatever he has. Players C and D have both been given two opportunities to raise, and neither has done so. Few players have the patience and sheer cold-bloodedness to slowplay a big pair through two raises at the table. You have to assume that both are nursing small pairs or drawing hands.

Now is the time to strike and go all-in. You'll almost certainly knock out Player C. Just because you've characterized a player as "aggressive" doesn't mean he has a death wish. You're forcing him to put his whole stack in jeopardy against a player who has raised him twice. That's not likely. Player D might call you in the side pot since he'll have only $300 left if he folds. But that's all right, since you're a favorite if he holds a drawing hand, and at worst you're a slight underdog if he holds a small pair.

If you can knock out both Players C and D with this move, you've gained a huge amount of equity. At that point, you'll have invested $325 for a shot at a pot of $1,275 where you're almost certainly a favorite.

Action: You go all-in. Players C and D both fold. The small blind turns over A♦9♥. Your A♠Q♣ holds up to win the pot.

In contrast to the last hand, this time you handled the aggressive players correctly. Loose, aggressive players at the table should only force you to cut down on the number of hands you play. However, when you do catch some strong cards, you have to play them decisively. Otherwise the loose players will simply wear you down.

Hand 2-7

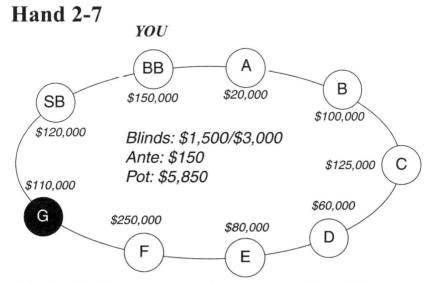

Situation: Ending stages of a major tournament. Player F is a very strong, young player with a super-aggressive style, capable of playing any two cards.

Your hand: A♣Q♥

Action to you: Players A through E all fold. Player F puts in $6,000. Player G and the small blind fold. The pot is now $11,850. It costs you $3,000 to call.

Question: *Do you fold, call, or raise?*

Answer: You must raise here. I'd recommend tossing in a significant raise of about the size of the pot, say $12,000 to $15,000. There are several reasons for making a good-sized raise here, some technical and some psychological.

1.   You have a legitimate hand. There's no harm in raising the pot when your cards are strong.

2.   You're out of position. If you and Player F both stay in the pot, you'll be acting first on every subsequent betting round. That's a big disadvantage, so you should make at least some effort to finish the hand early.

3.   You need to establish psychological dominance. You want players at the table to fear you, but if you can't get fear, at least get respect. As the big blind, this is your pot. Defend it. Show them you can't be pushed around.

4.   Player F is a tough player with a super-aggressive style. *Such players are extremely dangerous.* Because they can be playing any two cards, you won't be able to tell, after the flop comes, exactly where you stand. Right now, you know you have a good hand, so make a move. Against super-aggressive players you want to settle the hand quickly, win or lose.

Action: You just call. The pot is now $14,850.

Flop: 9♣6♥5♦

Question: *What's your move?*

Answer: This was a bad flop for you. Was it a bad flop for your opponent? Against a player who will cheerfully play any two cards, who knows? It might have missed him, or he might now have one or two pair.

The best way to handle this situation is just to make a bet and see what happens. Sometimes the bet will win the pot. Sometimes you'll get raised, and you can just throw your hand away. If you get called, you're still done with the hand unless you get very lucky on fourth street.

You want to play in such a way that you get information about your opponent's hand at minimum cost. If you have to act first, betting out is the only way to get that information. If you check, and he then bets, what do you know? Not much, except that you put him in a situation where he has an almost mandatory bet no matter what he holds, and he then bets.

Your dilemma illustrates why the raise before the flop was so important. You've missed the flop completely, and the argument for betting is still compelling. But if you had made the move before the flop, Player F would have thrown away a lot of hands which might now be winning.

Action: You just check. Player F checks as well. The pot is still $14,850.

An aggressive player checked when he could have bet. You should now be suspicious.

Fourth Street: 8♣

Question: *What do you do now?*

Answer: You still have nothing, and it's increasingly likely that something out there has hit Player F's hand. Since you just called before the flop and checked after the flop, your opponent is not going to believe that you have suddenly made your hand. Check and attempt to see the hand through cheaply.

Action: You check again. Player F also checks.

Fifth Street: 2♣

Question: *What now?*
   Answer: Keep checking, and hope that the hand is checked down.

Action: You check, and Player F bets $5,000. *What do you do?*
   Answer: It costs you $5,000 to see a pot of almost $20,000. Those are excellent odds. Of course, Player F knows that, and he gave you those odds anyway, so you're probably beaten. But just in case, I would call anyway.

Action: You call, and Player F shows A♦8♠ and wins with a pair of eights.

In retrospect, we can see what Player F was doing. When you called but didn't raise before the flop, he probably put you on a couple of high cards. When you didn't bet after the flop, he probably thought your high cards didn't include an ace, so you were probably holding something like king-queen or king-jack, maybe suited. By fourth street he knew his pair of eights were probably good, and also that he was unlikely to win a lot of money on the hand. At that point he probably decided a small bet on the end might be interpreted as a pot-stealer and get called, which was his best chance to make a little money.
   Note that the passive play of the player in your position cost him a pot he might easily have won.

Hand 2-8

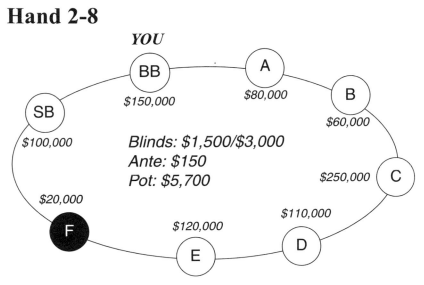

Situation: Major tournament, late in the second day. Player C is a very aggressive player who has been the "table captain" for some time.

Your hand: K♣Q♥

Action to you: Players A and B fold. Player C raises to $8,000. Players D, E, and F all fold. The small blind folds. The pot is now $13,700 and it costs you $5,000 to call.

Question: *Do you fold, call, or raise?*

    Answer: You should call, although raising is quite a reasonable alternative. In either case your goal is to defend your big blind against an aggressive attacker. Raising might win the pot right here, at the risk of costing you a bunch of chips if Player C actually has a hand. Calling, and then deciding on your right move after the flop, is the low-priced alternative. You'll be forced to defend your blind on many occasions during a tournament, and the best procedure is to vary between the raising and calling plays on a random basis.

Action: You decide to call. The pot is now $18,700.

Flop: K♦9♠2♣

Question: *What's your move now?*

    Answer: That's a perfect flop for you, and against this opponent, the right move is to check and allow him to continue to bet. You're going to employ the Hammer Defense against super-aggressive play.

Action: You check, and he bets $20,000. The pot is now $38,700. *What do you do?*

    Answer: He probably thinks you called with an ace, then missed the flop. As an aside, his bet is too large. If you indeed missed the flop, a bet of $12,000 or so should be plenty to chase you away. If you're trapping, he's just throwing away money. The risk/reward ratio for an overbet in this situation is especially poor.

    You, of course, should raise. Since you almost certainly have the best hand (top pair plus second-best kicker), make it a good-sized amount, about the size of the pot.

Action: You raise $50,000, and he folds.

The Hammer descends and wins a nice pot.

Part Three
Reading the Table

Reading the Table

Introduction

Some games can be played without paying very much attention to who your opponent is or what he's trying to do. If you're a chess master, and you're playing an amateur, you don't need to care what he's thinking, planning, or scheming. The position on the chessboard contains all the information you need to crush him. You just make one technically good move after another, he makes his inevitable errors, and you finally wear him down.

Backgammon is a similar game, but one which offers a little more scope for exploiting known weaknesses. If you're a strong player playing someone weaker, you can just play your normal game and grind him down in the long run. But you can also improve your results and win a little more if you have observed mistakes in your opponent's game. You might, for instance, offer a double which would be technically incorrect against a strong player (because he would know to take it) but which works against a weak opponent because you've seen him pass doubles in such positions before. Spotting such an opportunity lets you win money with a play that would be a mistake against a stronger opponent.

Poker, however, is not like these other games. When you play poker, you aren't just trying to make "objectively good" plays. You are also trying to keep the nature of your plays concealed from your opponents, while simultaneously trying to figure out what they are doing, so you can counteract it. Balancing all these competing goals is a tough business, and doing it well requires you to have a keen appreciation of what's been going on at the table. I call this "reading the table," and it requires watching for physical tells, betting patterns, and your own persona.

Physical Tells

In the wonderful poker movie *Rounders*, Teddy-KGB is undone when Matt Damon's character discovers his tell. If Teddy holds an Oreo cookie up to his ear, breaks it, and eats it, he has a monster hand. (He's psychologically devouring his opponent, you see.) If he merely listens to it break and puts it back in the tray, he's bluffing. As a result, the hero is able to break Teddy and survive with his bankroll and neck intact.

If only real life were that easy! Teddy's quirk is an example of a physical tell, a mannerism, expression, emotion or habit that in some way gives real information about your hand. Cataloging tells is a whole book in itself, and fortunately it's already been done. Find a copy of Mike Caro's classic *Book of Tells* and read it thoroughly. It's a good treatment of a difficult subject.

Rather than try to duplicate the material in Caro's book, I'm instead going to pass on some of my insights into spotting and using tells.

I group physical tells into three categories:

1.   Facial expressions

2.   General body language

3.   Hand motions

Of the three, I've found that hand motions are the most reliable and revealing. Although most players are keenly aware of the need to control their facial expressions, they don't pay as much attention to what they do with their hands, particularly as they move chips into the pot. While other players are looking at faces, I like to watch hands. Basically, I'm looking to see if players handle their chips and move chips into the pot any differently with strong or weak hands. If I see something, I assign it a high degree of reliability until I get evidence to the contrary.

In my experience, facial expressions and body language are more treacherous. I do watch for them, and you should too, but I need a bit more evidence before I'm willing to say I've spotted a true tell than with the hand motions. I do have two useful rules in this area, however. Here they are:

1. **If a player seems weak, I'll give more credence to a suspected tell**. This is just common sense. A good player will naturally have spent more time thinking about tells and concealing them than a weak player. So if I pick up what seems to be a tell, but the player is otherwise playing a strong game, I'm suspicious. If I get the same tell from someone who seems to be an obvious fishcake, I'll act on it more quickly.

2. **Weak means strong, and strong means weak**. This insight is straight from Caro's book, and it's the single best guide to evaluating the tells of a relatively unknown player. When humans want to conceal their true intentions, they tend to act the opposite of what they really mean. Dissembling is such a powerful innate drive that it can overcome a strong conscious desire to act in some randomly mysterious fashion. Just watch any televised tournament final, and you'll see that in almost every case where the players seem to be acting, they're acting in the opposite fashion from the real strength of their hand.

The skill of spotting physical tells is most important if you're a participant in a money game that meets on a regular schedule with the same players each time, or if you frequent a card club with a clientele that doesn't change much. In that case, you'll meet the same players over and over again, and you'll have plenty of opportunities to create a notebook on each player.

If you mostly play tournament poker the situation is a little different. Now you're going to see individual players much less frequently. With the explosion in the number of players showing up at tournaments, you might easily play in a tournament and not meet a single player that you've seen before. And of course, if you play online there are no physical tells to observe. The best you can do is to try and derive clues by seeing how long a player thinks to make a play, but this is easy to control and might simply represent internet delay times.

All serious poker players try to minimize their tells, obviously. There are a couple of ways to go about this. One is the robotic approach: where your face becomes a mask and your voice a monotone, at least while the hand is being played. With some practice, this approach is accessible to most players. The other is the manic method, where you affect a whole bunch of tics, twitches, and expressions, and mix them up with a river of insane babble. The idea is to overwhelm your opponents with clues, so they can't sort out what's really going on. This approach can be effective, but for normal people it's hard to pull off. (If you've spent part of your life in an institution, this method may come naturally.)

Betting Patterns

Another, and more reliable, way of getting information about your opponents is by studying their betting patterns. How many pots do they enter? When they have a good hand, do they make strong bets or weak bets? How about when they have a weak hand? When you reraise them, do they tend to back off, or fight for the pot?

Why do I think it's better to focus on betting patterns? It's pretty simple: No one has to twitch, but everyone has to bet!

One could argue, in fact, that *a player is nothing more than the sum of his betting patterns.* And those patterns are lying right out there to be observed. Every time a player bets, he tells you something about how he plays poker. You have to watch those patterns, deduce what you can, and file the memory away for future use. A top player can, in the space of an hour or two, compile a pretty good book on a collection of strangers at a tournament table. Your job is to try and do the same. It's tough work at first, but with practice and experience it will get easier. Here's my best advice on the subject of betting patterns, starting with some special advice for beginners.

Some Rules of Thumb for Beginners

If you're a true beginner, about to play in your very first no-limit hold 'em tournament, don't worry too much about observing the table. First-timers often arrive with the best of intentions for keeping track of the other players, only to find they're overwhelmed with the sheer amount of stuff going on around them — stacks, chips, cards, general hubbub. Just as you notice that the fellow under the gun has raised for the third hand in a row, the dealer is impatiently reminding you that it's your turn to bet. Real-life poker goes very fast, and you'll need a tournament or two just to get acclimated to the conditions of play.

When all that becomes second nature, you're ready to start learning about your opponents. Begin with baby steps. If you're playing at full tables, you'll have nine other players to watch. Don't try to keep track of all nine. In the beginning you just won't be able to manage that. Instead, focus on the players whose patterns will have the most effect on your fortunes — the players seated immediately around you. Watch the two players on your left (they'll act after you every turn) and the player on your right. If your table stays together for several hours, branch out a little bit and add the player three to your left, and the player two to your right. Now you'll be watching half the table, which will give you plenty to do.

What should you watch for? Here are a few key things to track in the beginning.

1. **How many hands do they play?** By counting the number of pots they play, you'll start to get some idea of the strength of their starting hands. If they play only one or two pots in each round of the table, they're conservative players. If they're involved in three or four pots a round, they're probably playing an aggressive or super-aggressive style. If they're playing more pots than that, they're giving their money away.

2. **What hands do they show down?** A hand shown down is a gold mine of information. You not only get to see the cards they initially held, but if you can remember how the hand was bet, you'll see how they responded to a bunch of different situations. Did they raise or call before the flop? If they raised, how much did they raise? How strong was their hand after the flop, and what did they do with it? Did they slow play a monster, or aggressively bet a weak holding? The more of this information you can remember, the better.

3. **Are they callers or raisers?** Do they like to enter a pot with a raise, or creep in with a call? A player who calls more than he raises is liable to be weak. A player who likes to raise may be strong and dangerous; at least his heart's in the right place.

4. **How do they respond when someone comes over the top?** Can they stand up to a big reraise, or will they meekly back away? That knowledge could win you a big pot later.

All this information is right there at the table, and it's free. When you're out of a hand, which will be most of the time, keep busy by observing and remembering. You never know which hand will teach you something that will save your neck later, so try to watch all of them.

Here's another tip for those just starting out. As you begin reading players and noticing their patterns, you'll find that some are much easier to read than others. After a few hours, you'll feel very pleased with yourself, as you become skilled at getting inside their heads and predicting their hands from their actions. But then you'll notice something very discouraging. Just as you've learned their habits inside and out, *poof!* — they're gone! Everyone else was learning to read them too, you see.

Example No. 1. Reading other players well is often a matter of blending physical tells with betting pattern tells, then making reasonable deductions to fill in the blanks. Here's a real-life hand that illustrates the whole process in action.

Discussion: I was playing in a major tournament in 2003, and we were a few hours into the opening day's play when the following hand occurred. I was in the big blind, and had a stack of $10,200 once I had posted the blind. We had all started with $10,000, so I wasn't doing particularly well. The blinds were $100/$200, and there weren't any antes.

The first player to act called the blind bet. I had two tells on this player that told me he had a marginal hand. The first tell came from his betting patterns. In the first two hours of play, he would raise in early position with any kind of strength, but would call with marginal hands. He never showed down a big hand after calling. This was a good tell in and of itself, but I had a second tell from his hand motion. When betting with a strong hand, he made a slightly different motion with his hands than when betting with a weak hand. The combination of the two tells made me 90 percent certain that he was on a marginal hand.

After the first player acted, four other players around the table called the bet. Although I didn't have tells on all these players, I wasn't really worried about them. In all likelihood, they were players with drawing hands who were attracted by the growingly favorable pot odds. (Remember that each new limper increases the pot, but not the bet, hence improving the pot odds for the next potential limper.) Almost no player, even the most inexperienced, would be foolish enough to limp into a pot against several players with a high pair (unless they were expecting a raise behind them). The right play is to raise and drive some of the players out, and that's a move that almost everyone understands.

When the action came around to me, the pot was up to $1,300. My hand was

Not a powerhouse hand, but not hopelessly weak either. If I didn't have any read on the first player to bet, I might have been inclined to just check the hand and see what happened on the flop. But knowing that the first player was weak gave me the edge I needed to make a good bet. Each player behind him in line had progressively more incentive to bet a strong hand, so they represented less and less of a threat. According, I stuck in a $2,000 raise.

There are players, particularly of the super-aggressive breed, who would make this move with any two cards, feeling that the chance of winning the pot outright more than compensates for the poor position they'll be in when someone calls. My approach is a little different. I want to have some kind of a hand, in case I get called or raised and have to play the hand down. King-jack suited meets my minimum requirements for this situation, so I was comfortable making my move.

As expected, the first player folded, as did the second, third, and fourth player in line. The only problem came from the button, who went all-in. He had me covered (his stack was bigger than mine) so his raise was the size of my remaining stack, which was $8,200. So the total pot at this point was $14,000. ($300 from the blinds, plus $1,500 from the five calls, plus my $2,000 bet, plus his $2,000 call plus his $8,200 raise = $14,000.) I needed to shove in my last $8,200 to win the $14,000 that's out there, which were odds of about 7-to-4.

I did have some information about the player on the button. He had gone all-in before in several situations where he might have been bluffing, and in each case the other player had laid down his hand. I'd also seen him make normal bets, showing down reasonable hands when called. Since you only get so many reasonable hands over the course of a few hours, it was certainly possible that this all-in bet was a move of his rather than a legitimate bet. I also noticed that he started to move his cards to the center of the table as the hand developed, then pulled his cards back as he saw everyone folding in front of him. That's the sort of involuntary nervous mistake that indicates a player expected others to move in, but now realizes he might be able to steal a pot.

I reasoned that I was probably facing one of three hands:

1. Ace-x.

2. A small pair.

3. A total bluff (two cards lower than mine).

I was unlikely to be facing a high pair, since those hands had a mandatory raise before the flop. If I was up against ace-x, I was about a 6-to-5 underdog in the hand (unless x was a king, queen, or jack). If I was up against a small pair, I was about a 11-to-10 underdog. And against a sheer bluff, I was about a 2-to-1 favorite. In each of these cases, the pot was offering me better odds than I needed to call, so I called.

My opponent showed

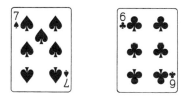

so my read on his move was correct. I had a nervous moment when the flop came

but I caught a King on the river to stay alive in the tournament.

Example Hand No. 2. My next example shows a hand with three players in action, all observing each other. Notice how each player needs to see the table through the eyes of the other players in order to draw the right conclusions.

Discussion: You're observing a major tournament, late in the first day. At the table you're watching the blinds are $600 and $1,200, with antes of $75. The total pot before any betting contains $2,550. The stacks at the table range from $6,000 to $29,000, with most in the middle of that range.

The first two players fold. Player A, third to act, has the small stack of $6,000. From your observations so far, A is a strong, solid player who's suffered a couple of bad beats. With the big blind at $1,200, he makes the minimum raise, putting in $2,400. The pot now contains $4,950. The next two players fold.

Player B, the sixth player to act, holds

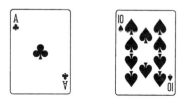

How should he think about what has happened at the table so far, and what should he do?

Before B looks at his hand, he should think about Player A's move. *How did the table look to Player A, and why did he do what he did?* A had only $6,000 left, just 2.5 times the pot. He had only a couple of rounds left before he's blinded away. With any kind of reasonable hand, Player A could easily have justified shoving all his chips in the pot and rolling the dice. But he didn't. Instead he made the minimum raise. That's what a player does when he wants others in the pot against him. He wants to make sure he gets some action before he gets all his own chips in. Conclusion? Player A has a very strong hand.

Now Player B can look at his own hand and see what he thinks. Ace-ten offsuit is a very borderline hand. You'd fold it in early position at a full table. If everyone had folded around to Player B in sixth position, it would be a very reasonable opening hand in middle position. But if you've deduced that Player A opened with a very strong hand, you've got to let A♣T♠ go. Player B, if he's bcen observant, will fold.

But Player B hasn't been observant, and he doesn't fold. Instead he raises, shoving in $5,000. The next player and the button both fold, as does the small blind.

Now the hand comes to Player C in the big blind, who has $11,000, and who has played very well throughout the tournament. He goes all-in! What do we think of his hand? Is he bluffing?

Again, let's stand behind Player C and see what he sees. Player A made a bet which indicated a very strong hand. We know Player B was asleep at the switch and didn't notice, but Player C can't know that. So Player C sees Player B toss in a reraise which must also indicate a strong hand. Player C now goes all-in with his $11,000, a move which will certainly be called by Player A with his limited chip count, and probably by Player B, who will have excellent pot odds. There's no chance that Player C will steal the pot with this all-in move, so his hand must be strong indeed.

Player A now in fact calls, moving in the remainder of his $3,600. (Just what we expected from his previous bet.) The action comes to Player B. Should he call?

At this point, we're done with the job of reading the table. An alert Player B will now know about all he can from pure observation. He's up against two very strong hands. Now we move into the realm of pot-odds analysis.

Player B, at this point, might have noticed his previous error and be regretting his decision to get in the pot in the first place. Far too often, this feeling will lead a player to fold a hand which has suddenly become playable by virtue of the huge pot odds that have been created. Don't ever fall into this trap. *If the pot odds are good enough, any hand might be worth a call.* We'll be discussing the theory of pot odds in the next chapter, so we'll run through the calculations quickly.

First we have to calculate the pot. The starting pot was $2,550. Player A has contributed his whole stack of $6,000, Player B has put in $5,000 so far, and Player C has moved in $11,000. That makes a grand total of $24,550, and it costs Player B another $6,000 to call, so the pot is offering him a shade better than 4-to-1. Those are huge odds. Against a single opponent, you might call even if you thought it was likely you were up against a big pair.

With two other players in the pot, however, your situation changes dramatically. Although you would almost never fold against a single opponent when looking at 4-to-1 pot odds, that's no longer the case against two players. Let's look at some possible holdings and see how the A♣T♠ is really doing.

If either Player A or Player C holds aces, Player B is just about dead. Against aces and queens, for example, Player B is 6 percent to win, or more than a 15-to-1 underdog. Even against a single ace, Player B doesn't have nearly the odds he needs. Against a combination of ace-king suited and queens, he's only 9 percent to win. In the unlikely event that one player is betting a pair lower than his ten, say a pair of nines, Player B gets just about the odds he needs. Against ace-king suited and nines he's 18 percent, just a 4.5-to-1 underdog.

If there's no other ace out there, Player B has some real chances. Against kings and queens, for instance, he's 24 percent, only about a 3-to-1 underdog. (His ace actually makes him second-best in this situation; the queens are just 19 percent.) But there aren't many hand combinations that fit this category. The betting made a holding like king-queen suited almost impossible for the situation. He might be up against kings and queens, or kings and jacks, or even queens and jacks, but that's about all.

On balance, Player B should fold. Even 4-to-1 pot odds aren't enough if an ace is out against him, and there aren't enough strong hands lacking an ace to balance out the odds. In fact, Player B called. Player A showed down

and Player C had

The Queens held up to win the hand.

Observing Yourself

While you're carefully observing the other players at your table, noting how many hands they play, what hands they show down, what their betting patterns look like, and any other information you can glean, make sure you pay attention to the most important player at the table — *yourself.*

Player X, sitting at your right, might only be involved in 10 percent of the hands you decide to play. But you're going to be involved in 100 percent of the hands you play, and what your opponents do in those hands will be partially determined by how they see you play. (The better they are, the more their play will be guided by your play.) So keep asking yourself these questions:

1.   How many hands have I been playing?

2.   What hands have I actually shown down?

3.   What would a keen observer think about me at this point?

Just because you're trying consciously to play in a certain style doesn't mean that you'll be perceived that way. The perception around the table may be quite different. Let's look at several hands where the key is understanding how the table perceives *you*, rather than how you perceive the table.

Example No. 1: It's the first table of your first major tournament. You've decided to start off playing a tight, conservative game, then gradually loosen up, building on your conservative image to steal a few pots as the blinds get larger. (A perfectly reasonable approach, so reasonable that most of the newcomers will be playing exactly the same way.) In the first 15 hands you have a huge run of cards — a pair of kings,

a pair of queens, and a couple of ace-kings. You lead out and bet these hands, catch some good flops, and win all four hands. In no case did you show a hand down. At the end of the first 15 hands, you've doubled your chip count.

Discussion: Now what? From your point of view, you've done nothing but play your normal, tight game. It's not your fault you had a great run of cards. But from the point of view of everyone else, you're a wild and crazy guy who's been bullying the table unmercifully. They haven't seen a single hand; they just know you seem to be in every other pot, raising and reraising.

If you stick to your original strategy and now try to loosen your playing requirements, it won't work. You'll start playing weaker hands just as your opponents have figured out that you have to be stopped. When you make a move with your suited connectors, the guy behind you will put you all-in with any reasonable hand. You might have started off playing tight, but your table image became loose. Go with it. The right move now is to continue to play tightly, maybe even more tightly than before, because your good hands will get paid off.

Example No. 2: You're a well-known super-aggressive player, quite willing to play any two cards to steal a pot. You're at the final table of six players, in the big blind. You pick up

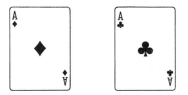

The first four players all fold. The small blind (an aggressive player himself, and one who knows you well) makes a modest raise. *What should you do?*

Discussion: Although I don't normally recommend slowplaying high pairs, this is a situation in which you could reasonably consider doing just that. You have only one opponent, he's making a move which may be a blatant steal, and if you just call, he might catch enough of a hand to lose more money to you after the flop.

That approach might work for a lot of players, but not for you. The essence of a good trap is to make a play *which looks routine for you*, and lull your opponent to sleep. If you have a super-aggressive table image, a call in this position won't look routine at all. A *reraise* would look routine. Players are used to seeing you raising all over, with all sorts of hands. Here's a spot where a reraise might just win the pot right here, and you're not reraising? What does that mean? When players get suspicious, you can't trap them. So just make your usual raise, and see what happens.

Example No. 3: It's relatively early in a major tournament. You have $23,000. The other chip stacks at your table vary from $5,000 to $28,000. The big blind has $19,000. The blinds are $300/$600, with antes of $25, so the pot starts with $1,150 each hand.

Over the last hour, you've been playing aggressively. You came into the pot with a $2,000 raise on four occasions, and each time you've taken down the pot uncontested. Each time you had a hand which, while not hopeless, was not a premium hand: 44, A5, K-J, etc. Now, in fifth position at a full table, you pick up

the best hand you've seen in awhile. **The first four players fold. You make your standard $2,000 raise.** Everyone folds to **the big blind, who goes all-in with his $19,000. If you call him and lose, you'll be reduced to just $4,000.** *What do you do?*

Discussion: If there were no history attached to this problem, you'd probably fold the tens. You made a bet of three times the big blind, you were reraised all-in, and now you'd be asking yourself "What kind of hand could make that move?" You're probably facing a high pair or two high cards, and while you're a slight favorite against the high cards, you're a substantial underdog against the higher pairs. You might be up against a bluff, but it's not likely enough to make you risk essentially all your chips. That's how you'd reason in the absence of any other information.

Once you know how the hand came about, however, your reasoning should change dramatically. The big blind has watched you steal four hands recently, and now you're on your way to stealing a fifth hand. No one else at the table has been standing up to you, so perhaps he's decided it's time to play sheriff. When a player thinks you're pushing the table around and wants to put a stop to it, he'll take any two reasonable cards and come over the top with them.

Note as well that an oversized raise is more likely to indicate a hand that doesn't want a call. Players with made hands are more likely to want you in the pot against them.

What does this mean? Simply that you can't assume any longer that his potential mix of hands consists of just high pairs and high cards. It's now a much broader group of hands, including low pairs, suited connectors, ace-x, and perhaps a few others. You're now either a small favorite or a large favorite against most of the hands he might show, and only an underdog against the high pairs. Because of the image you've created at the table, you're now compelled to call his bet.

Example No. 4: Let's say for argument's sake that you decided to fold, rather than call, that bet. Now it's exactly one round later at the same table. Once again you're fifth to act. Between your loss in that hand and a round of blinds and antes, your chip stack is down to $20,000. The other players are in roughly the same positions as before.

You have

The first four players fold to you. You once again raise to $2,000. The three players in back of you fold, but the small blind, with $18,000 chips in his stack and a history of making aggressive raises and reraises, reraises you to $5,000. The big blind folds. *What do you do?*

Discussion: Again, in the abstract this looks like a very strong bet. You raised triple the big blind, and a big reraise came from a player out of position. But now let's look at the table as the small blind sees it. He's seen you steal several pots over a short period of time. (Of course, he doesn't really *know* you stole them — you might have been betting with solid values. But it looks like you stole them, which is all that really matters.) A few turns ago, he saw you try to steal, then fold when the big blind came over the top. Now here you are again, probably trying to steal once more.

What kind of hand might he have? Under these circumstances, he could hold almost anything. Your A♠Q♥ might even be the best hand right now! I don't think you should fold, and I wouldn't even call. Instead, I'd reraise! Since any significant reraise would commit at least half your chips to the pot, you should just go all-in and see what happens. Most of the time, your opponent will throw his hand away. If he does call, you can still win the showdown.

All the decisions in this hand stem from the table images of both you and the small blind. If you had been presenting a solid, tight image, playing few hands, and the small blind had a similar image, you would have to throw away your A♠Q♥. Your bet would be interpreted as representing a hand at least as strong as what you have, and his raise indicates a better hand than that with a high degree of certainty. Under those circumstances, you would quietly beat a retreat.

If you do decide to fold in this position, you must be aware that your strategy for this table has to change dramatically. Your opponents have now seen you steal a few pots, then run and hide once someone steps up and reraises you. The next couple of times you get in a pot, you can be pretty sure you'll get action. So switch immediately to a conservative style, and make sure that when you open with a hand you're prepared to play a big pot. You won't be stealing any more cheap pots for awhile, but you may get some good chances to double up.

The Problems

Observing players is a key skill at the poker table. Problem 3-1 is an example of the observation process in action in what is otherwise a trivial hand.

The do's and don'ts of trying to steal hands based on what you have seen so far are covered in Problems 3-2 and 3-3.

Problem 3-4 is an example showing the importance of watching yourself.

Problem 3-5 shows the perils of not paying attention to the other players and their characteristics.

Hand 3-1

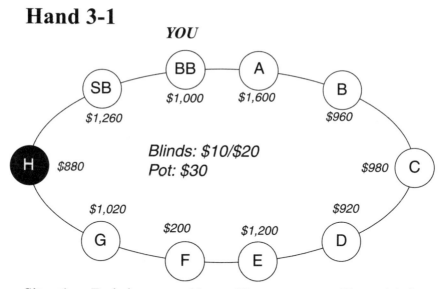

YOU

SB $1,260
BB $1,000
A $1,600
B $960
H $880
Blinds: $10/$20
Pot: $30
C $980
D $920
G $1,020
F $200
E $1,200

Situation: Early in a one-table satellite tournament. Player A is in a lot of pots. Two hands ago, Player A limped in and then called a small raise of twice the big blind. Player E has only played one pot, which he won.

Your hand: K♥7♥

Action to you: Player A and Player B both call $20. Players C and D fold. Player E raises to $80. Players F, G, H, and the small blind all fold.

Question: *Do you fold, call, or raise?*

Answer: You fold, of course. King-seven is a weak hand, suited or unsuited, and you're in bad position facing a guy who put in a big raise. Get out.

Action: You fold. Players A and B both fold. Player E rakes in the pot.

Question: *What is the significance of this hand? What did you learn?*

Answer: To the casual player, nothing really happened this hand. A couple of players called, one player stuck in a big raise, and everybody folded. Yawn.

A serious player would have learned something valuable, however. Player A, the player directly to my left, had previously limped in, then called a modest raise. Here, he limped in, then folded a raise of four times the big blind. He plays a lot of pots, so I know he's got to be limping in with a lot of weak hands. If this situation comes up again, and there hasn't been a big raise, I know I can probably steal the pot from him with a bigger than average raise.

Ask a casual player what separates him from the top players, and he'll probably have trouble giving you a good answer. Some think good players are just innately lucky. Others think they are just better bluffers. Still others think they can read your cards by dissecting every tick and twitch of your expression.

The truth is that good players are really good at remembering everything that goes on around the table, and making use of the information in a logical fashion. I've just made a mental note about a tendency that Player A seems to have. Player A is especially important to me because he's the player directly to my left. All my steal attempts have to go right through him, so I need to know as much as I can about how he behaves. Will this information help me steal a pot later on? Maybe.

Isn't that a lot of work and effort just for a better chance of perhaps stealing a pot or two down the road? Yes, it is. And that's the heart of good poker. Keep making these little mental notes, and after a couple of hours you'll know a lot about the players at your table. and your results will improve significantly.

Hand 3-2

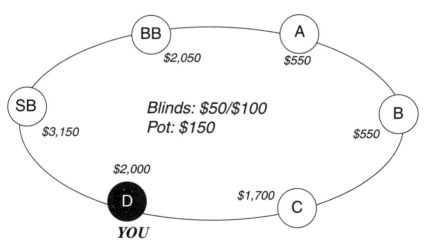

Situation: A single-table satellite for a major tournament. Four players have been eliminated, and we are down to the last six. The small and big blinds are loose, aggressive players who like to play a lot of pots. Players A and C seem very tight, with B about average.

Your hand: Q♠4♠

Action to you: Players A, B, and C all fold.

Question: *Do you fold, call, or raise?*

Answer: Many players who learned their poker from watching television think that you can steal a pot pretty much anytime you want, just by tossing in some chips and chuckling as the other players get out of the way. In the real world, it's not quite that easy. You need to pick your spots, find good situations, vary your betting patterns, and not overdo it.

In this hand, if I had no other information on my opponents, I'd simply let the hand go. When I steal, I like to have some kind of a hand to back it up. Even a hand like ten-nine unsuited has some straight possibilities working for it, so if I were in a position to steal, I might make a move with that hand. Q♠4♠ has a flush possibility, of course, but without the king or ace of the suit in my hand, there's also the possibility that I could make a flush and lose all my chips.

If I knew that the players behind me were tight, and I'd seen them fold small raises in similar situations, then I would make a move here. I'd try to raise whatever amount I had seen them fold in the past. If a bet of twice the big blind had chased them out in the past, that's what I'd raise. If they were calling bets of twice the big blind, but folding three times the blind, then I'd put in $300 here. This is just another example of how important observation is, even in hands that don't directly involve you. The information is usually lying around the table; you just have to pick it up.

But here you do have some information — and it's not good. The two players behind you are loose and aggressive, and they like to play a lot of pots. They're exactly the sort of opponents you don't want to try to steal from! That's all you need to know to fold this weak hand, even on the button.

But in the actual hand, the button tried to steal this pot. Let's see what happened.

Action: The button bet $200. The small and big blinds both called, putting in $150 and $100, respectively. Pot now $600.

Flop: J♠J♣9♠

Action: The small blind bets $200, and the big blind calls. Pot now $1,000.

Question: *What's your play?*

    Answer: Bad news and good news. Both blinds called your feeble stealing attempt, but the flop gave you a flush draw. Now there's $1,000 in the pot and it costs you $200 to call.

    The first point to notice is that this was a very good flop for you, all things considered. If neither player held a jack, which is likely (there are only two Jacks left in the deck) then the flop probably missed them completely. Since neither player raised before the flop, there are probably no big pairs out there. And since they're known to be loose, aggressive players, the bet and call don't mean as much as they might.

    Time now to forget about stealing the pot and start calculating pot odds. A flush will most likely win the pot. The odds of drawing a flush on the next card are about 4-to-1 against, and if you can stay for both fourth and fifth street, the odds drop to about 2-to-1 against. There are other sequences that might affect the outcome — two running queens, or two running fours, or someone else holding a better flush draw — but they're unlikely, so just stay focused on the main chance. The pot is now offering you 5-to-1 odds, so you're justified in calling, even if you only get to see one card. Don't even think about some wacky reraise. There's no reason to believe you can chase out either of these guys, let alone both of them.

Action: You call $200. Fourth street is the 2♣. The small blind bets another $200 and the big blind calls. Pot now $1,600.

Question: *What's your play?*

    Answer: You're 4-to-1 against getting the flush on the last card, and the pot is offering 8-to-1. Easy call, even given the possibility that your flush is no good.

Action: You call $200. Pot now $1,800. Fifth street is the J♥, putting three Jacks on the board. The two players in front of you both check.

Question: *What's your play?*

    Answer: Check, and be prepared to muck your hand when someone shows you an ace or a king. Betting is a waste of time and just puts more chips in jeopardy.

Resolution: You check, and the first two players show you K♦7♦ and K♣T♠, respectively. K♣T♠ wins the pot.

The button lost $600 on this hand, a just penalty for not observing the action more closely on previous rounds. Both his opponents were loose enough to call all the way down to the end with nothing but a king high. There's no way they could have kept those tendencies a secret through the first half of the tournament.

Hand 3-3

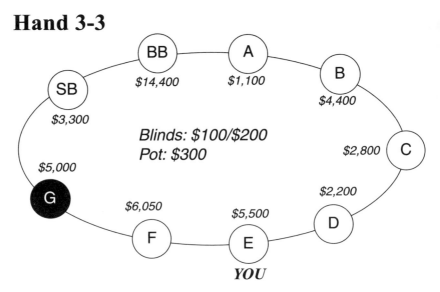

Situation: Major tournament, late in the first day. You have won two of the last three pots without showing down your hand. Player F is very aggressive and likes to come over the top. Player G, on the button, is also an active player. The big blind is an unknown quantity who has just joined the table.

Your hand: 8♠7♠

Action to you: Players A, B, C, and D all fold.

Question: *What do you do?*

    Answer: Suited connectors are a flexible holding, and under the right circumstances I might raise, call, or fold with this hand. Let's try to read the table here and see what you ought to do.

1.   Four folds to you. That's an argument for raising. If several limpers had come in, and you were in late position, you might be inclined to just call, see a cheap flop, and hope to flop a real monster. But here four of

the nine players are already out of the hand, so a modest raise might just take the pot, and your hand could still win if you are called.

2. Your suited connectors are relatively low. Eight-seven isn't nearly as exciting a holding as jack-ten or even ten-nine. That's an argument for folding.

3. You won a couple of recent hands, *without showing your cards*. That's an argument for folding. When you win hands by showing strong cards, players get intimidated. "I've got to stay away from that guy, he's just playing the nuts." But when you win hands without a showdown, they get curious. "Does he really have anything? I'd better call him and see. I can't be pushed around." Here, you'd be happy to raise and win an uncontested pot. But your recent couple of wins make that less likely.

4. There are active players behind you. That argues strongly for a fold. Ideally, you'd like to raise here with passive, tight players yet to act, for the obvious reasons. But here, the two guys right behind you have big stacks and like to play, while the last player to act, the big blind, is both unknown and one of the chip leaders in the tournament. This situation is very unpromising.

The weight of the evidence says "fold." So you do.

Hand 3-4

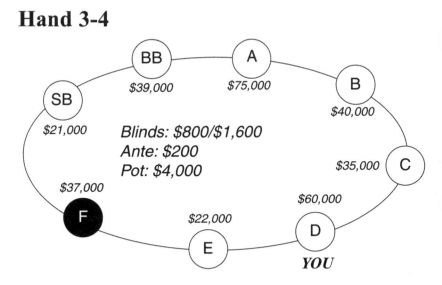

Situation: Major tournament, down to the last three tables, 28 players left. The table has been generally tight. You've been playing more aggressively than most. Player F has been a solid, tight player.

Your hand: Q♠Q♦

Action to you: Players A, B, and C all fold.

Question: *Do you raise, and if so, how much?*
> **Answer:** The standard raise with this hand is three to four times the big blind. You don't want drawing hands to come in cheaply, but unlike the case with jacks or tens, your hand is strong enough so that you don't want to discourage action entirely. Here $4,000 seems like a nice even number to raise.

Action: You raise to $4,000. Player E folds. Player F raises to $10,000. The blinds fold. The pot is now $18,000. It costs you $6,000 to call.

Question: *What do you do?*

Answer: Your first job is to figure out what this bet might mean. Your second job will be to decide if you want to put him all-in or not.

You can never tell, from a player's bet before the flop, exactly what he has. The best you can do is put him on a set of possible hands, then decide how you like your chances against each hand in the set. From that analysis you should be able to get a sense of what the right play is. Be very skeptical of players who claim they can look into their opponent's soul and do better than that. They're just messing with your head.

So what hands might he hold here? The first possibility, obviously, is aces or kings. If he holds those hands, you're a 4.5-to-1 underdog, and very unhappy.

The next possibility is ace-king. (Ace-queen is less likely since you hold two of the queens and he probably won't play ace-queen this way.) Here you're a slight favorite. On a strict probabilistic calculation, there are more ace-king combinations than pairs of aces or pairs of kings combined. (There are 16 ways to deal an ace-king from the deck, against just six possible ace-ace pairs and six possible king-king pairs. Ace-queen in this scenario has eight combinations but again is not something he would reraise with. Ace-queen suited has only two combinations here.)

The third possibility is a medium pair, say jacks though eights or even sevens. Here you have to consider both how likely these hands are, and how likely it is that he chose to raise with these hands. With aces or kings, he would almost certainly elect to raise. With pairs of jacks or tens, it's possible, but not at all certain, that he would have stuck in a raise. It's a little more likely than usual because you've been the aggressive player at the table. He might have decided that your initial raise was a bluff, and these were good hands for making a stand. (It's important to remember that in addition to noting how your opponents are playing at the table, you must also note how you appear to them. Sometimes that will provide a clue to interpreting their bets. If you've been giving action, lots of players will take any pair and come after you.)

The last possibility is that Player F holds some hand other than any of these. It's not likely, but it's by no means impossible. When stacks begin to get short in relation to the blinds, players will start making plays, and you have to factor this in. In your poker career, you'll end up many times agonizing over whether to call a tough-looking bet, only to find that your opponent had absolutely nothing! This case may not be very likely here, but you should give it some probability, perhaps about 10 percent.

Overall, it looks to me like you're a solid favorite here. You're a big dog against the two overpairs, and a big favorite against any underpair. There are many more possible underpairs than overpairs, so it's as much as 2.5- or 3-to-1 that he's actually holding an underpair. You're a small favorite against ace-king, and a big favorite against any random bluff.

Having reasoned that out, you should next look at the money odds, which turn out to be excellent. Right now there's $18,000 in the pot, and your opponent has $27,000 left. If you put him all-in and he calls, you'd be risking $27,000 of your own money to try and win $45,000 (the $18,000 currently in the pot plus the $27,000 he will have to put in to call). Those are great odds in a situation where you think you're a solid favorite. You won't be in good shape if you lose, but these kinds of decisions are the kind that win tournaments.

So go all-in.

Resolution: You put him all-in, and he calls and shows K♠K♣. The flop comes 8♠7♠3♠. Fourth and fifth street are the J♠ and the 4♣. His king-high flush beats your queen-high flush.

Note that you were destined to lose a lot of your money on this hand. Had you not put him all-in before the flop but just called, the flush draw would have forced you to put him all-in after the flop.

Hand 3-5

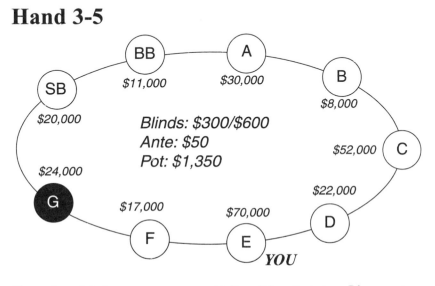

Situation; Major tournament, middle of the first day. Players A and C are pros who are both very aggressive and play many pots. Each is capable of bluffing deep into the hand. You are playing in your first major tournament, having just won an internet qualifier.

Your hand: K♣K♦

Action to you: Player A raises, putting in $3,000. Player B folds. Player C calls. Player D folds. The pot is now $7,350.

Question: *Do you call or raise?*

> **Answer:** You have to raise with your kings. Some players, especially newcomers, get carried away and decide to start trapping with kings. You might try this for variety against a single opponent, but it's too dangerous against multiple

opponents. The danger, of course, is that someone is calling with an ace and a small card, and if you let them stay in the pot cheaply, an ace on the flop will beat you. So raise here, and try to reduce the field to a single opponent.

Action: You raise, putting in $10,000. Players F and G and the blinds all fold. Player A folds. Player C calls. The pot is now $24,350.

Flop: 9♦7♠2♣

Action: Player C bets $12,000. *What do you do?*
> **Answer:** That was an excellent flop: three low cards in three different suits, with very remote straight possibilities. Your opponent is known to be aggressive. Here he appears to be making a standard continuation bet of half the pot. We'll discuss continuation bets more in Part Six; for now, just note that it's a post-flop bet designed to win the pot for the early leader who may not have improved.
>
> While you almost certainly have the best hand right now, you shouldn't automatically raise. That would be a good play against a tight player, but here you have position on an aggressive player with an excellent hand, and a better strategy is to bring out the feared Rope-a-Dope and just let him try to take the pot from you. A simple call is the right idea. You might want to spend a little time thinking about the call, just for some extra dramatic effect.

Action: You call. The pot is now $48,350.

Fourth Street: 3♠

Action: Player C bets $15,000. The pot is now $63,350. You have $48,000 left. Player C (after his bet) has $15,000 left. *What do you do?*

Answer: The fourth street card certainly didn't scare you, although it's possible that your opponent now has some straight or flush draws.

You should now put your opponent all-in. Some players get greedy here and just call, with the idea that they will bet on the river and collect all the rest of the chips when their opponent thinks they're pulling a desperation steal. I don't like that approach for two reasons:

1. Player C probably has something, and you'd be giving him a free chance to beat you.

2. If Player C is on a draw, he still has hope now. If he misses the draw on the river, all hope is gone, and he will fold.

Action: You actually just call. The pot is now $78,350.

Fifth Street: 5♥

Action: Player C checks. *What do you do?*

Answer: If Player C was going for a flush, his chance just evaporated. There's a remote chance that you're beaten by a low straight or a fluke set, but you don't have enough time in tournaments to worry about these things. You must accumulate chips and knock players out, and this looks like a good chance to do both. Put him all-in. If he's been nursing a small pair, he may call because the pot odds are very good and his stack is too weak if he folds.

Action: You actually check, and Player C shows a pair of eights. You take the pot.

Player C cost himself a lot of money when he made an elementary blunder before the flop. His original call of Player A's raise was fine; A was aggressive and might have had anything. But when a novice puts in a big reraise against two pros, you have to take it very seriously. He's not bluffing. That was the time for Player C to get out with his stack intact. A pro making that big reraise might have been attempting a squeeze play, and if you'd seen him make that move before, you might want to call. But a reraise from a novice indicates nothing but strength, and you can be very sure that your eights are beaten.

Part Four

Pot Odds and Hand Analysis

Pot Odds and Hand Analysis

Introduction

All successful gambling is based on one simple idea: making good bets at favorable odds. Assessing whether a bet is good or not involves knowing two key facts:

1.   What are the odds against your winning the bet?

2.   What are the payoff odds if you win?

When the payoff odds are higher than the odds against your winning, you have a good bet. Over time, if you kept making the same bet, you would win money, although the fluctuations might be severe. When the payoff odds are lower than the odds against your winning, you have a bad bet. In time, if you keep making such bets, you will lose money.

As a simple example, suppose that someone offered to wager on the roll of a single fair die. You're willing to bet $1 that you can roll a six. He bets $6 that you can't. You eagerly take the bet, because it's slightly favorable for you. There are six possible outcomes, one which wins for you and five which lose. The odds against your winning are 5-to-1. But your payoff odds are 6-to-1. Since the payoff odds are higher, the bet is profitable for you. (In six average trials, you will lose $1 five times and win $6 once, for a net profit of $1, or almost 17 cents per trial.)

When you walk into a casino, you are confronted with an avalanche of possible bets, almost all of which are unfavorable. Although most people who frequent casinos are aware that they are betting against the odds, only a few really understand what that means. Casual players mostly imagine that they lose when they place a bet and it doesn't win, or that the games don't let them win often enough. Actually, that's not the case. If you bet on the number 22 on a roulette wheel, the number will hit, in the long run, exactly as often as it's supposed to (one time in 38), and when the number doesn't hit, the casino is perfectly fair — it takes all your money, just as it's supposed to. In fact, in a sense *you lose only when you win*. When number 22 actually hits, the casino pays you less than required for an even-money bet — 35-to-1 instead of the even-money odds of 37-to-1. It's these tiny taxes on the winning bets that provide the casino with all its gambling profits.

When you walk through a casino into the poker room and sit down at a no-limit hold 'em tournament, the picture changes a bit. As the tournament goes on, you'll be confronted with a long string of possible bets. The good news is that some will be favorable and some will be unfavorable, but you get to skip the unfavorable ones and concentrate on the favorable ones. The bad news is that it won't be obvious at first which is which. Figuring that out is up to you, but the information in this chapter will put you quite a bit ahead of most of the other players. Becoming a better player is really a matter of recognizing and making your favorable bets, while avoiding the unfavorable or break-even bets.

Analyzing a Poker Bet: The Two Parts

To figure out if a bet is a good one or not, you need to know the payoff when you win, and the odds against your winning. In poker, the payoff when you win is revealed by the pot odds. How much is in the pot, and how much does it cost you to play? The odds against your winning comes from an intelligent analysis of what's happened in the hand so far.

Neither part is easy, but both are doable and can be learned. Of the two, calculating or estimating the pot odds is simpler, so we'll start with that.

Pot Odds

If your opponent has put you all-in, or has made a bet which is the last significant bet of the hand, then the pot odds are easy to calculate. Just calculate or make your best estimate of what's in the pot, and compare it to the amount required to call. The result is your pot odds to call.

Example No. 1. The pot currently contains $900. You have $600 left, and are in the hand with one other player. The other player moves his last $1,000 to the center, putting you all-in. *What are your pot odds?*

    Answer: Since you only had $600 left, your opponent can only actually put $600 in the pot. The pot you're shooting at is therefore $1,500, and it costs you your last $600 to call. Your pot odds are therefore $1,500-to-600, or 2.5-to-1.

Example No. 2. It's fourth street, and the pot contains $1,000. You hold the

and the board is

Your opponent, whom you believe to have a high pair, bets $500. You both have more than $3,000 in your stacks. *What are the pot odds?*

    Answer: This hand looks similar to the last one, but contains a few more ideas. We can quickly see that after our opponent's bet, the pot will contain $1,500, and it will cost us $500 to call, so the pot odds are 1,500-to 500, or 3-to-1. But unlike the last example, this may not be the end of the betting for the hand. There could be another bet on fifth street. How does this effect our calculation?

Expressed Odds and Implied Odds

    The odds of 3-to-1 we calculated in the last example are the *expressed odds*, the odds that are currently being presented by the pot. Just as important, however, are the *implied odds*, the odds that will eventually be offered by the pot after all the betting is done.

    In many hands, the expressed odds will not justify a call, but the implied odds will. In our previous example, for instance, you are drawing at the nut club flush. If you hit that flush, and you have estimated your opponent's hand correctly, you will win. If you miss, you will lose. But if you miss, you won't have to invest any more money in the pot, whereas, if you hit, you may win some more money from your opponent. That's not certain, since the third flush card will be visible on the board, and your opponent may not want to call a large bet. Suppose you believe that he will fold a large bet on the end if the flush card hits, but he will probably call a smaller bet, say one of $500. In that case your implied odds for your call on fourth street would be the $1,500 currently in the pot, plus the extra $500 you could win on fifth street, measured against the $500 required to call, or $2,000-to-$500, which is just 4-to-1. That's about the odds of making your hand, so the call is reasonable (but wrong because he will not always call the bet). To be more precise in your calculation multiply the size of your intended bet by the probability he will call it. The resulting "expected value" of his call should then be added to the pot to get your implied odds. Obviously you should also use this method to determine how much to bet in the first place. Normally you should choose the bet with the higher expected value, though in a tournament you might choose a slightly smaller expected value to get a surer call.

In no-limit hold 'em it is often correct to accept slightly unfavorable expressed odds to draw at monster hands that can win all your opponent's chips on the river. This is even more true of potential straights than of potential flushes, since straights are easier to conceal.

Hand Analysis

Calculating pot odds is a simple enough business. Look at the pot, look at the chips required to call, and make some rough adjustments if there could be more action in the hand. Divide one by the other, and you have your pot odds.

If pot odds is mostly a science, hand analysis is mostly an art. Here you have to figure out what hands your opponent might be playing that would account for his bets so far, and then how likely each of those hands is, and then figure out how likely you are to beat each of those hands, given the hand you have. At the end of this process, you'll have a probability that you can win the hand. It will necessarily be a rough estimate, based in part on what you know about *this* opponent in *this* kind of situation. But it will give you a number to compare to the pot odds you already know, and in most cases, comparing those two numbers will yield a clear decision from a murky situation.

Before we can proceed with some real-life examples, we need a couple of technical details. Let's take a look at some probabilities of winning certain hand match-ups and the technique of calculating outs.

Some Standard Pre-Flop Winning Probabilities

In no-limit hold 'em, certain pre-flop winning probabilities arise so often that you need to commit them to memory. If your opponent puts you all-in before the flop, you need to know the likelihood that you can win with your current holding against the various card combinations he may hold. Here are the most common, along with their probabilities and the odds of winning or losing when the hand is played to the end.

1. **Higher pair versus lower pair**. The higher pair is about 82 percent to win, or about a 4.5-to-1 favorite. The most favorable situation for the higher pair is to be close in value to the lower pair. For instance, a pair of kings is a slightly bigger favorite against a pair of queens than against a pair of nines, because the kings interfere with some of the straights that would help the queens pull ahead. The presence of common suits also helps the higher pair slightly. In pair versus pair with two suits in common, the higher pair gains about 1.5 percent in comparison to pair versus pair with no suits in common.

2. **Pair versus two higher cards**. This is the basic "race" situation that you see so often in all-in showdowns in no-limit hold 'em. The pair is about a 55-to-45 favorite. The pair does slightly better if it's close in value to the high cards, by eliminating some straight possibilities. The presence of common suits also helps the pair. (Obviously the unpaired hand is helped slightly if it is suited or connected.)

3. **Pair versus two lower cards**. Interestingly, if the two lower cards are close together in value this is only slightly more favorable than high pair versus low pair. The increased chance to make two pair and the increased chance to make a straight largely compensate for the loss of trip possibilities. The higher pair is about a 5-to-1 favorite.

4. **Pair versus a higher and lower card**. The pair is about a 5-to-2 favorite. The chance of a straight drops since the pair is taking away two key cards, but there's about a 30 percent chance of just pairing the overcard which is mostly good enough to win.

5. **Two higher cards versus two lower cards**. The two higher cards are about a 5-to-3 favorite. This statistic always

surprises beginners, who when they see ace-king against something like eight-six imagine that the ace-king must be a huge favorite. But whoever makes a pair mostly wins, and the edge for the ace-king just comes when no one makes a pair or both make a pair.

Calculating Outs

If after the flop you believe that your hand needs to improve to win, you'll have to calculate your outs. An "out" is simply a card which, if it hits on fourth street or fifth street, will improve your hand to a winning hand. Calculating your outs will give you some idea of how big an underdog you are at the moment.

When you calculate outs, always keep in mind that it's an imperfect business at best. If your opponent is bluffing, your hand, weak as it is, may already be best. If your opponent is trapping with a full house or four of a kind, what you believe to be outs may only be cards that cost you your entire stack. But with those caveats aside, it's still very useful to have some idea of how many cards could give you a likely winning hand.

Example No. 1. You hold

and the flop is

Your opponent called before the flop but now bets strongly, and you suspect he has at least a pair. How many outs do you have?

Answer: Since there is no pair on board, your opponent cannot have a flush or a full house yet. So if you make a heart flush, you can be reasonably sure of winning. (You hold the ace, so even if your opponent is also drawing at a heart flush, you have the nut flush.) There are four hearts visible to you and nine others remaining in the deck. We'll count those nine hearts as nine full outs.

If your opponent has only a lower pair, then an ace or a king will also qualify as an out. But if he now has two pair or a set, then hitting an ace or a king won't help you. His most likely hand here is a pair of jacks, but he could have called your bet with jack-nine, a pair of nines, or a pair of fives. You can't count the three remaining aces and three remaining kings as six full outs; probably counting them as an average of four outs is most reasonable.

There are sequences of two running cards that could also help you. A queen and a ten on the next two cards gives you the highest possible straight. The chances of that are pretty small, however. Although there are four queens and four tens, two of them were counted already — the Q♥ and the T♥. So you would have to hit one of the six remaining cards on fourth street, followed by one of five cards on the river. That amounts at best to a fraction of an out.

So our best estimate of your total outs is about 13. With two cards to come, that makes you a slight underdog in the hand.[5]

Certain common situations arise so frequently that you should become familiar with them. Here's a small table of these situations and their associated number of outs.

Number of Outs	Drawing Hand
4 outs	Two pair needing a full house or an inside straight draw
6 outs	Two over cards needing to make a pair
8 outs	Open-ended straight draw
9 outs	Flush draw
11 outs	Flush draw plus a pair needing to improve to trips
12 outs	Flush draw plus an inside straight
14 outs	Flush draw plus a pair that needs to hit its kicker or make trips

A good rule of thumb to remember is that if you have 14 outs, *and you know you can see both the turn card and the river card,*

---

[5] *See Small Stakes Hold 'em: Winning Big with Expert Play* by Ed Miller, David Sklansky, and Mason Malmuth for a good explanation of how to estimate your total outs.

then you're about even money to win the hand (as long as you will almost always win when you hit). The only time you can know that, however, is when you're facing an all-in bet after the flop. Now a call will let you see the hand down to the end, so 14 outs will indeed make you about even money. But if you're facing a bet after the flop and both you and your opponent have plenty of money left, that assumption doesn't hold. In that case, missing your draw on fourth street may mean that you'll be facing a large bet which, with only one card left to come, you won't be able to call.

With those technical parts behind us, we're now ready to look at some real hands and see how all these ideas fit together in practice.

Example No. 2: It's the second day of the World Series of Poker. You've managed to double your $10,000 buy-in to $20,000. Your table has one player with a stack larger than yours, at $26,000. All the other stacks are between $5,000 and $15,000. The blinds are now $150/$300, with antes of $25, so the pot starts at $700.

You're under the gun and you pick up

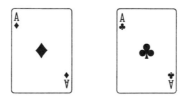

You elect to raise four times the big blind, putting in $1,200. Three players fold behind you. The player in fifth position, with the big stack, calls. All other players fold. The flop comes

of three different suits. You bet $3,000 with your aces. Your opponent puts you all-in. Up until now he has appeared to be an experienced solid, conservative player. Your table image is also that of a solid, conservative player. *Should you call or fold?*

Answer: The big mistake that most players make in this situation is not calling or folding, but calling or folding *quickly*. Their nerves fail them, and they say either "He's got trip nines — I'm beaten" or "Nobody bluffs me off of aces — I'm calling". Here's a better thing to say: "I've invested $10,000 and several days of my time in this tournament — I can afford to spend a few minutes and think this through."

So let's think this through together. As we know by now, our first job is to calculate the pot odds. Before your opponent raised, the pot contained $700 from the blinds and antes, plus $2,400 from the first round of betting, plus the $3,000 from your post-flop bet, for a total of $6,100. You've put in $4,200 so far, so your stack is down to $15,800. Your opponent called your $3,000 bet and raised you the rest of your stack, so he just put in $18,800, making the pot now $24,900. It costs you $15,800 to call that pot, so the pot is offering you odds of about 25-to-16, or just a little better than 3-to-2.

Those are pretty good odds. If you make a lot of bets with 3-to-2 odds in your favor, you only have to win 40 percent of them to break even. Win more than that, and you'll show a nice profit. But can you win more than that? Now we start the tough part, which is analyzing the actual hand.

There are only two hands your opponent can hold that scare you: a pair of nines and a pair of fives. (Very few players would make the mistake of calling a bet from an early raiser before the flop with a pair of deuces.) If he has one of those hands, he's now got a set and you're a huge underdog — about 10 percent winning chances with two cards to come.

If he made his raise with any other hand, you're a huge favorite. If he shoved his chips in with kings, queens, jacks, or tens, you're about a 92 percent favorite with two cards to come. If he's on a complete bluff with a hand like king-queen, then you're about 97 percent to win.

Now comes the really tough part. What is the likelihood of each of these possible hands? (Trips, smaller high pair, and bluff.) The common mistake that most players make is to try and figure out exactly what hand their opponents are holding, then make the play that suits that hand. If they decide he's holding trips, then they fold. If they decide he's bluffing, then they call. But can you ever "know" what he's holding? In my experience, the answer to that question is almost always "No." What you can do, with much greater reliability, is to make some educated guesses as to what hands he might be holding and the probability of each hand, then compare those guesses to the pot odds, and see if a clear decision emerges. In many cases, it will.

Let's start our guessing with the easy part. What's the probability that he's bluffing? I'm going to give you a good rule, which I've found works very well in real life. Call it *Harrington's Law:*

Harrington's Law of Bluffing: The probability that your opponent is bluffing when he shoves a big bet in the pot is always *at least 10 percent.*

At least 10 percent! It may be higher, depending on the opponent, but it won't be lower. Why not? Because people bluff.

They know they're supposed to bluff, they like the thrill of pulling off an outrageous bluff, so sometimes they do bluff. You've seen it happen all the time on television, and it will happen in your hands as well.

If you've pegged a player as "conservative," don't make the mistake of thinking that he can't be bluffing you when he shoves his chips in the pot. Bluffing is a big weapon for the conservative player, because it's so unexpected. Conservative players know that their bluffs will almost never be called because of their table image, so when they do make a bluff, they know they're making a very high-percentage play.

Poker players are very susceptible to a kind of error that affects everyone in real life: confusing perception with reality. When we meet someone initially, we form a first impression based upon a few clues from their mannerisms and behavior. Our first impression is composed of some useful adjectives that describe them in bold strokes: "reserved," "arrogant," "perceptive," "clumsy." These adjectives then guide our own responses. As we get to know the person better, we have time to take in much more information and we modify our perceptions, in many cases dramatically. For example, what we initially saw as "aloofness," we might later come to recognize as just a certain reserve in meeting new people. Over time, our opinions of others become much more subtle and nuanced. In real life, this process of forming initial gross impressions which are then transformed as more data become available serves us very well.

But at the poker table, this sensible real-life process breaks down. We're now confronted with people who are actively trying to mislead us, denying us the cues we need to modify our initial impressions. As a result, the adjectives we apply to describe their behavior tend to assume a weight that they don't really merit. Remember that words like "conservative" or "aggressive" are only adjectives, and the real person sitting opposite you may be a vastly more subtle and dangerous opponent. When you assume a player isn't bluffing because he's played conservatively up to now, you've fallen in love with the adjective and ignored the reality. Avoid this error!

What you should do when you think a player is conservative is to assign him a relatively low bluffing probability in your estimates for the hand. In this example, we'll give him the minimum bluffing probability, 10 percent.

We've still got 90 percent of our probability distribution to hand out to our two main categories of hands: The trips which are beating us badly, and the high pairs which we can beat. Just how we allot the remaining 90 percent is a tough judgment call, one of the toughest in poker.

Let's start by assuming he has trips, either nines or fives. In that case he's a huge favorite in the hand *and he knows it*. So why is he going all-in? Most good players would be worrying (correctly) about how to milk the hand for the biggest possible win. Shoving all your chips in will chase away most hands, while just calling will set up a bet on fourth or fifth street that should win at least a few more chips. Is this a nervous move by an inexperienced player? Up to now he's seemed to be experienced and solid. Can he know that we're going to call his all-in with a high pair? It's hard to believe he can know that, since most players would fold rather than put their tournament on the line. *Conclusion: If he has trips, he's made a pretty unusual play.*

Now suppose he has the other plausible holding, a high pair lower than yours. (KK, QQ, JJ, TT) Now his all-in move is a kind of sophisticated semi-bluff. Even if he reads you for another high pair, he could win the hand in three ways:

1. You read him for trips and fold.

2. You call, but his high pair is higher than your high pair, and his holds up.

3. You call, and your pair is higher than his, but he gets lucky and outdraws you.

This is pretty good reasoning on his part, and it's an interesting, aggressive way to play a high pair. There's a pretty good chance, perhaps more than 50 percent, that a player in your position will fold the hand even with a high pair, and otherwise the result may just be a coin flip. The only problem with this analysis is that, up to now, he's seemed more conservative than aggressive. But even a conservative player can make a move now and then. *Conclusion: If he has a high pair, he's made a somewhat unusual, aggressive play.*

Overall, it looks like he's made an unusual play in any case, but perhaps a little less unusual in the case where he has a high pair. Before we divide our remaining 90 percent probability between these two cases, let's note one other fact. There are four times as many possible hands in the high pair case (kings, queens, jacks, and tens) as in the trips case (just nines and fives) and four times the likelihood he has them because of card combinations.

So what's the right distribution of our 90 percent? This requires an intelligent guess. I'd make it 50 percent for the high pair, and 40 percent for the trips. This allotment takes into account the greater number of hands for the high pairs, and the more unusual nature of the all-in move in a natural trapping position.

Now let's combine our estimate of the likelihood of each type of hand with the winning probabilities, and see what we get for an overall likelihood of winning.

1. He holds a high pair: 50% times 92% = 46%

2. He holds trips: 40% times 10% = 4%

3. He's bluffing: 10% times 97% = 10% (Round numbers off whenever possible. These are all rough estimates, so just make the math as easy as you can.)

Our estimate of our total winning probability is 60 percent.

$$60 = 46 + 4 + 10$$

We're a favorite in the hand, and the pot is offering us a little better than 3-to-2 odds, so we call. In fact, it's a huge call, since with the 3-to-2 pot odds, we could call if we were better than just 40 percent to win.

How much would we have to tweak the numbers to make this a marginal call? If we moved his bluffing percentage down to zero (which can't be right) and made him 60 percent to hold trips versus 40 percent that he holds a high pair, we'd have a marginal call/fold decision. If we kept the bluffing percentage at 10 percent, which is more reasonable, then guessing 25 percent for the chance of a high pair and 65 percent for the chance of trips would make the call borderline. We'd have to go all the way down to 20 percent for the high pair and 70 percent for the trips before folding was a clear play. Those just aren't reasonable estimates, even if we credit your opponent with being generally tight. Even tight players make moves, and even tight players can go all-in with a pair of kings or queens.

If this seems like an intimidating amount of work to do for a single hand, don't be discouraged. It is a fair amount of work, but it gets much easier with a little practice. Besides, if your whole tournament may ride on the outcome, it's worth putting in some effort to at least make sure you made a reasonable play, rather than just a hasty decision that you'll regret for a long time to come. And if you ever wondered just what good players are thinking about when they pause for a long time — well, they're thinking pretty much like this.

What happened in the actual hand from which this problem was taken? The player with the aces called, and his opponent showed trip nines, and won the pot.

Example No. 3: You're playing an online tournament and just five players remain. The blinds are now $50/$100, and you

have $4,300, a bit less than half the chips at the table. On the button, you pick up

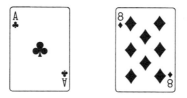

The two players in front of you both fold. You raise to $200. The small blind folds but the big blind, a solid player with $1,100, calls, putting in another $100. The pot is now $450. The flop is

The big blind checks, and you bet $250, a little over half the pot. The big blind raises you to $500. *What do you do?*

Answer: Your first thought should be to throw your hand away. You did your bit, but a check-raise indicates strength, and all you have right now is an ace-high hand.

But before you fold, notice that it costs you only $250 to play a $1,200 pot. With almost 5-to-1 odds staring at you, it's worth spending a little time calculating your outs. Let's see what they are.

1. An ace might be an out, and there are three aces left in the deck. But it's not an out if your opponent is holding a higher ace-x.

2.   An eight might be an out, and there are three eights left in the deck. But it's not an out if your opponent was slowplaying a higher pair.

3.   A four might be an out, and there are four fours left out there. But if your opponent has an ace like you do, then a four gets you only a split of the pot.

So how many outs do you actually have? If your opponent check-raised with something like

then you have ten outs. But that's a somewhat weak holding for a check-raise, and the truth is that you have no idea how many outs you have. Remember too your opponent may have actually made a strong hand, in which case you may have zero outs.

This looks like a fold to me.

Example No. 4: You're in the second day of a major tournament. Your table has nine players, and you have $6,900, slightly above average. The blinds are $200/$400 with antes of $25. The pot contains $825 to start. You're in second position. The player under the gun folds, and you look down at your hand, which is

Raising is certainly correct with a pair of queens. In early position, you should raise about three times the big blind with this hand. Of course, it's important to vary the bet around that number so as not to give away the hand. So on occasion, you should raise just double the big blind with this hand, and on other occasions, raise four or five times the blind.

Rarely just call with this hand and try to trap. The queens are in trouble if an ace or king come on the flop, so you want to discourage callers with your bet.

You raise to $1,200. The player on your left, a loose, aggressive player who likes to come over the top with marginal hands, calls. The player after him, a solid, tight player, calls. Everyone else folds. There is now $4,425 in the pot. The flop comes

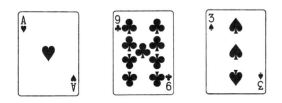

What should you do?

Answer: You weren't terribly unhappy that the player on your left called. In fact, his call, rather than his usual over the top raise, may indicate weakness. What's more bothersome is that the next player, a solid, tight player, called after a raise and a call in front of him. That probably indicates real strength.

You weren't happy seeing the ace on the flop, but even so you still have a high pair, and your opponents aren't guaranteed to have an ace. Since there's a good chance you still have the best hand at the table, you have to bet. A normal continuation bet here would be half the pot, but when the pot gets large in relation to the stacks, you have to modify your strategy a bit. A bet of half the pot would be $2,200, and since you only have $5,700 left in your stack, that would leave you with just $3,500. Let's downsize the bet a little bit, say to about $1,500. It's still a good-sized bet which should chase out worthless hands, but it leaves you with an exit strategy just in case. You can exit the hand if the tight player comes after you, but go to the end (if you choose) against the loose player.

You bet $1,500. The player on your left raises to $3,000, and the last player folds. The pot is now $9,925, and it costs you $1,500 to call.

This is a crucial play, as a mistake here could easily mean you'd be out of the tournament. You're happy that the last player left, since he was the player you most feared before the flop. But now we have to contend with the player on your left, who's just announced that his hand is better than yours. The trouble is that he needs only an ace for that to be true, and if he has one, you're in very bad shape here — more than a 9-to-1 underdog. He also could certainly have called before the flop with nines or treys, and now have trips.

If you fold, you've lost the $2,700 you've already invested in the hand, so your chip count will be down to $4,200. That's your fallback position. What happens if you decide to play the hand?

First point — if you decide just to call this bet, you're *pot-committed*. Calling for another $1,500 reduces your chip stack to a mere $2,700. With the blinds and antes at $825 per round, that's only good for three more rounds. It's hard to imagine any card that would come on fourth street that would make you throw the hand away if you decide to see the current bet. If that's the case, there's no reason to just call this raise. You should move all your chips in, which might win the pot if his raise is a complete bluff (unlikely, by the way — he probably has something), and at least ensures that you will double up if you win the hand. So your choices are fold, or go all-in.

If you go all-in, let's assume you get called. Sure, there's a small chance that his raise was a joke, but even if it was, the logic for calling is as compelling for him as it is for you. If you go all-in, he calls, and you win, the pot is $15,775. (Your $6,900, his $6,900, the last player's $1,200, the $825 in blinds and antes, less your antes and his of $50, which have been double-counted.) Call it $16,000 for a nice round number.

So you can fold and keep your $4,000, or risk it for a chance to get to $16,000. That's $4,000 in risk for a $12,000 reward, so you're getting 3-to-1 odds on your money. Mathematically, it's a good bet if you have one chance in four of winning, or 25 percent. Is it reasonable to think you could win that often? Let's take a look.

If you catch a queen on either of the last two cards, you'll almost certainly win the pot no matter what your opponent is holding. The chances of that are about 8.4 percent. That doesn't sound like much, but it's almost exactly one-third of the overall winning chance you need to go all in. That means that if there's just a 17 percent chance — about one in six — that your opponent is running a bluff, we can move at the pot. Since you know your opponent is a loose player, who's come over the top before with less than crushing hands, I'd say you have at least that much. (Remember too that he might have made his play with a hand that looks good but that you can beat — jacks or tens, for instance. It would be a gutsy play in the face of an ace on board, but it's not impossible to make a move here with a smaller pair. After all, you did!)

So just on the mathematics of it, I'd say you're justified in going all-in. But there's another issue that's equally important. If you fold here, you only have $4,200. That's far behind the leaders at this table and even farther behind the overall tournament leaders, who at this point probably have $40,000 to $50,000. What's worse, you only have enough chips to last about four more laps around the table. That's a situation that calls for a dramatic move — *when the price is right*. (We call this situation an inflection point, and we'll discuss it much more in Volume II.) Here the price is definitely right. You're holding a pair of queens, and have a chance to go from $4,000 to $16,000 chips. You have to accumulate lots of chips sometime, and this could be your last great chance. So move in now.

Most players try to handle these situations by taking a guess as to whether or not their opponent is bluffing. If they think he's bluffing, they call. If they think he has what he's representing, they fold. But it can be very hard to figure out if someone is really bluffing, and this approach leads to lots of big blunders.

I don't know if your opponent is bluffing in this situation. If I had to guess, *I'd guess he's probably not bluffing*. He probably has the ace he's representing, and you're probably going to be out of the tournament after this hand. But that's OK, because you're getting big odds on your wager, and if you're right, you'll have a real pile of chips to play with.

Remember this. In order to reach the final table of a big tournament, it's not enough to get paid off on your monster hands. At least once or twice during the event, you're going to have to come back from the dead. You're going to be all-in against someone who has you beat, and you're going to catch a card on fourth or fifth street that miraculously keeps you alive. I've been to a lot of final tables, but I've never been to one where I didn't have to hit a perfect card somewhere earlier in the tournament. That's a fact of life in all gaming tournaments, and poker is no different.

You go all-in, and your opponent calls. He shows

and your queens hold up to win the hand.

The Problems

Problems 4-1 through 4-6 show how to compute pot odds for your hand. Problem 4-2 also gives an example of deciding what pot odds to offer your opponent. In Problem 4-5 you have to adjust your pot odds when facing active players behind you.

Problems 4-7 and 4-8 show how to analyze hands based on the cards and betting you have seen so far. 4-8 also gives you some guideposts for extracting the most money from your opponent when you make a monster hand.

Problems 4-9 and 4-10 put the whole package together, testing your ability to blend pot odds and hand analysis to arrive at good decisions for your hand. Problem 4-10 shows how to handle a classically weak hand when confronted with great pot odds.

Hand 4-1

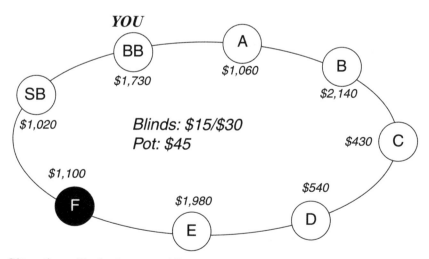

Situation: Early in a satellite tournament. Players B and E are active and aggressive.

144

Your hand: 7♥6♠

Action to you: Player A folds. Player B raises to $60. Players C, D, E, F, and the small blind all fold.

Question: *Do you fold, call, or raise?*

> **Answer:** Call. Your hand isn't much, but you're getting great odds here. It costs you $30 (remember, as the big blind you've put $30 in the pot already) to have a shot at a pot which is now $105. Those are 3.5-to-1 odds, and your hand, while weak, is only a bigger dog than that to a high pair. (Even if Player B is holding ace-king, you're only about a 2-to-1 underdog at this point.) Your implied odds make this an even stronger call.
>
> Get in the habit of computing the pot odds before throwing your hand away. Many times you'll find you have a compulsory call, virtually without regard to the cards you're holding.

Resolution: You actually fold.

Hand 4-2

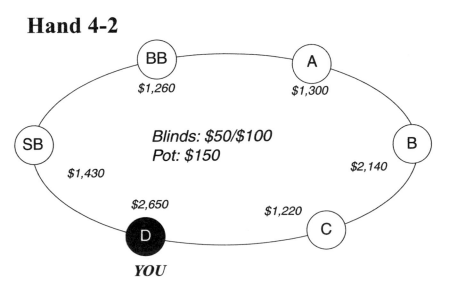

BB $1,260

A $1,300

SB $1,430

B $2,140

Blinds: $50/$100
Pot: $150

$2,650

$1,220

D

C

YOU

Situation: Single table satellite. Players began loose, but now appear to be playing tighter.

Your hand: Q♠Q♣

Action to you: Players A, B, and C all fold.

Question: *Do you raise $200, $300, or $400?*
    Answer: You're certainly going to raise here. There's no sense in calling, letting the small blind in cheap, then watching an ace or king come on the flop. Make your opponents pay to stick around. Queens are a fine hand, but they can easily get in trouble after the flop.
    The key question for this hand is — just how much do you raise? The two players left in the pot are the blinds, who already have some money involved. Since you have a strong hand right now, you want action. You don't want to bet so much that you chase moderate hands out of the pot. But you also have to remember The Fundamental Theorem of Poker.[6] You want to bet enough so that if they call, they'd be making a mistake given what you have.
    We can eliminate the $400 raise right away. It's too big, and it's likely to chase the mediocre hands away quickly. They might think you were stealing, but they don't want to put in a third of their stacks to find out.
    What about the $200 raise? Now the pot would be $350, and the big blind would have to put in another $100 to call. He would be getting 3.5-to-1 odds on his money. Those are good enough odds so that any hand containing an overcard (ace-jack or king-ten, for instance) is getting more than the proper odds to call. (Those hands are only 2.5-to-1 underdogs against a pair of queens.)

---

[6] See *The Theory of Poker* by David Sklansky for more discussion of The Fundamental Theorem of Poker.

The proper raise is $300. Now the pot is $450 and the big blind has to put in $200 to call. He's getting just 2.25-to-1 odds to call, which makes calling with an overcard an error against your hand. (The small blind has even worse odds, of course.)

Resolution: You bet $300. The blinds fold, and you take the pot.

Hand 4-3

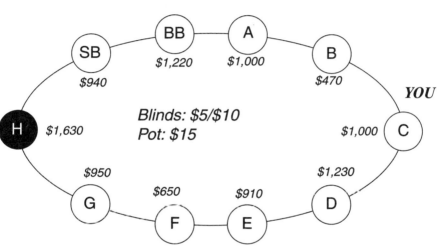

Situation: Early in a single-table online tournament.

Your hand: A♦K♠

Action to you: Players A and B fold.

Question: *Do you call or raise?*

   Answer: You usually want to raise with your A♦K♠. (Against loose-aggressive players it might be right to limp and then reraise all in.) Exactly how much to raise is the real question. In my view, three to five times the big blind is a good amount. If that chases other players out of the pot, so be it. Remember that ace-king is a good starting hand, but it will need to improve along the way to win; with no improvement, it's just an Ace-high hand.

In online tournaments, the players, being relatively new to poker, are looser and tend to call larger bets than they would in live play, so you can make bigger bets and expect to get called. I'd certainly want to make a bet at the high end of my normal range.

Action: You raise to $50. Players D, E, F, and G all fold. Player H calls. The blinds fold. The pot is now $115.

Flop: J♦7♣4♥

Question: You're first to act. *What do you do?*
   Answer: Given that you didn't hit your hand, that's a relatively good flop for you. No flushes, and no obvious straights. You now have to bet to find out where you stand. At a live tournament, you should lead out with a bet of about half the pot. Online, you have to bet a little more to achieve the same effect, perhaps about two-thirds of the pot.

Action: You bet $80. Player H raises to $160. The pot is now $355. *What do you do?*
   Answer: Your opponent has put the question to you, and you must answer. Let's quickly review what we know at this point:

1. It costs you $80 to call a pot of $355. Your pot odds are about 4.5-to-1.

2. To improve your hand on the very next turn, you have to catch one of the six remaining aces or kings. You've seen five cards so far, so there are 47 cards you haven't seen. Six of those are good for you, 41 are bad. Your

odds against improving on fourth street alone are about 7-to-1 against, much worse than your pot odds.

3. If you don't improve on fourth street, you'll usually face a bet that you won't be able to call. So it's mainly the odds of improving on the next card that you care about, not the odds that you might improve on fourth street and fifth street combined. (Those odds are about 3-to-1 against.)

4. Your opponent might be bluffing.

5. Your opponent might have flopped a set, so you can't win even if you hit. He might also have a holding like ace-jack or king-jack, which beats you now and negates some of your out cards.

    Early in a tournament, and lacking any information on your opponent's style, you should probably assume that the chance he's bluffing roughly cancels out the chances that he has a hand you can't beat, and treat this directly as a pot odds problem. You're not getting the pot odds you need to call, so you're done with the hand.

Action: You fold.

Hand 4-4

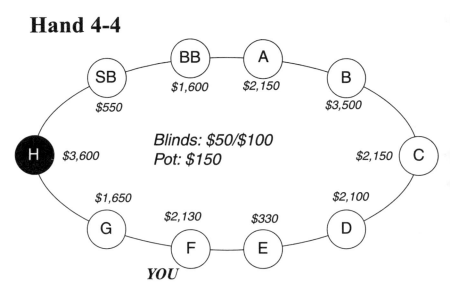

Blinds: $50/$100
Pot: $150

Situation: A few hours into a major tournament. The players are a mixed bag, but tend to be conservative. The small blind is a tight player who suffered a couple of bad beats about an hour ago.

Your hand: 5♥5♠

Action to you: Players A and B fold. Player C calls. Players D and E fold.

Question: *What's your play with this hand?*
　　Answer: A call here in good position is reasonable with a low pair. Your goal is to see a cheap flop and hit a set, after which you'll just need to figure out how to extract the most money from whoever is left. In addition, you may end up with position on your opponent, which might let you win the pot if you don't hit a set. If you don't hit your set and anyone shows strength, you'll need to beat a quick retreat.

Action: You call for $100. The two players behind you fold, but the small blind goes all-in for his last $500. The big blind and Player C now fold. The pot is $850, and it costs you $450 to call.

Question: *What's your action?*

Answer: The pot is now offering you slightly less than 2-to-1 odds on your money. Before you just shove your chips automatically into the pot, let's see if we can't do some simple calculations that might tell us if your call is clearly correct or not.

First question: What hands might your opponent have gone all-in with? We noted that the small blind was a tight player. We also noted that he lost most of his chips an hour ago, after which presumably he's been sitting tight and waiting for an opening. Although he's short on chips, he doesn't need to be desperate. He has enough chips to survive three more rounds, and since he's the small blind this hand, he won't need to put up any chips at all for the next eight hands. So we can dismiss the idea that this is just a desperate all-in bet with a couple of random cards. You're probably facing a pair higher than yours, or a couple of high cards.

If you're up against a high pair, it's a disaster, since you're 4.5-to-1 underdog in that situation. However, there are just nine pairs higher than yours, and six ways of drawing each pair, for a total of 54 possible hands.

If you're up against two higher cards, you're quite happy, since you're a slight favorite in the hand and you're getting almost 2-to-1 on your money. How many such hands are there? There are 16 different ways to construct a hand like ace-king (12 unsuited, 4 suited), and if you assume he would raise with any two cards above a ten, but not otherwise (pretty safe assumption for a tight player), then you're up against a total of 6 different unpaired hands (AK, AQ, AJ, KQ, KJ, and QJ), with 16 ways of drawing each one, for a total of 96 hands.

Let's assume that our tight opponent won't raise with any hand weaker than these. Of these 150 hands, how many can you win? You'll win about 10 of the 54 times he has a higher pair. You'll be a small favorite against the 96 unpaired hands, so let's say you win 52 of those. The total looks like 62 wins and 88 losses, not a bad result when you're getting 2-to-1 on your money. So you call.

Against a loose player, the call would be even easier, since you could guess that he would go all in with some hands like 22, 33, 44, A2, A3, A4, all of which would leave you a big favorite.

Resolution: You call, and your opponent turns over Q♥Q♦. He wins the hand.

Hand 4-5

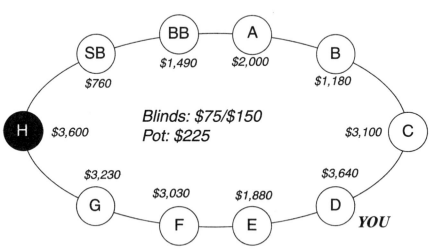

Situation: A major tournament, in the middle of the first day. You're the chip leader at a generally tight table.

Your hand: 5♠5♥

Action to you: Player A folds, B calls, and C folds. Pot now $375.

Question: *Raise, call, or fold?*
    Answer: You call as in the previous hand. A small pair is worth a call at this point, although a lot of action behind you will force you to throw the hand away.

Action: Players E and F fold. Players G and H (the big stack on the button) call. The small blind goes all-in for his remaining $685. The big blind folds, as does the original caller, Player B. The pot is now $1,510. It costs you $610 to call.

Question: *Raise, call, or fold?*
    Answer: If there were no other active players in the pot, this would be an easy call based on the pot odds, as we saw in our last example. But the presence of two live players with big stacks behind you changes everything. If you call, either one could raise and make you throw your now-expensive hand away. If you don't make your hand on the flop, you won't be able to stick around for fourth and fifth street unless the hand is checked around, which is unlikely.

    Always remember that the presence of active players behind you has a huge effect on your decision-making. Their presence makes many hands unplayable which are trivially easy calls in a one-on-one situation.

Resolution: You fold.

Hand 4-6

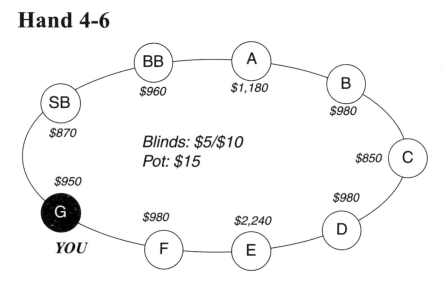

Situation: First round of an online tournament.

Your hand: Q♥Q♦

Action to you: Player A calls $10. Player B raises to $40. Player C folds. Players D and E call $40. Player F folds. Pot is $145.

Question: What's your play?

   Answer: This is the sort of action you like to see when you have a pair of queens on the button. The other players are building the pot for you, and the action is fast and furious. You should stick in a good-sized raise, about $200, and see what happens.

   There is a school of thought that advises just calling with the queens here, trying to see a flop, then making a move if no ace or king shows. It's not an unreasonable idea, and I've played that way myself on occasion. But my normal play is to raise.

Action: You raise to $200. The blinds fold. Player A folds. Player B puts in $160 to call, and Player D folds. Player E goes all-in for $2,200. The main pot is now $1,255, and it costs you $750 to call. (There's also $30 in a potential side pot between B and E, in which you will not be involved.)

Question: *Call or fold?*

Answer: If B folds and the main pot stays as it is, you're being offered 5-to-3 odds to call. If B gets in as well, the pot will be just over $2,000 and you'll be getting 8-to-3 odds.

Your first job is to make some guesses as to what Player E has. There are four possibilities:

1. He has aces or kings. Now you're about a 4.5-to-1 underdog, and you're not getting the odds you need to call.

2. He has ace-king. You're actually an 11-to-10 favorite, so the pot odds are very favorable.

3. He has a lower pair, something like jacks or tens. Now you're a 4.5-to-1 favorite, and you're getting odds besides!

4. He's bluffing, or playing something pathetic like ace-jack suited. Again, you're a huge favorite.

So unless you're sure, for some reason, that he's really holding aces or kings, the other three cases are so favorable that, on balance, you have to call. Keep in mind, also, that in online poker people are much more likely to shove all their chips in the pot with nothing, or just a low pair, than in live poker. That's just another reason to call, so call.

Action: You call, and so does Player B. Both players turn over ace-king, making you about a 2-to-1 favorite overall since their hands now interfere with each other, and your two queens help block their long-shot straight. The board comes Q♣T♠9♥8♠5♦, and you triple your chips.

Hand 4-7

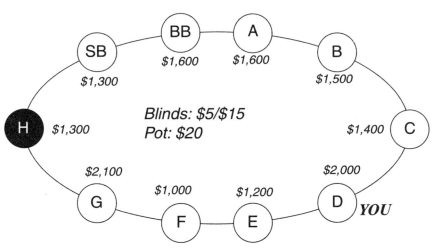

Situation: First hour of a major tournament.

Your hand: Q♦J♦

Action to you: Player A calls. Player B folds. Player C calls. The pot has $50.

Question: *Do you fold, call, or raise?*

    Answer: Beginners get excited about this hand, but they shouldn't. Queen-jack suited isn't an awful hand, but if anyone out there has an ace, a king, or a pair, you're playing catch-up. This is a nice drawing hand that you're happy to play cheap, but you should be quite willing to let it go if the pot generates some serious action. Because the cards are suited, you should be inclined to call here. With an unsuited queen-jack, you let the hand go after two early calls.

Action: In fact you raise to $60.

Too loose. You're trying to steal a pot, probably figuring that your hand has plenty of potential if you get called. That's not a bad strategy in late position when no one has opened the pot, but right now you have six players behind you who haven't acted yet, plus the two callers in front of you, both of whom probably have better hands than you do. What you're actually doing here is building a pot where you're an underdog, definitely not a recommended strategy.

Action: Players E and F fold. Player G calls. Player H folds. The blinds fold. Players A and C fold. The pot is now $170.

Flop: J♠4♦2♦

Question: *What now?*

Answer: You've had a mixed bag of good and bad news. The good news was that you forced out the callers in front of you. The bad news is that the player who called behind you often had you beaten. Remember, he saw two early callers plus a raise of four times the big blind, then he decided to call. That means he must have something, but probably not a premium pair, since he didn't reraise you. The flop is more good news, since you have top pair plus a flush draw.

You have to bet something here. You may well have the best hand, and you need to find out where you stand. I'd recommend you bet around two-thirds of the pot, say about $120. That's enough to chase him out if he has nothing.

Action: You actually bet $200, and Player G calls The pot is now $570.

Fourth Street: 6♣

Question: *What now?*
    Answer: You overbet the pot, and got called anyway. What does that tell you?
    Your first conclusion should be that he's probably holding a jack. He didn't raise before the flop or after the flop, so a pair higher than jacks is pretty unlikely. He might have called before the flop with a pair of jacks, and now be slowplaying trip jacks. That's so unlikely you should pay off to it if that's really the case. And trip fours or deuces are similarly unlikely, because calling a big raise before the flop with those hands, and plenty of active players yet to act, is just too weird.
    If he has a pair of jacks, what could his hand be? Queen-jack is the least likely possibility, because we have one of the queens. If he's holding king-jack or jack-ten, he should have folded before the flop. Likewise jack-x is very unlikely. That leaves ace-jack, suited or unsuited. I would have folded that hand before the flop, but lots of players would play it because of the ace.
    How about a pair of tens, nines, or even something lower? He might have called with those before the flop. Would he keep calling against an overcard on the flop followed by a big bet? That's a pretty gutsy call, but a few players would do it. He might think that your overbet really showed weakness, and be calling based on that.
    How about A♦K♦? That matches all his plays so far. The call before the flop makes sense, and after the flop he has two overcards plus a flush draw, for a total of 15 outs twice. (Three aces plus three kings plus nine diamonds, total of 15 cards.) He's a small favorite with 15 outs twice, so his call after the flop makes sense too.

Ace-king, ace-queen, or king-queen unsuited is a real stretch. He can call after the flop with that hand only if he's certain you're bluffing, and nobody's that certain.

So his most likely hands are ace-jack, which beats us, and A♦K♦ or similar hand, which is now an underdog after missing on fourth street. A bet of some kind looks necessary here. We can't let any flush draws have a free card. I'd bet about $300, which doesn't give him a call if he does have the A♦K♦, a hand with only 12 outs.

Action: You actually check, and Player G checks.

Fifth Street: 7♦

Question: Now what?
Answer: You have the flush, so you have to bet something. But without the ace or king of diamonds, you can't be completely confident. I'd bet about $400 here. If my opponent comes back with an all-in raise, I'll have to think about throwing the hand away.

Action: You actually bet $500, and Player G calls. He shows K♦8♦, and takes the pot.

Bad luck. Your opponent made bad calls everywhere and got rewarded for it. Just make sure you don't go on tilt when this scenario occurs. Be glad you're still alive in the tournament, because this guy sure won't be for very long.

Hand 4-8

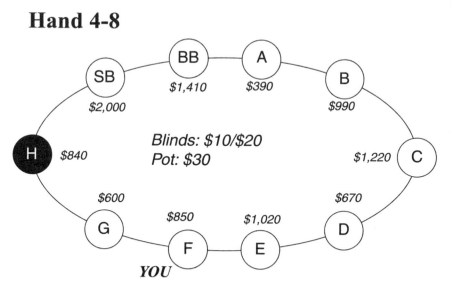

Situation: Early in a one-table satellite tournament.

Your hand: K♥K♦

Action to you: Players A and B fold. Player C calls $20. Player D folds. Player E raises to $40. There is now $90 in the pot.

Question: *Do you raise, and if so, how much?*
   Answer: You certainly want to raise a goodly amount, but not so much as to discourage action. A roughly pot-sized bet looks about right here.

Action: You raise to $100. Players G and H and the small blind fold. The big blind calls for another $80. Player C, the original caller, calls for another $80. Player E, the original raiser, calls for another $60. The pot now contains $410. You will be last to act next round.

Flop: A♥6♦4♥

Action: The big blind checks, Player C bets $20, and Player E calls. The pot is now $450. *What do you do?*

Answer: *It's good to get in the habit of recapping the action in your head before you make a move.* The first thing to notice is that Player C has made a strange sequence of plays. He called the blinds in third position, then after a raise and a big raise behind him, he just called again. No hand that merited just limping in the pot could also justify calling two raises. So either he's making some sort of weird trap with a big hand, or he's a fish who doesn't know what he's doing.

You should be unhappy that you couldn't narrow the field more with your raise, but such things happen. (Make a mental note for the future that with this group, a bigger-than-normal raise is necessary.) The ace on the flop, however, is a big problem. With three callers, at least somebody should have an ace out there, so you've got to be very cautious. On the bright side, you have a back-door flush possibility, even though that's a real long shot. Right now, you're happy to just call and see a cheap card. Hopefully, the big blind won't do a check-raise.

Action: You call, and the big blind also calls. The pot is now $490.

Fourth Street: J♥

Action: The big blind bets $65, Player C calls, and Player E raises to $130. The pot is now $750. *What should you do?*

Answer: The jack seems to have helped this crowd, and everybody is saying they have something. What do you do? The first job is to assess your situation carefully.

There's some chance that you have the best hand right now. If no one had an ace, your kings are probably still good. The ace on the flop was scary, but the betting on the flop was anemic, so there is some possibility that you don't need to improve to win.

If you do need to improve, it's time to start counting the cards that will improve your hand. The jack helped you here, because it's the fourth card to your nut flush. With no pair on the board, there are no full houses out there, so hitting the flush will certainly win the hand. Four flush cards accounted for gives you nine outs. The two outstanding kings might win the hand for you, but they might not; you could already be facing a flush. You can't count them as two outs — maybe one out is about right. That gives you 10 outs out of 46 cards. You're a 36-to-10 underdog, or about 3.5-to-1.

You have to put in $130 to call this pot, and the pot has $750 in it. That means the pot is offering you a tad less than 6-to-1. So far, it looks like calling is a no-brainer.

But there's some additional good and bad news to consider.

The bad news is that you're not guaranteed to see the river card for just $130. The big blind and player C are still alive behind you. Neither has shown much this hand, so you're probably not going to see a raise out of them. But it could happen, and if it does your pot odds are wrecked.

The good news is that if you hit your flush on the end, you're going to win a lot of money. At least one and perhaps two of them will hit a flush at the same time, and whoever does might lose most of his chips. So your implied pot odds are huge. It's hard to quantify the good and bad news here, but on balance it still looks good for you. So call.

Action: You call. The big blind folds, and Player C calls. The pot is now $945.

Fifth Street: 9♥

Action: Player C checks, and Player E bets $20. *What's your play?*

Answer: Be calm. You've hit the flush, and since you have the king and the ace is on board, you have the nut flush. And since there's no pair on board, there are no full houses against you, so you have the lock hand. The beginner in this situation is so delighted with having won the hand that he just shoves all his chips in the middle of the pot. Resist this temptation. Your job now is to extract the most money from your opponents. How to do that is often a tricky problem.

Your first job is to check out the remaining stacks. Player C started with $970 and now has $720 left. Player E started with $750 and now has $480 left. You are down to an even $600. By the way, this is a key skill to develop if you start out playing online poker and then move to live poker. You can't just look at the screen to gauge how many chips remain; you have to estimate it from the stack sizes. Don't worry — it's a skill that improves with practice.

The bad news here is the betting action so far. Player C only checked, and Player E bet $20. With four hearts on board, this action indicates one of three things:

1. No one has a heart.

2. Someone has a heart, but they're afraid of a higher flush.

3. Someone has a heart and has decided to trap.

Case (3) is unlikely. It's foolish to check a flush after the last card, because of the danger that the hand simply gets checked down. Cases (1) and (2) are more reasonable. If it's Case (2), and you make a modest bet, the player with the flush will look you up. He might look you up even if you go all-in, although I've seen good players fold in that situation.

If Case (1) applies, even a modest bet may not get called here.

I like to think of a range of plausible bets, then shade my decision toward the top and bottom of the range, depending on whether my opponents have acted loose or tight. Here the right range looks like $100-to-$200. It's small enough so they're getting great pot odds to call, and it's also small enough so they'll have reasonable sized stacks left if they call and lose. In a situation like this, I definitely don't want to bet more than half of anyone's stack. Losing more than half your stack is a real psychological barrier, and I don't want to push anyone across that barrier. Seems like $150 is about right. Players C and E seem a bit on the tight side, just from the action this hand, so this is probably the best you can do to pick up a few extra chips.

By the way, in online play you can be much more aggressive here. The rounds are so short, and players are under such pressure to accumulate chips quickly, that even an all-in bet has a reasonable chance to be called.

Action: You bet $150, and Players C and E both fold. You take the pot.

C'est la vie. Don't waste any time second-guessing the size of your bet. Just take your chips and get on to the next hand. The time for second-guessing is after the tournament is over.

Hand 4-9

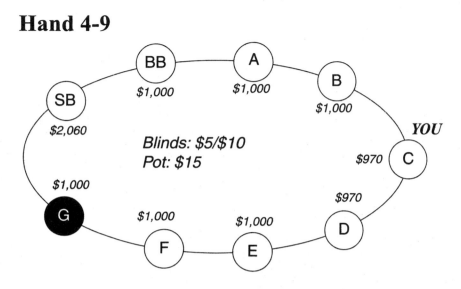

Situation: Early in a single-table online tournament. You don't have any solid information about the other players.

Your hand: A♥K♠

Action to you: Player A calls, Player B folds. The pot is now $25.

Question: *Do you call or raise?*

> **Answer:** Your hand is certainly strong enough for a raise. Three, four, or five times the big blind would be a good amount.

Action: You raise to $40. Player D folds. Player E calls. Players F and G fold. The small blind calls for $35. The big blind folds. Player A puts in another $30 to call. The pot is now $170. There are four players in the pot, and you will be third to act after the flop.

Flop: K♣9♥3♣

Action: The small blind and Player A both check. *What should you do?*

 Answer: You have top pair with top kicker, so you're in excellent shape. You're going to take the lead and bet. The only real question is: how much?

 Your hand is quite strong, so you don't want to bet so much that everyone runs away. But there are two clubs on board, so you don't want to bet so little that the flush draws have the proper odds (including implied odds) to stick around. This is a very common situation after the flop, and the right bet is something in the range of three-quarters of the pot to a little more than the pot. In this case, you should consider betting between $140 and $200.

 Keep in mind also that you can increase your bet depending on the number of players you're facing. Against a single opponent, choose a bet at the low end of your range. Against several opponents, pick an amount at the high end of the range. The more opponents, the greater the chance that someone will come in against you.

Action: You actually bet $100. Player E calls. The big blind and Player A fold. The pot is now $370.

 You bet too little. If Player E is on a club flush draw, he got the proper pot odds to call.

Fourth Street: K♦

Question: *What should you bet now?*

 Answer: With your trip kings, it looks like you'll win the hand easily unless he's on a flush draw and hits his flush on the end. You need to bet enough so that he's not getting the right odds to draw to his flush, but you also want to extract some more money in case he's chasing you with some lesser holding and is inclined to play. You both have much more than the pot at this point — your chip count is $830, his is $860.

A gainst most opponents you should bet about $250 here. To call, he would have to put in $250 for a pot of $620, about 2.5-to-1 odds. He's more than 4-to-1 to hit his flush, so it's a blunder for him to call if he knows what you have.

Action: You actually bet $200, and he calls. The pot is now $770. You have $630 left, he has $660.

Fifth Street: J♣

Question: Three clubs are now showing on board. *What do you do?*

Answer: Now you've reached a genuinely tough decision. Let's work through it and see what should go into your thinking in these situations.

The first question you should ask yourself is this: "If I check and he makes a substantial bet or goes all-in, will I throw away my trip kings?" If the answer to this question is no, then you should tend to bet now. By betting, you'll make some extra money when he calls with some hands that he wouldn't have bet if you had just checked. For example, if he was holding J♥9♥ to start, he wouldn't necessarily bet on the end, but he'd almost certainly call a bet by you. The same reasoning holds true if he's been playing hands like ace-jack or queen-jack, or even slowplaying aces or queens.

If you would throw your trip kings away after a bet, then you should tend to check now. In no-limit tournaments you don't throw these hands away. Your time is severely limited. The blinds keep crawling up behind you, and you have to keep accumulating chips to stay ahead of them. A set of kings against a possible flush is just too good a situation to throw away.

The real choice is between going all-in right now and betting something like $200. The $200 bet will win some more money from hands like a single pair that might have folded an all-in bet, and against stronger hands you will get all-in eventually anyhow. A bet like that would be my top choice, but it's a very tough judgment call.

Action: You actually go all-in and get called. Your opponent shows 8♠8♣ and loses to your trip kings.

In online poker, players are much more likely to play all the way with a low pair. When you make the move from online to live tournaments, be aware that in general your opponents will show down much stronger hands.

Hand 4-10

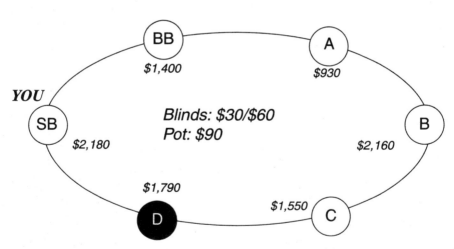

Situation: Late in a single-table online tournament. Players B and D are very aggressive.

Your hand: 9♣2♣

Action to you: Player A folds. Player B calls. Player C folds. Player D calls. Pot is now $210.

Question: *Do you fold, call, or raise?*
Answer: Obviously 9♣2♣ is so weak that you can just throw the hand away. But there are a couple of reasons why you might play a hand like this occasionally.

1. The first reason is simply to vary your play so that your opponents can't read you so easily.

2. The second and more important reason is to take advantage of the huge pot odds you're being offered in the small blind. You have to put in only $30 to play a pot of $210. Those 7-to-1 odds are quite compelling. Even a very weak hand has more chance than that if it can play to the end. Your 9♣2♣, for instance, is about 25 percent to win against two hands dealt at random. If the two hands contain a common high card, the winning chances rise to about 33 percent.

This is not the whole story, of course. The big blind hasn't acted yet, and he may chase you out with a raise. You're probably not facing random hands, but hands that are somewhat better than random. And those quoted winning chances are based on being able to play the hand down to the end. If you miss your hand on the flop and are then confronted with a big bet, you won't be getting the odds you need to continue playing. But there's no harm in playing a hand like this, occasionally, as a speculation. With those caveats in mind, you can call here.

Action: You elect to call for $30. The big blind just checks. The pot is now $240.

Flop: 5♦4♣3♣

Question: You're first to act. *What should you do?*
    Answer: You should usually make a significant bet of about half the pot. You now have a decent hand, with a flush draw and an open-ended straight draw. The flop probably missed your opponents, who may all be sitting there with a couple of high cards. A good-sized bet here may win the pot right now, and you have plenty of outs if it doesn't.

Action: You bet $120. The big blind and Player B call. Player D raises to $240. The pot is now $840. *What do you do now?*
    Answer: Your first thought here should be to slow down and take some time, because you could be making a crucial decision. The pot is getting big, you're drawing at potentially monster hands, and this could be a pot where several players go broke. A lot of decisions in poker can be made quickly, but this isn't one of them.

    You should be thinking about three things here:

1.   **Pot Odds**. It costs you $120 to call a pot of $840. Those 7-to-1 odds look very good. The big blind and Player B are still able to act behind you, but you're still getting very good odds.

2.   **Potential Outs**. You're drawing at a straight and a flush. Both are strong hands, but neither is guaranteed to win. If someone is out there with two clubs, one is likely to be higher than your 9♣. There are nine clubs still out, plus three aces (you can't double-count the A♣) and three sixes (don't double-count the 6♣), for a total of 15 potential outs. That's plenty of outs, given the pot odds you're offered.

3. **Your opponents.** You were called by two players and raised by a third, which was certainly unexpected given the nondescript flop. Players B and D are known to be aggressive, so you can discount their plays a bit, but not entirely. You might be facing a set of trips somewhere, but you might just be up against a pair. A made straight is unlikely; someone would need to be holding ace-deuce, or seven-six, or six-deuce, all unlikely hands to be playing before the flop.

Once you've reasoned this far, it's time to make a judgment. Given this set of facts, you should call. The pot odds are just too enticing given the number of potential outs. Calling is better than reraising because you would like to get in as cheaply as possible, and calling may draw in the two players behind you, improving your pot odds.

Action: You call. The big blind calls. Player B folds. The pot is now $960.

Fourth Street: 9♠

Question: *What's your move now?*
Answer: You now have top pair on board, plus the straight and flush draws. With the pot at $960, you should start looking at the remaining stacks. You have $1,880 left, while the big blind has $1,100 and Player D has $1,490.

You should make a strong, pot-sized bet here. That's a large enough bet so that anyone who is drawing will not be getting the right odds to call. It also shows your opponents that they have to be willing to go all-in to play.

Action: You in fact check. Player D bets $500. *What do you do?*
    Answer: You should call. You can't be sure about the quality of any of your outs, but you have so many of them that it's worth calling. The nine clubs are probably outs, the six additional aces and sixes that are not clubs are probably outs, and the two outstanding nines may be outs. There are 46 cards left in the deck and 17 of them may be outs for you. (Don't forget that you may not *need* any outs; your pair of nines could still be good here.) It costs you $500 to see a pot of $1,460, so you're being offered almost 3-to-1 odds. Take them.

Action: You call. The pot is now $1,960.

Fifth Street: 6♣

Question: *How should you bet on the end?*
    Answer: If Player D had a drawing hand, he certainly didn't bet like it. It's reasonable to assume your flush is now good, and you should go all-in.

Action: You go all-in and Player D calls. He shows 7♥6♥, and your flush beats his straight.

    Player D should have bet a lot more on fourth street, so that any flush draws would not have had the proper odds to call. In all, however, an interesting hand.

Part Five

Betting Before the Flop

Betting Before the Flop

Introduction

A no-limit hold 'em hand opens with the betting before the flop. Here you make a claim on the pot with your good hands, toss away your junk hands, and try for cheap steals when the occasion warrants. This phase of the hand offers the most scope for style and ingenuity. Once the flop appears and common cards are exposed, there will be generally correct and incorrect plays, and a good player is supposed to know what's correct and do it. But before the flop the players are looking at a blank canvas, and, within reason, they can do pretty much what they want.

How you play before the flop will depend on your basic approach to the game. Each of the three styles I described in Part Two has a different way of handling the pre-flop play.

1. The conservative player wants to enter just a few pots. When he does play, he wants either a hand that rates to be the best, or one that's being offered great odds to play. He's trying to minimize the number of difficult decisions he will face after the flop.

2. The aggressive player is willing to play more hands with somewhat weaker cards. He wants to see more flops than the conservative player, and he's confident in his ability to read the table and extricate himself from second-best hands.

3. The super-aggressive player will enter a lot of pots, perhaps as many as 30 percent. He's looking to steal some pots or see some flops cheaply. He's counting on his skill to enable him to let go cheaply of a hand that's beaten, while collecting

huge pots on either his legitimately strong hands, or his random hands that hit great flops.

Basic Strategy

In the next few pages I'm going to describe a basic strategy for betting before the flop. It's a generic strategy, which describes how I would play under the following circumstances:

1. I'm at a full table of nine players, in the early to middle part of a tournament.

2. I don't know any of the players particularly well.

3. As far as I can tell, the players are all playing a somewhat solid, conservative game.

4. There are no very big or small stacks.

5. We all have plenty of chips compared to the blinds and antes.

This is not as unusual a set of conditions as you might think. Tournaments are so large now that it's not unusual to sit down at a table where I recognize only one or two faces. Most players who've paid out $5,000 or $10,000 to enter a major tournament tend to play conservatively, at least for a while. And the stack sizes tend to stay in a fairly close range until some players start calling the occasional all-in move.

The strategy I'll describe is more aggressive than a straight conservative strategy, but more conservative than a lot of the play you will see. It's designed to keep you out of trouble, while making sure that when you do get involved in a hand, you have some solid values to play. At a live tournament this strategy will be just slightly more conservative than the average player around you. In online tournaments, you'll definitely be one of the tighter players at the table.

When you implement this strategy, don't be concerned if there appear to be long stretches that you are just throwing your hands away. It happens to all players when they're playing well. If you get a little bored and anxious throwing lots of hands away, remember these two facts:

1. While television poker is real poker, most of the hands aren't shown. There are lots of hands that one player bets, and everyone else folds. On television, those hands don't make the cut.

2. In no-limit hold 'em, all your chips are in jeopardy every time you enter the pot. A player who splashes around in a lot of pots is much more likely to be flushed away quickly than one who enters fewer pots, but chooses them carefully.

After I lay out the basic strategy, I'll describe some of the adjustments you need to make as these preconditions change. If you're a newcomer to tournaments, don't worry too much about those adjustments. If you can simply learn and implement the basic strategy, you'll already be playing better than many of the players at your table. After you're fully familiar with the strategy, you'll be ready to start making modifications based on the playing styles of the players or the changing stack sizes.

As I describe the strategy, note that I refer to the player who is first to act after the blinds as being in first position, all the way around to the button, who is in seventh position. Then follow the small blind and the big blind. Although I'm describing the action at a nine-handed table, just remember that at a ten-handed table, you need to play with slightly tighter requirements.

Who is in the Pot?

What hands you use to raise, call, and fold depends to a huge extent on the action you have seen in front of you and your position. You need one set of criteria if everyone has folded to you, and quite another set if two players have already raised and reraised. It would be completely impossible to cover all the possible combinations of raisers, callers, and folders for each position at the table. Instead, I've boiled the situations down to five, which will give you a good overview of the various possibilities:

1. No one has entered the pot yet.

2. The player in third position has made an opening raise of three times the big blind. You are in fifth position. The players in first, second, and fourth position have folded.

3. The player in third position has called the big blind. As before, you are in fifth position, and the players in first, second, and fourth position have folded.

4. You are on the button. The player in third position raised three times the big blind, and the player in fifth position raised nine times the big blind. All other players folded.

5. You are on the button. The players in second, fourth, and sixth position all limped in (called the big blind). The players in first, third, and fifth position folded.

While you'll rarely be in these exact situations, the discussion should show you how you're supposed to think about the problem of entering the pot.

Case No. 1: No one
has entered the pot yet.

This is the most favorable case, since no one at the table has shown any strength, and a bet may simply win the pot. Let's see how the various types of playable hands should be treated.

AA, KK, QQ: With these premium pairs, you can raise from any position. In online play, I would always raise with these hands, since it's highly unlikely that you will meet the same players often enough for them to get a read on you. In real tournaments, where the good players try to keep track of what they see other players doing, you always have to vary your play somewhat. With these hands, I would try to raise 80 percent of the time, and just call the other 20 percent.

You should be clearly aware that slowplaying these hands is usually a theoretical mistake that would cost you money *if you could be sure that your opponents weren't studying your style*. But they will be studying you, so you have to adopt a balanced style, varying your approach somewhat at random. This advice will apply to all the hands we discuss throughout this chapter. When I mix two different approaches to the same hand, I'll try to give you the percentage distribution for each play.

You should be aware that in top-class poker you will encounter many players who, after each session, go home and write down everything that they've seen at the table in their notebooks. There are players with enormous written notebooks on the habits of hundreds of other players. So when I tell you to select your plays on a random basis, I'm not kidding! Any move or play that you make on a constant basis will soon find its way into these databases.

What about the size of the raise? The number I like to raise with these hands is about three to four times the size of the big blind. Again, I need to vary this amount in a random pattern, so my actual bets might look like this:

- 35 percent: Raise three times the big blind
- 35 percent: Raise four times the big blind
- 15 percent: Raise twice the big blind
- 15 percent: Raise five times the big blind

(Note that before the flop I like to describe raises as multiples of the big blind rather than as multiples of the pot. After the flop, I think in terms of fractions or multiples of the total pot. It's a somewhat arbitrary distinction, but if you hang out on the poker circuit for awhile, you'll realize this is how the players talk and think.)

Should you ever go all-in with these premium pairs? It's a very rare play, because with hands this strong you very much want to encourage action from a single opponent and try to build a big pot. Going all-in normally just chases people away and leaves you merely claiming the blinds and antes. You might consider the play if you find yourself at a very active table where you have seen all-in bets called. (Even in that case it would be an unusual move.)

In late position (sixth to act) or on the button you don't want to raise more than three times the big blind. Your bet is now more likely to be interpreted as a stealing attempt and less as a value bet, and you want to encourage action, since the hands that call you will be a little weaker than usual. In this situation you also want to limp a little more than usual, especially if you have noticed that the big blind will defend his blind aggressively by raising. Give him a chance to try to chase you away.

JJ, TT, 99: In early position, you need to play a mixed strategy of raising and calling with these hands. I like a mix of 70 percent raises and 30 percent calls. When you do raise, you should raise a larger amount than with the premium pairs, since you prefer to win the pot right away. While they are probably the best hand at the table right now, they become difficult to play when they are called and overcards appear on the board. With these hands, I like to raise four to five times the big blind.

In middle position, you want to raise aggressively with all three of these hands, especially in fourth or fifth position. (You should be a bit more conservative in third position.) Treat them as premium hands, and raise three to five times the big blind. Unlike the premium hands, however, you should almost never limp with these cards. Because these hands are so weak when high cards come on the flop, you can't allow players with face cards to limp into the pot behind you.

In sixth position or on the button, you still want to raise with these hands, but you can now afford to blend more calls into the mix. Continue raising three to five times the big blind, but use a ratio of about 75 percent raises and 25 percent calls.

88, 77, 66: These hands are noticeably weaker than the previous group, and must be played accordingly.

You will still play these hands in early position, but with more caution. You predominantly want to limp in with these low-middle pairs, but you need to mix in a few raises for the sake of deception. I like a mix of 20 percent raises, 80 percent calls.

Middle position is a little trickier. I play third position the same as one of the early positions. In fourth position I will start to raise with eights, but continue to limp with the two lower pairs. In fifth position I switch over to a mostly raising strategy with all three pairs.

In late position these are all raising hands. I use a mix of 75 percent raises and 25 percent calls.

55, 44, 33, 22: Low pairs are inherently dangerous cards for two reasons. Low pairs are, of course, beaten by high pairs. In addition, however, low pairs can be *counterfeited* when high pairs appear on the board. Suppose, for instance, you hold

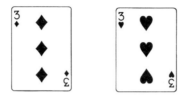

and the board comes

Right now you have two pair, nines and treys. But if the turn card is a five, you don't get credit for having three pair! Your pair in the hole just disappears (we call this counterfeiting) and your hand just becomes the board plus a trey kicker. You must play these hands very carefully.

In early position, usually throw these hands away.

In middle position, limp with fives and fours, but throw the treys and deuces away.

In late position, mostly raise with your fives and fours, and call with your treys and deuces. If the blinds seem weak, raise with all of these hands.

AK, AQ, suited or unsuited: Now we get to the hands that don't contain a pair. Of these, ace-king (Big Slick) and ace-queen are by far the strongest, and can be played much like the high pairs. Note that these hands are strong enough so that, unlike the case with the weaker unpaired hands, you can make the same plays whether they are suited or unsuited.

In early position, you want to mostly raise with these hands. I use a mixture of 75 percent raises, 25 percent calls. When you do raise, three to five times the big blind is a good amount, varying the bet randomly, of course.

In middle position you raise even more frequently, perhaps 85 percent raises and 15 percent calls. Note that you are quite happy to just win the pot with these hands (especially when there are antes as well as blinds in there). Remember that when you get action and don't hit your hand on the flop, you are a big underdog to any low pair.

Late position is handled the same as middle position. Raise most of the time and don't be sad to win the pot.

AJ, AT suited: In early position with ace-jack suited, use a mixture of half raises and half calls, with your raises being three to five times the big blind, as before. Ace-ten suited in early position is a very marginal hand. At a tough table, I would often just throw it away. At a table of feebs, I'd limp.

In middle position, I would just make a normal raise with ace-jack suited. With ace-ten suited I would mix it up a little, with perhaps 75 percent raises and 25 percent calls.

In late position they are good hands, and I would raise strongly with them.

AJ, AT unsuited: I would just throw away ace-ten unsuited in early position. At a tough table, I would throw away ace-jack unsuited as well. At a not-so-tough table, I would play ace-jack with a mixture of half raises and half calls.

Middle position gets a little complicated. In third position I would still fold ace-ten, but I'd play ace-jack with a mixture of 70 percent raises and 30 percent calls. In fourth position I'll play ace-jack the same way, but I'll start to be active with ace-ten as well, with an equal mixture of raises, calls, and folds. In fifth position I'll mostly raise with both.

In late position I will raise strongly with both.

A9, A8 suited: As we get down to the weaker suited aces, we're entering dangerous territory. Unlike previous hands, hitting the ace is now a mixed blessing, because the chance is increasing that we are facing an ace with a better kicker. The real strength of these hands comes when we flop either the nut flush, a draw to the nut flush, or two pair, any of which could win a huge pot.

I like to think of ace-eight as the crossover hand with aces. If I'm facing an opponent who will play against me with *any* ace-x, then there are five ace-x combinations that are higher than mine (AK, AQ, AJ, AT, and A9) but six that are lower (A7, A6, A5, A4, A3, A2). In that limited sense, I'm still likely to be a favorite with ace-eight, whereas ace-seven would make me an underdog.

In early position these hands must be discarded (unless the players are weak and there is little raising preflop).

In middle position things are again a little complicated. If I were in a good mood at a weak table, I might call in third position with these hands. Be aware that to make calls with these marginal hands, you must be able to play very well after the flop. In fourth position I would definitely play with a mixture of half raises and half calls. In fifth position I would raise a lot.

In late position they are also raising hands.

A9, A8 unsuited: Throw away these hands in early position.

In third and fourth position, throw them away as well. You can start playing these hands in fifth position. When you do play, you mostly want to raise, to cut down on the chance that you'll actually have to see a flop. Use a mixture of 70 percent raises and 30 percent calls.

In late position you are again mostly raising with these hands. Use 90 percent raises and 10 percent calls, because now you are very happy just to get the pot.

A7 and lower, suited and unsuited: At a tough table, I would throw all these hands away unless I was on the button or one off the button. On the button I would raise with any ace. One off the button, I would raise with ace-seven and ace-six only. The remaining advice applies only to weak tables, or when the blinds have been unwilling to defend their position.

Ace-seven suited I would play from fifth position on, with a mixture of 50 percent raises and 50 percent calls. Ace-seven unsuited I would play from sixth position on, with the same mixture of raises and calls.

The hands between ace-six and ace-deuce I would only play in late position, raising in all cases to steal the blinds. If the blinds have shown some toughness, however, I would just throw these hands away.

KQ, KJ, QJ, suited or unsuited: These hands are very treacherous for beginners, who see two face cards and think they have a fine hand. While the hands are playable in certain positions, they must be handled very carefully.

In early position, just throw away king-jack and queen-jack, suited or unsuited. With king queen, suited or unsuited, fold in a tough game. In a weaker game with king-queen suited, raise 50 percent of the time and call 50 percent of the time. With king-queen offsuit, call 50 percent of the time and fold 50 percent of the time.

In middle position these hands do a bit better. With king-queen I would play in all middle positions, with a mix of 60 percent raises and 40 percent calls. In third or fourth position I would play king-jack with a mixture of 50 percent raises and 50 percent calls. In fifth position I would bump the raises up to 60 percent and call with the rest. I would play both these hands the same way whether suited or unsuited. For queen-jack, I would fold the hand in third position, play it suited in fourth position with equal chances of raising or calling, and mostly raise with it in fifth position.

In late position I would be raising with all three of these hands to win the blinds.

All percentages in this section, are, of course, just general guidelines based on my experience. Remember too that the quality of the table (tight or loose, weak or strong) will affect whether you play these hands.

Suited connectors: I have one unusual play I like to make with any suited connectors. If I'm in first or second position, I'll raise with them about 15 percent of the time, representing a top pair. I need to bluff some percentage of the time in early position, and by using suited connectors as my randomizer, I ensure that my bluffs can't be read. When the connectors turn into a big hand on the flop, it's almost impossible for anyone to put me on that hand, and when I finally show down the winning hand, my opponents remember it for a long time.

The rest of this section covers normal value betting with suited connectors.

We've already covered the high suited connectors, down to queen-jack.

I would limp in with jack-ten suited in early position at a passive table. In middle position, I'd be a little more aggressive, with 50 percent raises and 50 percent calls. In late position I would certainly raise.

With ten-nine suited, I would fold in early position, limp in middle position (with just a few raises), and raise in late position.

With nine-eight suited and eight-seven suited, I'd fold in early and middle position, limp in sixth position, and raise on the button.

With seven-six and six-five suited, I would usually fold except on the button, where I would raise if I had seen that the blinds were folding.

I would usually fold five-four, four-trey, and trey-deuce suited in any position. The cards are just too low to play.

Miscellaneous weak hands: In sixth position I would play king-ten suited, king-nine suited, and queen-ten suited. I'd play these hands with a mixture of 50 percent folds and 50 percent raises. When I raised, I would still put in a normal raise of three times the big blind.

On the button, I would raise with a few more hands of this type: king-ten suited or unsuited, king-nine suited or unsuited, queen-ten suited or unsuited, queen-nine, suited or unsuited, and jack-nine suited.

With these very marginal hands, much depends on what I have managed to learn about the players in the blinds. You can see why studying the three players to your immediate left is so important. The player second to your left is always in a blind when you're in one of the two late positions. The player immediately to your left is the small blind when you're on the button, and the player three to your left is the big blind when you're one off the button.

Small blind versus big blind: Here's my general strategy for small blind versus big blind situations:

1.   Play any pair.

2.   Play any ace or king.

3.   Play any queen down through queen-five.

4.   Play jack-ten suited or jack-nine suited.

When you play, you want to limp half the time and raise half the time. When you raise, raise five times the big blind. The reason for the bigger-than-usual raise is that you'll be out of position the whole hand, and thus you need to discourage action.

The Gap Concept and the Sandwich Effect

The case that you're contemplating being the first player in the pot is the simplest to analyze. Your play depends only on the cards you hold and your position at the table. In all our other cases at least one person has entered the pot ahead of you. Before we discuss these cases, let's introduce two key ideas: the Gap Concept and the Sandwich Effect, both of which will influence your play in multi-player pots.

The Gap Concept was first defined by David Sklansky in his excellent book, *Tournament Poker for Advanced Players*. If you're thinking of entering a pot that has already been opened, you need a stronger hand to call than you would need to open the pot yourself from that position. Suppose, for example, you're in fifth position with

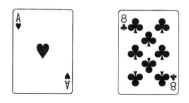

unsuited. If the first four players folded, you think that ace-eight unsuited is one of the minimum hands with which you would open the pot. But after the first two players fold, the third player opens with a raise and the fourth player folds. Should you call with your A♥8♣? No! You need a better hand than the minimum opening hand to get involved in a pot with a known opponent. The distance between the hand you need and the minimum opening hand is what Sklansky calls "The Gap," and it varies depending on circumstances. (In this situation, I would want an ace-king or an ace-queen suited to call.)

The logic behind the Gap Concept is easy to understand. Consider these two ideas.

1. When you open a pot, part of your vigorish is the possibility that the remaining players will just fold their hands, and you'll pick up the blinds and antes without a fight. Once the pot is opened ahead of you, that vigorish disappears.

2. The player who opened ahead of you opened in earlier position and therefore (at least theoretically) needed a stronger minimum hand to open. But he may have opened with a *much* stronger hand than that; you have no way of knowing. If you call with a minimum opening hand from your later position, you're probably going into the pot as a solid underdog. You would need big pot odds as compensation, and you're probably not getting them.

The Sandwich Effect is a related idea. Suppose there is one active player who has raised the pot, all other players have folded to you, and you are last to act. In this case you have all the information you need to calculate your pot odds and make your decision. But suppose instead that the pot has been opened, you are next to act, and there are several potentially active players behind you. Whatever you do, some or all of them may enter the pot behind you. Now you're operating in the dark. You don't know how many players will finally be involved in the pot, or, since you could be facing a raise, what your actual pot odds may be. You're caught in a *sandwich*, and as with the Gap Concept, you need a stronger hand as compensation.

With these ideas in mind, let's take a look at my starting requirements in some typical cases where the pot has already been opened.

Case 2: The player in third position opened for three times the big blind. You are in fifth position.

As you might expect, your strategy has to take into account the nature of the raiser.

If the raiser is a known super-aggressive player, *you reraise with any hand that you would use for an opening raise from your position.* The Gap Concept does not apply against a player who can make a move with any two cards. You also call with any hand that is slightly stronger than a hand that could make an opening call.

If the raiser is a solid, conservative player, however, the Gap Concept does apply, and you need to be more circumspect. Now you need stronger hands to reraise. To call, you need a hand that is slightly better than required to open an uncontested pot. Here are my detailed rules.

Holding pairs: With aces or kings, you want to call occasionally and mostly reraise. I would use a mix of 85 percent reraises and 15 percent calls. When you reraise, you want to put in two to three times the amount that your opponent put in.

With queens, you play, but with a larger percentage of calls. I would reraise 70 percent and call 30 percent.

With jacks and tens, you still play but again increase the percentage of calls. Now I would reraise only 20 percent and call the other 80 percent of the time.

The medium pairs, nines through sevens, are typically calling hands.

The small pairs, sixes through deuces, are not playable. Just throw them away.

Holding Ax: Ace-king is worth a call whether suited or unsuited.

With ace-queen, I would call if suited, and throw it away if unsuited.

Fold any smaller ace-x holding against a strong player. Against a player who is both aggressive preflop and weak (a delicious combination!) reraise with ace-king through ace-ten to isolate him.

Holding KQ, KJ, QJ: These are simply trap hands following an early raise. Throw them away.

Holding suited connectors: Fold them all.

Case 3: A caller in third position. You are in fifth position.

Facing a caller is much less threatening than facing a raiser. A call doesn't indicate nearly as much strength, so you don't need nearly as good a hand to play.

Here's your general rule: *With a few exceptions, you can play the same hands against a single caller that you could use to open.* Let's run through the candidate hands and see how they should be handled.

AA, KK, QQ: You should raise with these premium pairs. As before, a good raise is three to five times the big blind. Although I recommended a very occasional call with these hands in an unopened pot, I don't recommend that here. Limping in after one limper has already entered will just encourage several other limpers to come in after you, and that creates exactly the situation you *don't* want with a premium pair: a small pot with many players. You'll be the favorite, but unless the various hands have common cards, you'll be an underdog to win. Important exception: Limp if a raise behind you is fairly likely.

JJ, TT: Treat these hands like the premium pairs, and put in a healthy raise. As before, you don't want to encourage a multiway pot. Here's a sobering statistic: a pair of jacks, facing four opponents with randomly weak hands (ace-small, king-small, and two low flush draws) is only about 30 percent to win if the hands are played down to the end.

99: Play the hand, but with a 50/50 mixture of raises and calls.

88 through 22: In this situation, the small pairs benefit from what's called the *umbrella effect*. With one extra caller in the pot, calling with the small pairs gets you slightly better pot odds. As a result, you can call with eights, sevens, and sixes. On the button instead of fifth position, I would call with all these pairs. With the lower pairs, you're hoping to flop trips or catch an otherwise exceptionally favorable flop.

AK, AQ: With ace-king raise whether the hand is suited or unsuited. With ace-queen, I would raise only with suited cards, and call with unsuited.

AJ, AT: Call with ace-jack whether suited or unsuited. With ace-ten I would call only if suited. Fold an unsuited ace-ten.

A9 through A2: Fold all these hands. This may seem an exceptionally conservative strategy, but if you are playing these hands, you'll often find yourself up against an initial caller who had ace-x and x is a higher kicker than yours. You're a huge underdog in these hands, and you'll find yourself losing many big pots when an ace flops.

KQ, KJ: With a suited king-queen I would call. Fold an unsuited king-queen. I would play a suited king-jack only if I thought the opener was a loose or weak player.

Suited connectors: Fold them. The problem here is that you don't have enough players in the pot yet. Be alert, though, for the ideal hand with suited connectors: you're late to act and several limpers have already entered the pot. In that case you want to limp in as well. You'll mostly be throwing your hand away after the flop, but when you do hit your flush or straight, you'll have a chance to win a very large pot.

Case 4: You are on the button. The player in third position raised three times the big blind, and the player in fifth position raised nine times the big blind.

One player announced he had a strong hand. Knowing that, a second player announced he had an even stronger hand. Under these circumstances, what do you need to hop into the pot? Answer: You need a monster hand. The first player just might be bluffing, but the second player certainly isn't. Don't forget, too, that the blinds have yet to be heard from, and the first player still has the right to reraise no matter what you do.

AA, KK: Reraising with aces is obvious; this is the dream scenario for a pair of aces, and you may win a huge pot.

You can still reraise with kings, however. Sometimes one of your two opponents will be holding a pair of aces, and you'll be unhappy. But many times the two players are holding queens and ace-king, or something even weaker. Raising with the kings will still show a profit in the long run.

QQ: A pair of queens is usually worth a call here. If you don't improve on the flop, or you end up facing an all-in bet, you'll have to make a tough judgment call. But enough oddball situations can occur to make the call a reasonable play.

Long ago I saw a hand with a pair of queens all-in before the flop against three other players. The other three players all turned over ace-king! The queens held up.

All other hands: Fold. No matter what else you have, you don't belong in this pot.

Case 5: You are on the button. Three limpers in front of you.

This situation occurs all the time on online play, but not so much in live poker. It presents some interesting opportunities that the other situations do not.

AA through TT: Raise strongly with these hands, perhaps four to five times the big blind. This is a great situation for you. Your raise will often be mistaken as an attempt to steal the pot from some hands that haven't shown real strength, and you'll sometimes find yourself reraised by the small or big blind.

99 through 22: With these hands you should just call. If you flop trips you can look forward to winning a big pot. If not, you can let the hand go without having invested too much.

AK, AQ: With ace-king you can raise whether the hand is suited or unsuited. With ace-queen I would usually raise only with a suited hand. I'd usually just call with ace-queen unsuited.

Ax: With ace-jack and ace-ten I would call whether the hand was suited or unsuited. With a kicker smaller than a ten I would call if the cards were suited but fold them if they were unsuited. There's too much danger that one of the limpers holds an ace-small combination as well.

Suited connectors: Suited connectors are a great holding in this situation, and I would call with all the connectors down to five-four suited. You have a chance to see a cheap flop with a big pot, which is giving you the right odds and position for your suited connectors.

Before playing your suited connectors, make sure that the limpers aren't on short stacks. It's the big implied odds when you hit your straight or flush that makes this an attractive call, but if your opponents are short-stacked, you won't be able to win enough chips to make the play worthwhile.

Unsuited connectors: In this situation I would also call with the unsuited connectors down to five-four. I'm hoping to hit a straight or a straight draw, and I'm not paying much to do it. The big implied odds when I hit the straight makes the play worthwhile.

Other hands: King-jack, suited or unsuited, is worth a call here. I'd fold king-ten, however.

Making Adjustments
for Play in the Real World

The strategies I laid out here will work well at a full table of somewhat conservative players, all of whom have reasonable sized stacks. The real world, however, is not quite so neat. Real tables have tight players, loose players, crazy players, big stacks, little stacks, and everything else you can imagine. So let's look at the kinds of adjustments you have to make to survive in real-life poker.

As the number of players at the table shrinks, your playing requirements become looser. You can (and must) play more hands and play them more aggressively. I'll have much more to say about this topic in Volume II.

Real tables will have mixtures of tight players, loose players, and players with styles that are hard to characterize. If your table is mostly tight or mostly loose, the very useful general rule is that *you want to play in a style opposite to that of most of the players at the table*. At a table of tight players, you should loosen your requirements (opening not calling), because pots will be easier to steal, and you'd like to steal some of them. At a table of loose players, you theoretically want to play tightly, with better starting hands than normal, because you'll win fewer uncontested pots.

The "loose table" rule, however, is a more complicated case. Let's say your table is loose because Gus Hansen and Daniel Negreanu are on your left, and Phil Ivey is on your right. Now you have a strong incentive to play tightly, because when you get involved in pots with marginal hands, these guys will outmaneuver you after the flop. But suppose you're at a table with three guys who think they're Gus, Daniel, and Phil, but in reality they're Larry, Curley, and Moe. Now it's very important that you *not* be tight; instead you want to get involved in pots with them

196

with some marginal hands. The reason is simple. Over the first few hours of the tournament, Larry, Curley, and Moe are going to be losing their money to the stronger players at the table. Do you want to try to win the money now, while they still have their hands on it, or win it later, when the good players have it? I vote for the former.

Responding to
a Raise Behind You

What happens when you enter the pot with a nice call or raise, and a player sitting behind you reraises? There is no easy answer to this question, but there are a number of issues you have to weigh in deciding on your next move. In some cases, all (or most) of the issues will point in the same direction, and your decision gets pretty easy. In other cases, the issues will point in different directions, and you'll have a tough decision.

Let's look at the issues first. What should you take into consideration when you're reraised?

1. **Your hand**. Did you come into the pot with solid values, or were you making a call or raise with a marginal hand for your position?

2. **How many players were in the pot?** A raise from a player facing only one opponent in the pot is usually less significant than one from a player who has already seen two or more players enter the pot. There are at least four different situations, which must be judged differently. (1) You call the blind. A raise behind you indicates some strength. (2) You raise. A reraise behind you indicates more strength. (3) There is a call in front of you, and then you raise. A reraise behind you indicates even more strength. (4) There is a raise in front of you, and you reraise. Now a reraise behind you represents a real powerhouse.

3. **How many players are yet to act?** A reraise from the button or one of the blinds may just be an attempt to defend the blind or foil a steal. A reraise from a player in early or middle

position, who faces the possibility of several players yet to act behind him, indicates more strength.

4. **Will you have position on the reraiser after the flop?** If the reraiser is one of the blinds, you will act behind him after the flop. You can call with weaker hands than if the reraiser will act after you.

5. **What are the pot odds?** Be sure to calculate the pot odds before making your move. You should be much more willing to enter a pot with good odds rather than bad odds.

6. **How aggressive is the reraiser?** A reraise from a conservative player has to be given somewhat more respect than a reraise from a player who plays many pots. But don't press this analysis too far. Many aggressive and super-aggressive players like to steal unopened pots, but their reraises may be quite sound and normal. Until you have evidence that a player will try to reraise with minimal or weak hands, don't be quick to assume that's the case.

7. **What's the situation in the tournament?** If it's early in the tournament, and both you and the reraiser have plenty of chips in relation to the blinds and antes, you want to play more conservatively. You should be much less inclined to get involved in a situation that could knock you out of the tournament quickly. As your stack shrinks and the blinds pressure you more, your willingness to make a big move increases.

Those are a lot of issues to weigh. Let's look at a few examples and see how these decisions work out in practice.

Example No. 1. It's a nine-handed table, with blinds of $100/$200 and antes of $25. The pot is $525 to start. You're in

fifth position with $14,000. The stacks range between $6,000 and $17,000. The first four players fold to you. You have held good cards and have played several recent pots. You hold

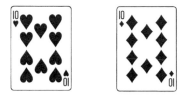

and raise to $600, making the pot $1,125. The rest of the players fold to the big blind, who has $12,000 and who has played somewhat aggressively. He puts in $1,000, making it $600 to you. The pot is now $2,125. *Should you fold, call, or raise?*

Answer: Let's walk through our criteria and see where we stand with this hand.

1. Your holding itself is very good. A pair of tens is an underdog only to the top four pairs. *Favorable.*

2. The reraise came from the last player to act, and there were no other players in the pot. *Favorable.*

3. You will have position on the reraiser after the flop. *Favorable.*

4. It costs you $600 to call, and there is $2,125 in the pot. You're being offered almost 3.5-to-1 odds to call. *Very favorable.*

5. The reraiser is known to be aggressive, and your recent activity creates the appearance that you may be on a steal. *Favorable.*

6.   Both you and the reraiser have plenty of chips in relation to the hand. *Neutral to favorable.*

Your first decision here is pretty easy; nearly all factors are favorable, and you're going to play the hand. Your real decision is a tougher one. Are you going to just call, or are you going to reraise?

You might think at first that with nearly all factors favorable, this must be an easy reraise. But that's not the case. A pair of tens is not really a great hand for putting in a third raise, and how you want to handle the hand depends a lot on the flop. If a couple of overcards appear on the flop, you're in bad shape. If low cards appear, you're in great shape. I like to base my decision on my position and my chip strength. If I'm out of position, I like to wrap the hand up quickly. If I have position, I like to let the hand play out more slowly, so that my positional advantage has time to operate.

My chip strength also affects my decision. It's early in the tournament, and I have plenty of time. The value of hands like jacks and tens drops in this situation, since those hands often end in coin flip situations against hands with two higher cards. That also argues for playing the hand more slowly. Considering both position and chip strength, I'd recommend a call.

Example No.2. Same table as before, with the same structure of blinds and antes. Once again, you have $14,000. A couple of players have a little more; most have less. The pot is again $525 to start. You're in third position with

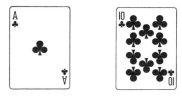

The first and second players fold. You elect to call. The fourth player folds, but the player in fifth position, with $10,000, raises $1,000. Since he is a new player who just joined the table, you know nothing about him. You have been playing aggressively and have won several recent small pots. The players behind him and the blinds all fold. The action is to you. The pot is now $1,725, and it costs you $800 to call. *What should you do?*

Answer: Let's walk through our criteria once more and see where we stand.

1. Your hand, A♣T♣, is a relatively weak holding for third position. Your call here was a little frisky. *Unfavorable.*

2. When your opponent raised, there were still four active players behind him. That indicates some strength. *Unfavorable.*

3. You will be out of position after the flop. *Unfavorable.*

4. It costs you $800 to call, and there is $1,725 in the pot, slightly better than 2-to-1 odds. Not as good as last time, but not bad either. *Slightly favorable.*

5. You know nothing about the raiser. Therefore he knows nothing about you. The fact that you have been aggressive lately is irrelevant, because he can't know that, having just arrived at the table. (Did you notice this?) He's probably giving you credit for being conservative, since that's what most players do by default. Therefore he'll imagine that your hand is better than it actually is. *Unfavorable.*

Not much doubt here. All factors except for the pot odds are unfavorable. Fold.

Limping into Pots

One characteristic problem of weak no-limit hold 'em players is calling too much before the flop, particularly in the early stages of tournaments. Their motivation is easy to understand. Calling is very cheap compared to their chip stack. Any hand can theoretically turn into a monster on the flop. When a weak hand flops a monster, it's more likely to be disguised than a strong hand. (Imagine you have

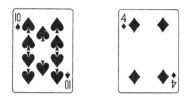

and the flop comes

Who will suspect you have an extremely strong hand?) So why not play a lot of weak hands on the cheap and see if you can flop a hand that lets you double up?

This argument sounds reasonable, but it has a few severe, practical problems.

1.   Players behind you may not be cooperative with your clever plan, since they've seen it all before. What happens when you and three others limp into a pot cheaply, and the big blind

makes a big raise? If you call you're putting all your chips at risk on a marginal hand, but otherwise you've just wasted a few more chips.

2. When you don't flop your monster hand (which will be almost always), you'll find yourself facing difficult decisions. Suppose you play a

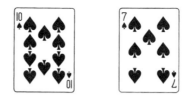

and the flop comes

Did a good player call with an ace-king, trying to trap you? Will you be able to lay down your pair of sevens? These are tough decisions. One virtue of playing good cards before the flop is that the decisions after the flop get easier.

3. Most flops miss most hands. Even when you don't run into one of the first two problems, you may simply spend a lot of chips trying to hit a big hand.

There is a time for playing more flops with weaker hands. It comes when you're a strong player at a table of weaker players, and you want to win their chips before they give them away to someone else. Even here, you want to choose your starting hands carefully and pick cards that hold some promise. Don't lose sight of the fact that, when the blinds are very small relative to the chip stacks, the theoretically correct way to play is very tight. In order to deviate, you need a very clear idea of what you're doing.

The Squeeze Play:
Exploiting the Sandwich Effect

The existence of the Sandwich Effect allows for a special kind of move called the "Squeeze Play." Imagine you have an early raiser, who may or may not have a strong hand, followed by a caller. When a player in late position now tosses in another raise, the original raiser is caught in a squeeze. The player in late position has shown strength and may have him beaten. But if the original raiser calls to see a flop, the caller, who might have been trapping with a strong hand, can raise as well. Under the circumstances, the original raiser needs a huge hand to continue playing, and will often elect to throw his hand away.

Here's a complex example of a squeeze play in an important tournament.

Sample Hand: Final Table of the 2003 World Series of Poker. The Players and their chip counts are as follows:

Small Blind	Amir Vahedi	$1,500,000
Big Blind	Tomer Benvenisti	$700,000
1	Sam Farha	$1,460,000
2	Yong Pak	$320,000
3	Jason Lester	$1,050,000
4	Dan Harrington	$575,000
5	Chris Moneymaker	$2,800,000

The blinds are $15,000 and $30,000, with $3,000 antes. The starting pot is $66,000. I'm in fourth position, and my hand is

This was an unusual hand from the 2003 World Series of Poker. Sam Farha raised 60,000 from first position, and I knew from his style and the number of pots that he had been playing that his raise represented a weaker hand than usual from the starting position. When Jason called I still hadn't looked at my hand, but I decided to pull a squeeze and come over the top as long as I had any kind of reasonable holding, like a low pair or suited connectors.

When faced with this move, the initial raiser gets squeezed between a reraiser and a caller who might have real strength, and almost has to throw his hand away unless he's latched onto a monster. The caller is then faced with a situation where he's out of position against a reraiser who's shown great strength. He'll often throw his hand away as well. I'll make this play unless my hand is really hopeless, like seven-trey or eight-deuce. As long as my hand has some outs, this is a great move.

When I looked at my cards and saw that I was holding kings, I realized that I'd stumbled into an incredibly favorable situation. I decided to raise to $200,000, overbetting the pot.

Chris Moneymaker, Amir Vahedi, and Tomer Benvenisti all fold. Sam Farha folds. Jason Lester (with 7-7) calls for another $140,000.

This hand made it to TV, and Jason was criticized later for his call. But in my opinion his call was perfectly justified. He's played with me a lot, and he knew that I was perfectly capable of making this move in this position. He figured my most likely holding was something like ace-queen or king-queen, so his sevens were likely to be good at this point.

And I knew he knew, which was why my bet before the flop was just a little larger than usual, to get more money into the pot.

The flop comes

Jason goes all-in.

On the tape, this looks foolish, going all-in with just a pair of sevens. But he made the right move. Most of the time I'm going to be sitting there with two unpaired high cards, and I'm going to have to throw my hand away. His real fear is that one of my unpaired high cards is a jack, in which case he's in trouble. But that's a minority of the cases, and mostly his play will just pick up the pot, crippling me in the process.

Some hands can't be understood without some knowledge of who the players are and what they have done against each other in the past. To the uninitiated, Jason and I look like a couple of amateurs here. I make a too-large raise with my kings, practically announcing I have a large pair, and Jason foolishly calls, then compounds his error by going all-in against a monster hand. But if you know both players well, the whole hand makes perfect sense.

I call, and my kings hold up.

All-In Before the Flop

In the late stages of a tournament, all-in moves before the flop are not uncommon. Players with short stacks find that making a smaller bet would commit them to the pot anyway, so they put all their chips in, or someone else at the table does it for them

In the early stages of a tournament, when players have plenty of chips relative to the blinds, all-ins before the flop are much more unusual. Of course, you'll occasionally see two very big hands butt heads, with one player getting all-in as a result. But most pre-flop all-ins result when weaker players get overenthusiastic.

It's easy to see why all-in bets should be rare. If you have plenty of chips and your hand is very strong, say aces or kings, then you want to use the hand to make a lot of money. An all-in bet will mostly chase the other players out of the pot, and you'll only make the blinds and antes. Not an optimal result. On the other hand, suppose you have a hand that's pretty good, but you'd like the other players to go away, say tens or nines. You could bet all your chips, which will chase away the riff-raff, but if a really big hand is waiting behind you, you're in serious danger of losing everything. A bet of four or five times the big blind is still big enough to chase the weak hands away, without jeopardizing your whole stack when someone behind you has a monster.

To see just how bad a play the quick all-in bet can be, let's take a situation in which a beginner might go all-in and do some math.

Example No. 1. It's the first hand of a major tournament, and you're in first position with

Your stack is $1,000, and the blinds are $5 and $10. You elect to go all-in with your queens. *How much do you expect to win, on average, with this play?*
Answer: Let's make a few quick, but reasonable assumptions.

1. If someone's waiting behind you with aces or kings, he will call.

2. No one else at the table has queens.

3. Smaller pairs will fold rather than risk all their chips.

4. Someone holding ace-king is an underdog to any pair and will fold.

So how often will you run into a pair of aces or kings? You'll draw a pair of aces, on average, about once every 220 hands. The same is true for a pair of kings. So let's say an individual player will get aces or kings about once every 110 hands, and we'll round off to every 100 hands just to make the numbers easier. There are nine players behind you, and each one has about a 1 percent chance of holding aces or kings. A quick approximation says that you'll end up facing aces or kings about 10 percent of the time; the other 90 percent, you'll win the pot uncontested. In the 10 percent of the time when you do face a big pair, you lose about 8 percent and win about 2 percent. Here's a summary of your results:

1. 90 percent of the time you win the blinds. Your expectation is 90 percent times +$15 which equals +$13.50.

2. 2 percent of the time you face aces or kings but win anyway. Your expectation is 2 percent times +$1,015 which equals approximately +$20.

3. 8 percent of the time you face aces or kings and lose. Your expectation is 8 percent times -$1,000 which equals -$80.

Your average result is just the sum of these three expectations which is -$46.50.

$$-\$46.50 = \$13.50 + \$20.00 - \$80.00$$

On average your play is a loser, costing you about three times the size of the current pot! Not too good, but also more than a little surprising. Most players would evaluate an all-in move with a pair of queens as non-optimal, but not really a large negative-equity play.

The lesson here is pretty clear. The chance of losing your whole stack to aces or kings is large enough to overwhelm the value of picking up the piddling blinds out there.

How big would the blinds have to be to make the all-in move a reasonable play? If we keep all our expectations the same but raise the blinds to $70 (from $15) then the play becomes a break-even move. That's not to say it's correct, only that it doesn't actually cost you money, on average. (Logic dictates that there must be some way of playing queens from first position that actually shows a profit.) As a rough guess, I would say that blinds somewhere in the range of $120-$150 would make the all-in move about as good as any other play.

The Problems

The problem section for this chapter is quite extensive. Problems 5-1 through 5-8 show a group of hands that cause a lot of trouble for beginners: unpaired high cards, ace-x, and king-x, suited or unsuited. Pay particular attention to how these hands should be treated. If you find yourself in too many tough situations after the flop, your trouble is probably rooted in your choice of starting hands.

Problems 5-9 through 5-13 deal with the techniques of handling a big pair before the flop. Pay careful attention to Problem 5-9, which explains some key tactical nuances.

Problems 5-14 through 5-17 focus on handling medium pairs. Problem 5-16 discusses some alternative strategies to the basic raise.

Problem 5-18 gives some extra insight into betting very low pairs before the flop.

Big Slick (ace-king) is a very tricky hand in no-limit hold 'em. Problem 5-19 gives an example of playing this hand.

Problem 5-20 talks about the similar ace-queen holding, this time when facing an all in from a short stack.

Problems 5-21 through 5-23 cover some miscellaneous topics. Problem 5-21 shows the dangers of an ill-considered steal attempt. Problem 5-22 shows how to use a raise to eliminate a positional disadvantage. Problem 5-23 illustrates the Sandwich Effect.

Hand 5-1

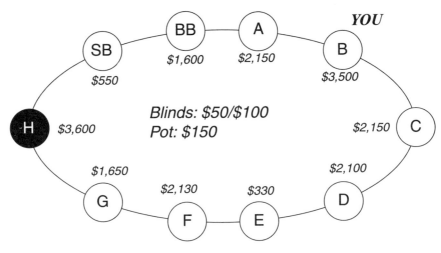

Situation: A few hours into a major tournament. The players are a mixed bag, but tend to be conservative.

Your hand: K♣6♣

Action to you: Player A folds.

Question: *What's your play with this hand?*

   Answer: In early position, you have to let this hand go. There are eight players still left to act, and you have no idea what they have or how many will enter the pot. This isn't really an aggressive/conservative question. You are in poor position with a mediocre hand, and your chip position is quite good, so just throw it away.

   In late position, you might consider doing something with this hand. If everyone folds around to you, and you're, say, one off the button, you could put in a small raise with the hand. Only three opponents remain, so you might steal the pot, and if you don't, you will have position plus some outs, and a shot at a flush, a potential monster hand. If there were several limpers in front of you, the combination of the pot odds, good position, and the flush possibility would make a call reasonable. Before you put in your call or raise, be sure to make a quick glance at the players still to act behind you. If anyone is reaching for his cards, that's a good sign. Anyone reaching for their chips is a bad sign. If I saw someone reaching for his chips, I'd switch gears and reach for my cards instead.

Be aware that to make such plays, you must know what's going on at the table, and be very cautious after a questionable flop. If you call against four people, and the flop comes A♦K♠T♣, you're in big trouble. To make the call in the first place, you have to be cheerfully able to let a situation like that go.

Resolution: You fold.

Hand 5-2

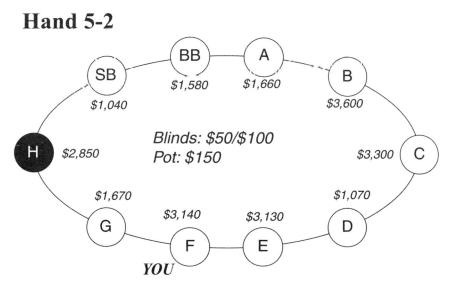

Situation: A few hours into a major tournament. Players B and C seem like solid, tight, good players. Player G is very loose. Other players tend to the conservative.

Your hand: A♣4♥

Action to you: Player A folds, B and C call $100. Players D and E fold. Pot is now $350.

Question: *Do you fold, call, or raise?*
> **Answer:** Fold. You have to get used to letting these hands (ace-small) go, especially in multi-way pots. What, actually, are you rooting for on the flop? Since the other players are also trying to stay with aces, and since another ace is likely to have a higher kicker than yours, hitting an ace on the flop could be very expensive. If not, you're really pulling to flop a small straight, which would win but which is very unlikely. The risk-reward ratio here is terrible. Let it go.

Resolution: You fold.

Hand 5-3

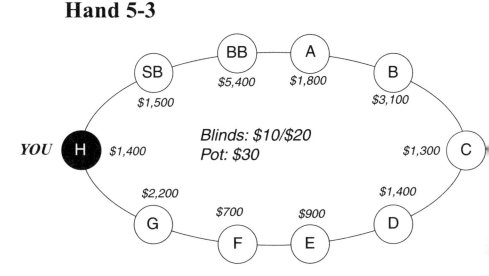

Situation: Major tournament, early in the first round. Player B likes to play a lot of pots, and has won a couple of big ones so far. No information yet on Player D. Player E has shown down a couple of good hands, and seems to bet what he has. The big blind has just arrived from another table.

Your hand: A♠8♦

Action to you: Player A folds, B calls $20, C folds, D calls $20, E raises to $80, F and G fold. Pot now $150.

Question: *Do you fold, call, or raise?*

> **Answer:** Despite the good position, ace-eight isn't that strong a hand. Here it's up against two callers and a raiser, with the big stack yet to be heard from. You should simply fold.
>
> If the action had been folded around to you, then you could raise with this hand.
>
> If you were up against only one caller, and he seemed to be a tight player, then venture a call.
>
> The minimum hand you should call with in this position would be ace-jack or ace-ten. You could also call with any pair.
>
> With ace-king or ace-queen you can reraise on the button.
>
> In the actual hand, Player H does elect to call.

Action: You call. The small blind and big blind fold. The original two callers put in another $60 each. Pot now $350.

Flop: T♥7♦3♠

Action: Player B checks, Player D bets $20, and Player E raises to $160.

Question: *What do you do?*

> **Answer:** The flop missed you completely, and a solid player says he has something. Believe him and fold.

Action: You fold.

Hand 5-4

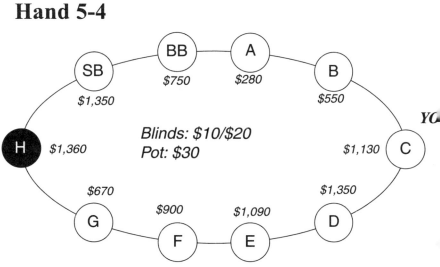

Situation: Early in a one-table satellite tournament.

Your hand: A♦T♣

Action to you: Player A folds, Player B calls $20. Pot is now $50.

Question: *What do you do?*

> **Answer:** You're in early position with a hand that is not that strong. One player is already in and seven players are yet to act behind you. You fold.
>
> Ace-ten is one of those seductive hands that traps many players into losing a lot of money over time. Remember this about kickers — they're on an accelerated depreciation schedule. Ace-king is a fine hand. Ace-queen is a little weaker, but still good. With ace-jack, you're already sliding rapidly down a slippery slope. With ace-ten, you've slid down the slope, fallen off the cliff, and lie in wreckage at the bottom with hands like ace-five and ace-six. When you

evaluate a kicker, remember that it has to be able, on occasion, to win the hand for you on its own, when no ace appears on the board. So a king is just fine, but a ten looks pretty weak when kings, queens, or jacks appear. You should fold this hand without giving it much thought.

But the player we're watching decides to play, so let's see what happens.

Action: You call for $20. Players D, E, F, and G all fold. The button calls. The small blind folds and the big blind checks. There's now $90 in the pot, and you're third to act out of four players.

This was an excellent result for you. There were no raises, and your position after the flop is relatively good.

FLOP: T♠9♥3♥

Action: The big blind bets $40, and Player B folds. The pot is $130, and it's $40 to you.

Question: *What's your play?*

Answer: That was a very good flop for your hand. You have top pair with top kicker. The big blind's bet doesn't necessarily mean anything. It looks like what we call a probe bet — a bet of about half the pot or less, designed to win the pot cheaply or gather some information. You should raise here both to define your hand and to chase out Player H. If your bet draws a big reraise, you're probably done with the hand.

Action: You raise to $80. The button folds, and the big blind calls. The pot is now $250.

Fourth Street: 5♠

Action: The big blind checks. *What do you do?*

Answer: The big blind is certainly acting like he's on a draw, perhaps to a spade or heart flush. If that's the case, he's about a 4-to-1 underdog to make his hand. (There are 9 spades outstanding, out of a total of 46 cards that the players hasn't seen yet. So he has 9 winning cards and 37 losing ones, making him a 37-to-9 underdog, or about 4-to-1. Remember this number for flush draws with one card to come.)

If he's on a flush draw, you want to make sure he's not getting the right odds to draw to his hand. You need to bet enough so the odds aren't right, but there's no need to overbet the pot, just in case you had misread the situation, or he's trapping. I'd bet about $150 here. Then he'd have to put in $150 to win a pot of $400, so he's getting less than 3-to-1 on his money — not enough.

Action: You actually bet $250, and he calls. The pot is now $750.

Fifth Street: 6♣

Action: He checks. *What do you do?*

Answer: If he was drawing for either flush, he just missed them. Possibly he's been playing with some combination of a low pair and a draw, in which case you have him beaten, but he might still call a small bet. If he has a stronger hand, he's played incredibly passively throughout.

You have about $700 left, while he has only about $400. There's not that much left to be won, but you should bet something in the neighborhood of $150. You need to accumulate chips whenever you can, you've got plenty of reasons to think you have the best hand, and the pot odds of about 5-to-1 should be irresistible to him, particularly since he'll still have a few chips left if he calls and loses.

Action: You check, and he shows down 8♠7♠, for a winning straight.

An unlikely holding, but certainly good enough. He had an open-ended straight draw on the flop, and that plus a flush draw on fourth street. With 17 outs (nine flush cards plus eight straight cards), he almost had the money odds for a proper call on fourth street.

Were you unlucky? Yes and no. It was an unlikely holding given his bets, and he didn't win as much as he could have. But you had no business being in the pot in the first place. The problem with playing marginal starting hands in early position is that you get caught in a lot of these predicaments — difficult hands, difficult decisions, and a lot of chips committed to what turn out to be toss-up situations.

Hand 5-5

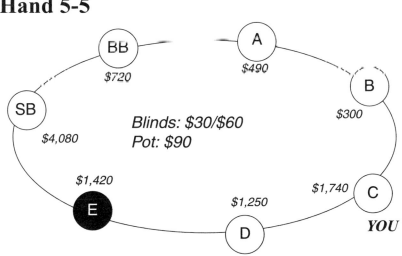

Situation: Middle of a one-table satellite tournament.

Your hand: A♦T♠

Action to you: Player A calls for $60, Player B raises to $120. Pot is now $270.

Question: *Do you fold, call, or raise?*

 Answer: Ace-ten is a hand that fools a lot of players. It looks like you have something strong, but, as in the last problem, in reality you just have an ace with a weak kicker.

 Here you're facing a bet and a raise from the two small stacks. In itself, that's not scary. But the four other large stacks are yet to act behind you, and you don't know what any of them are going to do. That's scary.

 Late in a tournament, with a dwindling stack, you'd make a stand with this hand. Not here. Just let it go.

Action: You fold.

Hand 5-6

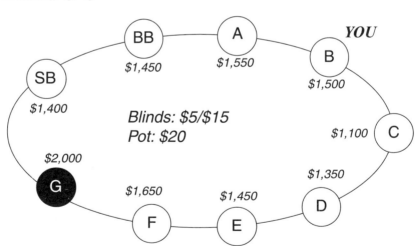

Situation: Early hand of a major tournament.

Your hand: A♠J♠

Action to you: Player A folds.

Question: *Do you fold, call, or raise?*

    Answer: As a practical matter, you should call with this hand. Theoretically, it's not quite strong enough to play in such an early position. But there are enough weak players in the early rounds of tournaments that it's not a bad strategy to see a few cheap flops with marginal hands, just to see if you can catch something and maybe double up.

    Note that the weaker a player you believe yourself to be, the less you want to employ this strategy. If you think you're inexperienced or overmatched, just fold the marginal hands and try to play with solid value. Fooling around with marginal hands is just a tool for the player who knows how to let a hand go when he gets in trouble (which will often be the case!).

    Raising is a mistake unless the table has been so quiet that you think there's a good chance you may buy the pot. When you play ace-jack from early position, your goal is to see a cheap flop and evaluate, not to build a big pot before you actually have anything.

Action: You actually raise to $60. Players C, D, E, and F all fold. Player G raises to $460. The blinds fold. The pot is now $540 and it costs you $400 to call.

Question: *What do you do?*

    Answer: You throw your hand away. You represented a strong hand to begin with, and your opponent promptly raised you another $400. Unless he's just bluffing, what hands justify that play? Not very many — just the high pairs, ace-king, maybe ace-queen suited. Every hand that could reasonably make this move has you beaten, and even some of the other hands (tens, for example) are slight favorites. So if you call, it's just with the hope that he's bluffing. Is it worth risking a third of your stack for that possibility? Not to me. Just let it go.

Action: Actually, you call.

Flop: J♦8♣5♥

Question: You're first to act. *What do you do?*
Answer: Check. You now have a pair of jacks, but your opponent has said he's got a real hand. Let him make a move and then decide.

Action: You check. Player G bets $820. *Do you call?*
Answer: Now calling makes no sense. He's representing a hand better than yours. If you think he's bluffing, put him all-in so you at least get the rest of his chips. (If you call, the pot odds are so big that he's going to get the rest of yours.) If you believe him, then fold.

Action: You call.

Fourth Street: 2♠

Action: He puts you all-in for your last $220. *Do you call?*
Answer: Sure. You've reached what's called an inflection point. We'll say lots more about inflection points in Volume II. For now, just note that your choice is between leaving the hand now and remaining with just $220, or trying to double up and get to $3,000. Any chance at all that he's bluffing makes the call worthwhile, since you really don't want to try to survive with a tiny stack when the blinds are creeping up behind you.

Action: You call, and he shows Q♥Q♣. His hand holds up on fifth street.

The big mistake here was getting involved in the hand at all. A good player would have tossed in a $20 call, then folded his hand after the big bet before the flop. By falling in love with your A♠J♠, and ignoring what your opponent was telling you, you lost all your chips.

Hand 5-7

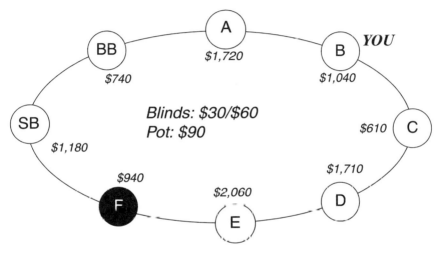

Situation: Halfway through an online single-table tournament.

Your hand: K♦J♥

Action to you: Player A folds.

Question: *Do you fold, call, or raise?*

    Answer: No single group of hands gets beginning players in as much trouble as these hands — two unsuited high cards without an ace. They see king-queen, king-jack, queen-jack and think "Wow, two face cards, I must have something pretty good." Actually you have a hand which, lacking an ace, is just okay.

At a table of eight players, like we have here, you should fold K♦J♥ in first position (Player A). On the button or one off the button (Players E and F), you should definitely open if no one has yet entered the pot. In middle position (Players B, C, and D) you have a marginal opening hand, and you might want to play. You would base your decision on how you see yourself interacting with the table. If you think you're the strongest player, you definitely want to play. If you have control of the table and the other players are responding to your moves rather than vice-versa, you also want to play. If you're playing passively and the other players are pushing you around, then you're better off folding this hand.

Action: In fact you call with your K♦J♥. Players C, D, E, and F all fold. The small blind puts in $90, raising you an additional $60. The big blind calls for $60. The pot now contains $300. It's $60 to you.

Question: *What do you do?*

Answer: Here's another chance to make an error. Every now and then, in the middle of a hand, a player will realize that he didn't belong in the hand in the first place. While he might try to keep a straight face, inwardly he's thinking *"Dumkopf! Why did I call??"* Then he "corrects" his error by throwing his hand away.

Don't fall into this trap. Once you're in a hand, every subsequent decision has to be determined by your hand, the pot odds, and the total table situation. *Every betting decision is a new problem.* Don't forget that.

Here the pot is offering you 5-to-1 odds to call. Your K♦J♥ may not have been a great entering hand, but you're nowhere near a 5-to-1 underdog here and you have position. So call.

Action: You call. The pot now contains $360.

Flop: K♥6♠2♦

Action: The big and small blinds both check. *What do you do?*
Answer: That's a great flop for you. You have top pair with a decent kicker, so you're going to bet. You want to bet a decent amount, because it looks like you have the best hand. You don't want to bet too much, because you'd like to encourage, rather than discourage, action. I'd bet something in the range of $200-$220.

Action: You actually bet $300. The small blind calls, the big blind folds. The pot is now $960.

Fourth Street: 7♣

Action: The small blind checks. *Should you bet or check?*
Answer: Time to look at the stacks that are left. You have $620, he has $760. The fourth street card eliminated all flushes, and there is no plausible straight draw out there. The only significant bet you can make is to move all-in. It still looks like you have the best hand, so do it. If he's sitting there with ace-king, that's poker. You have to win your chips sometime, and this looks like the time.

Action: You actually bet $200, and he calls.

Too small a bet.

Fifth Street: J♣

Action: He checks. *What do you do?*
Answer: You still go all-in. If he has trip jacks, that's just incredibly bad luck.

Resolution: You go all-in, and he calls with 8♦8♣. You win the pot.

You might have been surprised to see your opponent show down a mere pair of eights on the end. Although he did misplay the hand, his play wasn't completely hopeless. From his point of view, you were in stealing position throughout the hand, and might have been simply trying to steal the pot. Had you been playing ace-queen instead of king-jack, all your bets would have made sense and his eights would have been the best hand at the end. Optimistic thinking on his part, perhaps, but not crazy.

He did make an error, however, in not leading out with a bet after the flop. With a medium pair and an overcard showing on the board, he could have defined his hand with a bet, as well as giving you a chance to fold. You would have called or raised of course, and he would have known that he was facing some sort of real hand, and his eights were most likely no good. By not defining his hand after the flop, he never knew where he stood until the showdown, at which point he had lost all his chips.

Hand 5-8

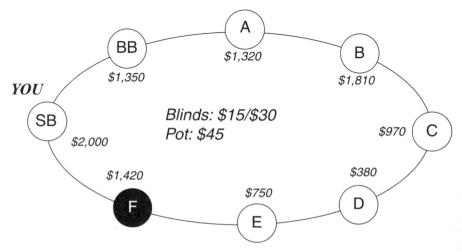

Blinds: $15/$30
Pot: $45

Situation: Early in an online tournament. The button has been playing aggressively and stealing some blinds.

Your hand: K♣8♠

Action to you: Players A through E all fold. The button raises to $60. The pot is now $105.

Question: *Do you fold, call, or raise?*

    Answer: The button may be trying to steal, or he may have a hand. Your actual hand, however, is pretty weak. At this point, you are the big stack and the button is the third-biggest stack, so getting mixed up in this hand could be expensive. *Do you want to risk it?*

    I think the worst play is just to call. Now you're involved in the pot with bad position, a weak hand, and knowing nothing about what Player F really has. That way gets you in a lot of trouble.

    If I think he's bluffing (or just want to find out for sure), I'll venture a raise to about $180. If I get called I know I'm up against something, and if I get reraised, I'm definitely throwing the hand away. But this way I've defined my hand and I'll have some idea of where I stand after the flop. I'll also make this play against someone who's put in a few raises from the button without being called. I've got to make a stand against that sort of player at some point, and while I'd like to do it with a better hand than K♣8♠, it's just good enough for my purpose.

    In the absence of any information about the button, the best play is just to throw the hand away.

Action: You actually call for an additional $45. The big blind folds. The pot is now $150.

Flop: 8♦5♠3♥

Question: *Bet or check?*
> **Answer:** Pretty good result. You now have top pair plus an overcard. If you don't bet this, why are you in the hand? (Note, by the way, that you could check-raise an aggressive player who is known to make continuation bets.)

Action: You bet $100. Player G raises to $200. The pot is now $450. *What do you do?*
> **Answer:** You must call. You still have top pair, and the pot offers 4.5-to-1 odds. Don't get trapped second-guessing yourself about whether you should be in the hand in the first place. In poker, we don't care how we got to this spot. We just care about the situation currently on the table.

Action: You call.

Fourth Street: 9♦

Question: *What do you do?*
> **Answer:** Check. The card hurt you, since it's an overcard to your pair. You don't need to make an informational bet, since he's already told you, with his bet last turn, that he has a good hand. So check and see what happens.

Action: You check. He bets $150. The pot is now $600. *What do you do?*
> **Answer:** You call. You're getting offered 4-to-1 odds by the pot, and you may still have the best hand. Remember that you're only beaten if he was playing an overpair to the board from the beginning, or had something like ace-nine, and just hit a pair of nines. One of those two things is possible, and at this point it's probably even likely, but it may not be the case and you're getting good odds to call.

Action: You call. The pot is now $750.

Fifth Street: 7♣

Question: *Any reason to bet on the end?*
    Answer: No. Just check and see what happens. If he makes a big bet, you're going to throw your hand away. If he makes a small enough bet, you'll call.

Action: You check and he checks. He wins the hand with a pair of jacks.
    Answer: A tough hand that ended up costing you a lot of money. As we've seen before, it was only the initial move into the pot that was a mistake. After that, all plays were reasonable, given the pot odds. This hand and many of the others we've seen show how important that initial decision to play the pot really is, and why it's so dangerous to get involved with sub-par starting hands.
    Note also that the jacks missed an opportunity to make a little more money by betting on the end. Weak players lose a lot of money over the course of a tournament by missing these high-percentage situations. Good players don't.

Hand 5-9

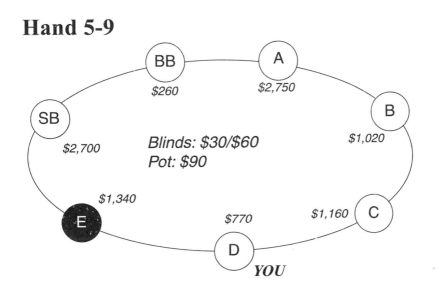

Situation: About halfway through a single-table online tournament.

Your hand: A♥A♦

Action to you: Player A calls. Players B and C fold. The pot is now $150.

Question: *Do you raise, and if so, how much?*

Answer: With a pair of aces, the question is never "Will I get involved in the hand?" but "How can I get the most money into the pot?" This can be a tricky business. Here are some tips to keep in mind.

1. *You want more money in the pot, but not more players in the pot.* Aces are a big favorite against a single opponent, but winning chances start to drop drastically as more players get involved. Against two opponents, your aces might be no more than 60 percent to win a showdown. True, you will triple up when that happens, but 40 percent of the time you'll be out of the tournament, which is a high price to pay. Ideally, you want lots of money in the pot and a single opponent.

2. *Rarely slowplay aces!* This is a key insight which beginners frequently violate. Slowplaying creates a smaller pot with more participants — exactly what you *don't* want.

3. *Watch the stack sizes of your potential opponents carefully.* Unlike the case with most other hands, with aces you don't need to be concerned with staying away from stacks that can break you. Here the big stacks are your natural prey, since they will be the most willing to play with you. Also remember that you can make a

slightly bigger bet against a big stack, since they can call you more readily.

Here you have one player already in the pot, and that player is the biggest stack at the table. You should probably raise about $180-$200. That should discourage other callers from getting involved, while being a pretty easy raise for Player A to call.

Action: You actually put in only $120, a raise of $60 to Player A. Player E folds. The small blind calls, putting in $90 more. The big blind puts in $120, raising the pot another $60. Player A folds. The pot is now $480. The big blind has $80 left. The small blind has $2,580 left. You have $650.

Question: *What do you do?*
> **Answer:** A cute situation has arisen. The big blind will be all-in this hand, but with a very small stack. You're not really concerned about him any more. Your real target is the small blind, who has enough chips for you to double up. Your real problem is keeping the small blind in the hand, and for that you need to just call here. A raise is just too likely to chase the small blind away.
>
> Doesn't this violate our principle of trying to play aces against just a single opponent? No, it doesn't. If the two opponents have very different stack sizes, you're not really facing two different players. *As long as you win the large side pot against the big stack, you'll show a nice profit in the hand, regardless of how well you do in the main pot against the small stack.*

Action: You actually go all-in. The small blind folds, and the big blind calls for his last $80. The big blind turns over K♥K♠, and your aces hold up to win the pot.

If the small blind had stayed around, he might have beaten you. But you need to accumulate chips sometime, and what better time to go up against a big stack than when you have aces?

Hand 5-10

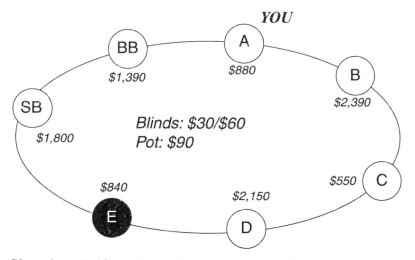

Situation: Halfway through a one-table satellite. Player D looks like a strong player. Player E has been wild.

Your hand: Q♠Q♣

Action to you: You are first to act.

Question: *How much do you raise?*

 Answer: You should certainly raise with Q♠Q♣ in first position. The only question is: How much?

 With aces or kings, a good raise is $120, twice the big blind. It's a significant bet, but not so large that it discourages action. You welcome action with hands that strong.

 With queens, it's a little different. Now you're not so eager for action. If players call you with ace-x or king-x and an ace or king flops, you're in big trouble. So you've got to cut down the number of drawing hands, and that means you're going to bet more with queens, to make the pot less interesting to anyone on a draw. You want to bet three to four times the big blind here — perhaps $180 to $220. Anyone who wants to get into the pot against your queens has to pay for the privilege.

Action: You in fact raise to only $120. Players B and C fold. Player D raises to $180. Player E calls the $180. The blinds fold.

Question: *What do you do now?*
Answer: This is a great result for you, particularly with your small chip count. You should now move all-in for your last $760. You're a favorite against ace-king, and only aces and kings have you beaten. Against all other hands you're a huge favorite. Player E is very loose, so even an all-in bet might get a call from his presumably weak hand. If Player D calls you, he'll show down a strong hand.

One last point — you're still in bad position versus the other two players. An all-in bet neutralizes your positional disadvantage.

Action: You put in another $200, raising the other players $140. They both call you. The pot is now $1,050.

Flop: 7♠3♠2♠

Question: *What's your move now?*
Answer: Now it's clear to go all-in. The flop was good for you. If your opponents called with two high cards, they didn't get helped. Your Q♠ gives you some insurance against the flush possibility, and unless someone is sitting there with two spades, your bet is incredibly scary to call. In addition, you're down to your last $560 and you're not folding if anyone bets, and someone certainly will if you check. So you're really

committed to the pot here, and an all-in bet is the last leverage you have. Use it.

Action: You go all-in for your last $560. Both players call. Player D shows A♠K♦, Player E shows T♥7♣.

The Board: Fourth street is the 2♦, fifth street is the A♦. Player D wins.

A tough beat, losing to an ace on fifth street, although any king or spade would also have beaten you. Player D's draw at the nut flush gave him 14 outs on each of the last two cards, so he was actually a slight favorite after the flop. His plays were all correct. Player E was completely brain-dead, of course. You should be very nice to Player E, who's no doubt a fine fellow when he's not trying to play poker, and welcome him to your game in the future.

Hand 5-11

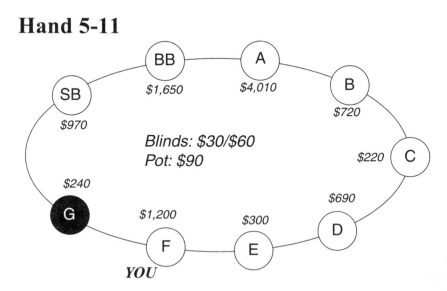

Situation: In the middle of a single-table tournament.

Your hand: K♥K♦

Action to you: Players A, B, and C all fold. Player D calls $60. Player E folds. The pot is now $150.

Question: *As you move for your chips, you notice Player G behind you moving toward his chips. How much do you raise?*

Answer: If you knew this was a two-player hand, your normal raise would be to something like $200. But the knowledge that the small stack behind you is ready to presumably go all-in changes your strategy a bit.

You're not afraid of an all-in from the small stack, of course. He's desperate and could be playing with anything, and your kings are undoubtedly good. But you can use this information to crush Player D and drive him out of the pot. Just raise $120. Now Player G will follow up with an all-in to $240, and Player D will be sandwiched between the two of you. If he calls G's bet, you're still active and can raise him any amount. So he'll likely toss in his cards and you'll be heads up against G, with only one hand to beat rather than two, and a fair amount of dead money in the pot.

Action: You raise $120. Player G goes all-in for $240. The blinds fold. Player D folds. You call the all-in. The pot is $630. Player G shows a Q♥T♦, and your kings hold up.

Hand 5-12

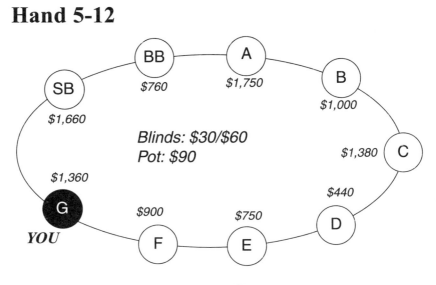

Blinds: $30/$60
Pot: $90

Situation: Early in a one-table satellite.

Your hand: Q♠Q♦

Action to you: Player A folds. Player B raises to $120. Player C folds. Player D raises to $440, all-in. Players E and F fold. The pot is now $650.

Question: *Do you fold, call, raise, or go all-in?*

 Answer: Here's a common situation where a lot of players make a routine mistake. Player B raised twice the big blind. By itself, that doesn't mean much. He has some kind of a hand, but it's unlikely to be a favorite against queens. Now Player D, with the short stack at this point, goes all-in. We'll deduce that he has some sort of a hand, he's desperate, and he's making his move. Again, there's no reason to think his hand is better than your Q♠Q♦.

 So what's your play? The common mistake when faced with an all-in bet is just to call. But if you call, there's a good chance that Player B will call as well and get to see the flop.

Although your queens are probably a favorite against either of the two hands out there individually, you're probably less than 50 percent to win playing against two reasonable hands simultaneously. For instance, if one of the hands is ace-jack and the other is nines, your winning chances in a three-way pot dealt down to the end are just 58 percent, even though you're better than 80 percent heads-up against the nines and 70 percent heads-up against the ace-jack.

So instead of calling or putting in a small raise, now is the time to go all-in. This way you chase out Player B (probably) and isolate on Player D. Your chances of winning the pot go up, and if you do lose, the loss won't hurt you that much. If you let Player B hang around and he outdraws you, you could lose most of your chips.

Resolution: You raise all-in and Player B folds. Player D turns over T♣T♥. Your queens hold up to win the pot.

Hand 5-13

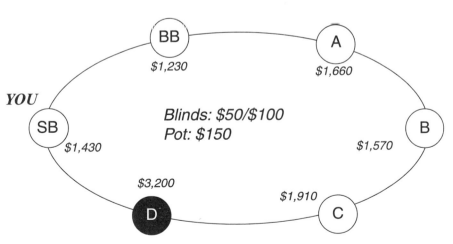

Situation: Halfway through a single table satellite.

Your hand: K♠K♥

Action to you: Players A and B fold. Player C raises to $200. Player D folds. The pot is $350.

Question: *Do you raise, and if so, how much?*
　　Answer: You want to raise here, obviously, but you don't want to raise too much. You want him to call so you can make some money. I'd recommend a raise to about $600. If he calls and an ace comes on the flop, well, that's the way it goes sometimes. But you don't want to chase out some medium pair here.

Action: You actually raise $800. The big blind folds. Player C puts you all-in for your remaining $580.

Question: *What do you do?*
　　Answer: You're delighted, and you call.

　　A lot of players will tell you stories about the times they folded kings because they knew their opponent was raising with aces. Here's my story. About a year ago, a tight player in the big blind raised me. I actually thought he had aces. I was in early position with a pair of kings. I made a modest raise and he reraised me. I thought a long time and called. The flop came three small cards, and he bet a modest amount and I called. He actually had the aces.

　　I almost threw the hand away, but I couldn't do it. Just not savvy enough. Even bets and raises that seem to indicate great strength can have a variety of explanations, from moderately strong hands to outright bluffs. And here's a little secret from the world of top-class poker. Nobody else is that savvy either, no matter what they tell you.

Action: You call. Your opponent shows you A♣A♦, which holds up.

About one time in 24, when you hold kings at a full table, someone at the table will be holding aces. If you try to figure out exactly when that occurs, you'll end up folding a lot of hands when you're actually facing queens, or ace-king, or something even weaker. So don't bother. Just play your kings like you have the best hand, and you'll do better in the long run. (Note that when you raise with your kings, get called by one or two players, *and then an ace flops*, is a very different situation.)

The simple truth is that everyone remembers the times that their kings were beaten by aces, but they forget all the other times that they were afraid the other guy had aces, but he turned over jacks or queens instead. You have only a limited amount of time in tournaments to make money before the blinds devour you, so put the whip to your genuinely good hands, and let them carry you home.

Hand 5-14

YOU

BB — A

SB $2,270 $1,550 B

$1,260 $940

H $3,170   Blinds: $15/$30 $1,870 C
         Pot: $45

$1,290 $1,690

G $2,090 $1,900 D

F — E

Situation: A major tournament, an hour or so into play. You're in first position, and behind you is a random mix of loose and tight players.

Your hand: T♠T♦

Action to you: You are first to act.

Question: *What's your play?*

Answer: As with the other medium pairs, you probably have the best hand before the flop, but, unless you flop your set, you could be in difficulty after the flop. Traditional (and correct) strategy is to make a nice sized bet before the flop, trying to narrow the field to a single caller, against whom T♠T♦ will play well. My standard bet here is three to four times the big blind.

But here's the problem with this and all such advice. Your opponents are always watching you, looking to pick up betting patterns. Even though you may think that three or four times the big blind is the "correct" play, you have to vary your actual bets around that number, so that your opponents can't get a read on exactly what you're doing. About a third of the time, I'd just limp in with this or another medium pair. Perhaps 10 percent of the time, I'll take the bet up to five or six times the big blind. The rest of the time, I'll make my standard play, and hope that the other players won't know exactly what it means.

Resolution: You raise $150, and everyone else folds.

Hand 5-15

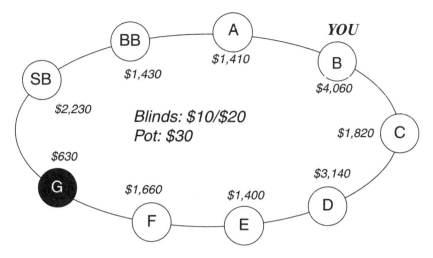

Situation: Major tournament, early in the first round. You have already won several big pots, showing down strong hands.

Your hand: T♥T♦

Action to you: Player A folds.

Question: *What's your play?*

    Answer: There is no "correct" way to play a medium pair in early position, but there are two plays that make good sense. Choose between them based on the circumstances, or just vary your pattern at random to throw off your pursuers.

    The problem, of course, is that the hand rates to be the best at the table right now, but does not rate to be the best after a flop comes. So you don't want to play this hand against a lot of players for a significant amount of money.

    One approach is just to call, hoping to see a cheap flop against some number of opponents, and then make a decision later to commit more chips. If you hit the third ten, you have a monster hand and can win a lot of money. If you don't hit the ten, but three low cards come on the flop, your hand is probably still best and you can play accordingly. If you miss the flop and high cards come, you can throw the hand away for just the price of a call.

The second approach is to make a significant bet now (say three to five times the big blind), and hope to either win the pot or narrow the field to just one opponent. Now you can survive a high card on the flop, although two high cards would still make you very nervous.

Which approach should you use here? Note that here you've already won some big pots at this table by showing down some very strong hands. That fact will determine your play. Let's see how.

When people notice you showing down strong hands, they remember it. Unconsciously, they start to assume that those are the only hands you play. They also remember if you're showing down winning hands. In their heads, they start to associate you with the thought "I need to stay out of pots that this guy is in. He's dangerous."

Given the likely perception of you at this point, the raising play doesn't look quite so good now. It's true that you're more likely to steal this $30 pot with an $80 or $100 bet. But any hand that does call you is likely to be stronger than average for this situation, and you shouldn't like that risk-reward ratio. So you should settle for a simple call here.

Action: You call for $20. Players C and D fold. Players E and F call. Player G, on the button, goes all-in for $630. The blinds fold. The pot is now $720, and it costs you $610 to call.

Question: *What's your play?*

Answer: An all-in raise from the short stack shouldn't scare you. You certainly want to play this hand with your pair of tens. Your concern now is the two live players behind you. A normal play is to toss in another raise here, say to $1,200, with the idea of showing more strength and discouraging either Player E or Player F from calling. After they fold, you're heads-up against the button, which is just what you want.

That's the standard play in this situation, but here there's a problem with the stack sizes. Both Player E and Player F have about $1,500. If they're willing to call a $600 bet with those stacks, would they really fold for a $1,200 bet? Probably not. They might just view this as a fine chance to go all-in and double up. You shouldn't be terrified of that result, but you also shouldn't yet want to risk that big a portion of your stack on T♥T♦. If you call, and they call, you'll know they've got something, but you've left yourself a way out of the hand. That's a good play.

Action: You call for $610. Player E folds, but Player F puts in another $610 to call. The pot is now $1,940.

Flop: Q♦Q♣6♥

Question: *What do you do?*

Answer: First, note that the flop is a good one for you. It's much better that two queens came rather than, say, a king and a queen, because it's much less likely that your opponent holds a card that matches the board. (If king-queen flops, there are a total of six kings and queens outstanding. But there are now only two queens outstanding. Remember these little factoids — they matter!)

You must bet here to protect your hand. To see why, imagine that you check instead. He may then check as well, and you may have given him a free card that beats you. That's a mortal sin in poker.

How much should you bet? The standard rule for a continuation bet, half the pot, doesn't apply here. The main pot is capped, and the side pot between you and Player F currently has zero chips in it. Instead, look at your chips and Player F's chips. You've got $3,430 left, and F has $1,030. You want to bet enough so that he's not getting the right odds to call, but little enough so that he's enticed to call. A bet of $500 seems about right.

Action: You bet $500, and Player F folds his hand. The button turns over 4♥4♦, and fourth and fifth street come the 8♥ and the 5♦ respectively. You win the pot.

Hand 5-16

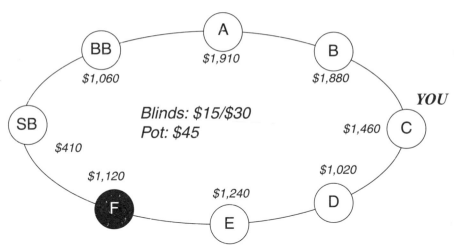

Situation: Early in a one-table satellite.

Your hand: T♥T♦

Action to you: Players A and B fold.

Question: *Do you raise, and if so, how much?*

    Answer: As we've discussed, you certainly want to raise, and you need to put in a good-sized raise, because you really don't want to see calls behind you. Three to five times the big blind is a good amount, varying the bet so it's not so obvious what you're doing.

Action: You raise to $150. Players D, E, F, and the small blind all fold. The big blind puts in $240, making it $120 to you. The pot is now $435. *What do you do now?*

    Answer: The pot's offering you between 3-to-1 and 4-to-1, and your T♥T♦ might be the best hand since he could be raising with something like ace-king or ace-queen. You're only a little more than a 4-to-1 underdog if he actually has an overpair, so the price is right to call, and on those occasions when you hit your third ten, you may win a lot of money after the flop.

Action: You call. The pot is now $555.

Flop: Q♠9♣4♥

Action: The big blind bets $85. The pot is now $640. *What do you do?*

    Answer: If you're up against a top player, a little bet like this could be an attempt to trap you and get more money in the pot. In low-level tournaments, it usually means "I've missed my hand, and I want to stop you from betting at me." You might still be beaten, but you have a hand and the pot odds are almost 8-to-1, so calling is at least mandatory.

    However, there is a good tactical alternative to calling. You could raise about $200. You might, of course, win the pot with that raise. But you're also giving your opponent a chance to make a blunder by calling, which by definition is good for you. If your opponent is holding ace-king, he's about a 6-to-1 underdog to improve his hand on the turn and the river. By raising $200, the pot will be offering him only about 4-to-1 odds to call. If he reraises strongly, you can be almost sure you're beaten and just throw your hand away.

Action: You call. The pot is now $725.

Fourth Street: Q♣

Action: The big blind checks. *What do you do?*
    Answer: That's a good card for you. If the first queen missed your opponent's hand, then the second queen didn't help him either.
    You need to bet here to see where you stand and not give him a free card. If you get called, you can check on the end. If you get raised, you can throw your hand away. I'd recommend a bet in the neighborhood of $220 to $250.
    It's tempting to just check, but then you won't know anything and you won't know what to do if you face a big bet on the end. Get the facts out now.

Action: You just check.

Fifth Street: 8♥

Action: The big blind bets $110. *Do you call?*
    Answer: Yes. He probably has something like ace-king or ace-nine or maybe jacks. The pot odds are huge, and given his betting sequence, you're probably about even money to have the best hand.

Action: You call, and he shows J♦J♣, and takes the pot.

His bets make sense. He was scared when he saw the queen come, which pointed to a pair or draw underneath the queen, although ace-king was always a possibility as well.

Hand 5-17

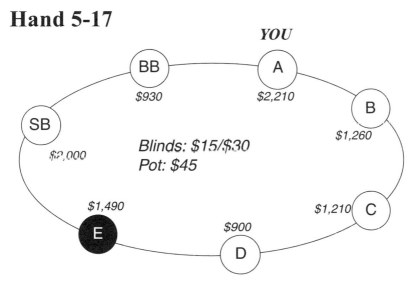

YOU

BB
$930

A
$2,210

B
$1,260

SB
$2,000

Blinds: $15/$30
Pot: $45

C
$1,210

E
$1,490

D
$900

Situation: Early in a single-table satellite tournament. Player C is very aggressive, check-raising or raising any attempt to steal. The small blind has a similar style.

Your hand: J♥J♦

Action to you: You are first to act.

Question: *Do you call or raise?*

> **Answer:** The standard play is, of course, to raise a good amount (three to five times the big blind). The real question here is whether the presence of a couple of live wires behind you makes you want to just call in the hope that someone will try to steal the pot, and you can reraise them later.
>
> It's a creative play, but not really a good idea. There's too much danger that your call might just induce a series of calls behind you, and you'd be in the worst possible situation for your jacks — facing a group of limpers and out of position.

Just make a good-sized raise here, and let the aggressive players decide what they want to do.

Action: You raise to $100, and everyone folds.

Hand 5-18

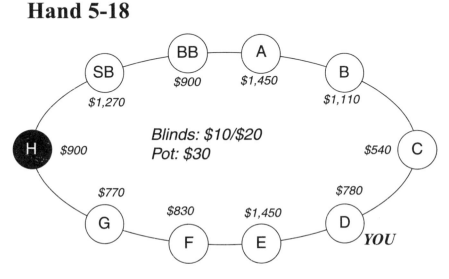

Situation: Early in a single-table online tournament. Many players have been limping into pots to see a flop.

Your hand: 2♠2♦

Action to you: Players A and B call. Player C folds. There is $70 in the pot.

Question: *Do you fold, call, or raise?*
    Answer: Many players give up on a pair of deuces, remembering all the hands they've played where deuces were worthless after the flop, or were counterfeited by other cards when the hand was played down to the end. However, deuces are a pair, and they do have some value. But they also require very careful treatment.

The optimal time to play deuces is sitting in late position, behind a bunch of limpers. In that case, you can just limp into the pot with everyone else and see if you can flop a set. If you flop a set, the implied odds should let you win a big pot. If not, you can mostly throw the hand away, except in some special circumstances. If, for instance, you were on the button and the flop came 7♥7♠3♣, and the players in front of you checked, you could make a bet of two-thirds of the pot. That flop likely missed the other callers, and you might well have the best hand.

Here you're in earlier position than you'd like, but the table has been showing a pattern of many players limping into pots. Overall, it seems like the situation is favorable enough, so you should call.

Action: You call. Player E folds. Player F calls. Player G raises to $40. The button folds. The small blind calls for $30. The big blind folds. Player A raises $130. Player B folds. The pot is now $310, and it costs you $130 to call.

Question: *What do you do?*
Answer: This is much more action than you wanted to see, and the pot odds are now highly unfavorable. The pot is offering you about 2.5-to-1, and it's about 7-to-1 against improving to trips on the flop. It's hard to imagine you can win without improving, so fold.

Action: You fold.

Hand 5-19

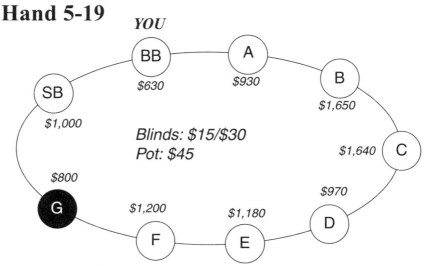

YOU

BB $630

A $930

B $1,650

SB $1,000

C $1,640

$800

G

$970

F $1,200

E $1,180

D

Blinds: $15/$30
Pot: $45

Situation: Early in a single-table online tournament. Players B and G seem to be slightly conservative.

Your hand: A♠K♥

Action to you: Player A folds. Player B raises to $60. Players C, D, E, and F all fold. Player G calls. The small blind folds. The pot is now $165, and it costs you $30 to call.

Question: *What should you do?*

> **Answer:** With the short stack and a strong hand, you're obviously going to play the hand, and play strongly. So what's the proper way to play it?
>
> One approach is to go all-in right now. A lot of tournament players would argue that's the right play. The pot ($165) is large enough so it's not a trivial amount to win, and an all-in bet gives you the best chance to take the pot right now. You're also out of position, and going all-in eliminates position as a consideration on any further betting rounds. Finally, you have a good hand, but not a made hand. Right

now you've just got an ace-high, and you might have to improve to win, so taking the pot right now isn't a bad result.

Those are all good arguments, but I'd still play the hand differently. My preference is to raise somewhere between $200 and $250. It's a good enough hand so that I want to strike a balance between winning the pot and encouraging action. The all-in play minimizes action. A slightly more than pot-sized bet might still win the pot right here if no one has anything, but it also gives me a better shot at doubling up if one of my opponents has some kind of a hand. I'm not too worried about the positional consideration, because if my bet is called, the pot will be larger than my stack. In that case it's highly likely that I'll eventually get all my chips in anyway.

Action: You actually go all-in, and the button calls and shows 8♦8♣. The board comes K♠5♥4♠9♦7♣, and your kings take the pot.

Question: *Should the eights have called?*

Answer: When I was learning no-limit hold 'em almost 20 years ago, the classical answer was "No." The argument at the time went as follows. "About half the time you'll be up against ace-king, ace-queen, or two other high cards, and you'll be a slight favorite. The other half of the time you're up against a big pair, and you're a 4.5-to-1 underdog. So you don't want to get your money in."

But that's an argument from money game players, and when you're playing for money, people tend to have those big pairs like aces, king, or queens when the money actually goes in the pot. However, in tournaments nowadays there is a spectrum of hands that you might see here that you would never have seen in the old money games: hands like ace-six suited, or small pairs, or even stone bluffs. Adding those hands into the mix makes calling with a pair of eights more like an even-money call. Now you just have to factor in the table situation. "Is he aggressive?" "Does he have a short stack?" Here you're the short stack at the table, so there's definitely a higher chance that you made a move with nothing. So I like his call.

Hand 5-20

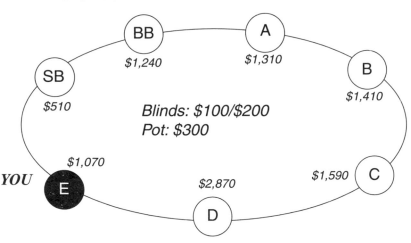

Blinds: $100/$200
Pot: $300

BB $1,240
A $1,310
SB $510
B $1,410
YOU E $1,070
C $1,590
D $2,870

Situation: Middle of a one-table satellite. The big blind is a solid player who occasionally makes aggressive moves. Over the past couple of rounds, initial bets of three times the big blind have won many pots without a contest.

Your hand: A♦Q♦

Action to you: Players A, B, C, and D all fold.

Question: *What's your move?*

   Answer: As a tournament plays out, *you want to pay attention to the size of an initial raise that will cause players at your table to fold.* It will vary from table to table. At some tables, a minimal raise of double the big blind might chase players out. At other tables, it might take three or four times the big blind before marginal hands will decide to throw their cards away. Practice focusing on the size of the first bet, and notice whether that bet claims the hand or not. After awhile, you'll begin to see patterns emerging. It's just another one of the several things you must train yourself to observe when you're out of a hand.

You'll use this knowledge when a hand has been folded around to you, and you're about to act. First decide if you want to *discourage* action (because you're going to bet but your hand isn't that strong), or *encourage* action (because your hand is almost surely the best hand remaining). If you want to discourage action, bet the amount that seems to be claiming the pot. If you want to encourage action, bet somewhat less than that.

Your A♦Q♦ is a good hand and may well be the best hand remaining at the table. But it's not a strong enough hand that you should be looking for a fight. You want to discourage action in this situation, and since a bet of three times the big blind has been chasing people away, that's what you should bet.

Action: You in fact raise to $400, twice the big blind. The small blind folds and the big blind calls for another $200. The pot is now $900.

Flop: 9♥4♥4♦

Action: The big blind goes all-in for the last $840. You have $670 left. *What do you do?*

Answer: Pretty easy call.

The pot now contains $900 plus $670, or $1,570. (Don't, by the way, ever make the mistake of overcounting your opponent's bet. His all-in bet is only as large as your chip stack, not his chip stack. Seems like an elementary point, but I've seen players make this error in the heat of battle.) You need to put in $670 to call, so you're getting better than 2-to-1 on your money. Those are good money odds, and even without further consideration you should be inclined to call.

Looking at the flop, however, makes the call even easier. It's a flop that's very unlikely to hit a player who either raised or who called a raise. So it's a good flop to bluff with. If you had been first to act with that flop, you would have been happy to bet since it would probably have missed your opponent. But instead he's first to bet, so give him credit for being able to make the same move you would have made.

Once you've decided the pot odds are good and a bluff is reasonably likely, your work is done. It's clear that much of the time, your hand is right now the best at the table, plus you have aces, queens, and two running diamonds to give yourself a possible lock. Just shove your chips in and see what happens.

Action: You call. He turns up K♦2♣, a stone bluff hand. The turn and river are the 8♦ and the 9♦ respectively, and your flush wins.

These flops that come with a low pair and another medium card create some tantalizing traps. You look at the flop and says "Hey, that probably didn't hit his hand. I'm making a move here." But if your opponent is awake, he'll realize that by the same logic, it probably didn't hit *your* hand either.

Hand 5-21

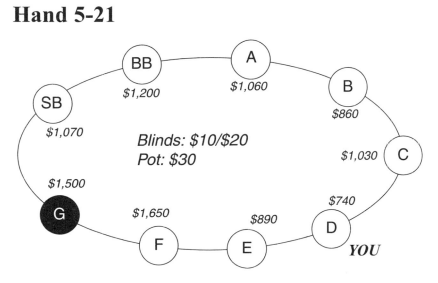

Situation: Early in a single-table online tournament. Player G and the big blind are aggressive players, involved in many pots.

Your hand: T♣8♠

Action to you: Players A, B, and C all fold.

Question: *Should you fold or attempt to steal the pot by raising?*
   Answer: There are several obvious reasons for not trying to steal a pot here. The most important is that five players behind you have yet to act, and two of those are known to be aggressive players who are unlikely to fold. A second key reason is that, while you have only $740 and are in last place among the nine players, your chips total 25 times the blinds, so you're not yet in a desperate situation. T♣8♠ unsuited is certainly a mediocre hand, and you have time to wait for something better.
   On the button with everyone having folded to you, this would be a semi-daring steal. Here, it's just a foolish play.

Action: You decide to steal the pot and raise to $50. Players E and F fold. Player G calls. The blinds fold. The pot is now $130.

Flop: 5♦4♣3♠

Question: You act first. *What do you do?*

Answer: Your bet was too small to succeed in online play. You should have bet a minimum of $100, perhaps as much as $150, to have a chance at a successful steal.

The flop was a mixture of good and bad news. Only one player called, and the flop was all low cards, so you have two overcards to the board. However, there are two spades on board, so a player with the ace of spades may elect to keep playing.

Here you should take another shot at winning, and make a bet of about half the pot. The 2-to-1 odds are favorable, and the bet has some chance of succeeding. (If you bet half the pot, you only have to win one-third of your bets to break even; winning one bet out of three wins the amount of the pot, while losing twice costs you half the pot each time.)

Action: You bet $60. Player G calls. The pot is now $250.

Fourth Street: K♠

Question: What do you do now?

Answer: Bad moon rising. The king is a scary card, and Player G doesn't seem to be going away. You should cut your losses right here.

Action: You check, and Player G bets $130. You fold, and Player G takes the pot.

Hand 5-22

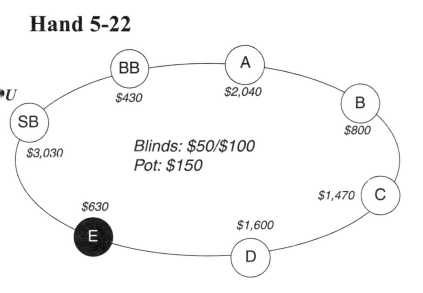

Situation: In the middle of a single-table online tournament. Players A and D are very aggressive. Player B seems solid.

Your hand: A♦K♣

Action to you: Player A folds. Player B raises to $200. Players C, D, and E fold. The pot is now $350.

Question: *Do you call or raise?*

 Answer: You have a fine hand, of course, and you certainly want to raise some amount. Just how much you raise is actually determined by the relative chip stacks and your position at the table. Currently you have $2,980 left and he has $600. You're also out of position relative to Player B throughout the hand. If you raise him a moderate amount, say $200 to $300, and he calls you, he'll have so few chips left that he'll be committed to the pot. If he doesn't immediately reraise you, he'll probably get the rest of his chips in after the flop. Under these circumstances, you should go all-in and put him to a decision for all his chips right now. This move eliminates the positional disadvantage of acting first next round, and gives you the best chance of chasing him away (if that's possible) and winning the pot right now. Ace-king is a nice hand, but remember you're an underdog to just a simple pair of fours. You wouldn't mind taking the pot right now.

Action: You raise all-in, and Player B calls, showing 7♥7♦. The flop comes A♣K♠5♠, and your hand holds up to win the pot.

Remember that all-in with an ace-king is a common play against a much smaller stack when you can use the move to eliminate a position disadvantage, and guarantee that you'll be able to see all five cards on the board.

Hand 5-23

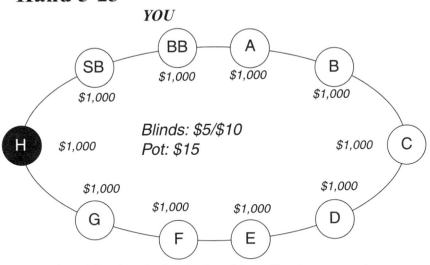

Situation: First hand of a single-table online tournament.

Your hand: Q♥J♦

Action to you: Player A folds. Player B calls. Players C, D, and E all fold. Players F and G call. Player H raises to $30. The small blind folds. The pot is now $75. It costs you $20 to call.

Question: *Do you fold, call, or raise?*

   Answer: Under slightly different circumstances, you'd be delighted to play this hand (Q♥J♦) in the big blind. Suppose, for instance, Player B had raised to $30 and Players F, G, and H had just called. Now the pot would contain $135 and you'd need to put in an additional $20 to call. You'd be getting almost 7-to-1 pot odds, and your hand would easily be worth a bet at that price.

   What's different about this hand? Although the pot odds are worse (you have to put in $20 for a shot at a pot of $75, slightly less than 4-to-1), that's not the main problem. The real difficulty is that you're caught in a sandwich. If you call, Players B, F, and G are all still active behind you, and they can all raise. You don't really know what it will cost you to play this hand, or how many players you'll be up against. You'll also be in the worst possible position after the flop. Under the circumstances, queen-Jack offsuit just isn't good enough to stick around. It's clear to fold.

   Note that if the pot odds were much better, say 6-to-1 or 7-to-1, then you could call even in these unfavorable circumstances.

Action: You fold.

Part Six

Betting After the Flop

Betting After the Flop

Introduction

The flop is a defining moment in a no-limit hold 'em hand. In one swoop, 60 percent of the eventual board gets revealed. You may have already flopped a monster hand, or perhaps your opponent did. More likely however, is that you made no improvement, or only a modest one, and the same is true of your opponent.

When watching the hands unfold on television, much of the betting, if not all of it, is now completed. It happens because we're often at the end of a tournament and the blinds and antes are large compared to the amount of chips in play. But at most other spots, this isn't the case. You're going to have to analyze the texture of the flop and play your hand on the flop: This includes betting, calling, raising, and deciding on how much each of these options is worth.

Put another way, there's a lot more going on here than what most new players think. Play on the flop (and the later streets) can get very complex. So read this section carefully.

Texture of the Flop

When you stay in a hand and the flop comes, there are two things that you'd like to have happen.

1. You want the flop to improve your hand.

2. You don't want the flop to improve your opponent's hand.

You can tell right away if the flop improved your hand. But you have to deduce if the flop helped your opponent or not. In poker, we call this *analyzing the texture of the flop*. Good texture (for you) means either the flop was unlikely to help a hand that might have reasonably called you before the flop, or the flop probably helped another hand, but not as much as it helped you. Bad or dangerous texture means a flop that might well have helped other players, but not you. Let's look at a few examples and see what good and bad texture look like.

Example No. 1. You're on the button with

A player in middle position makes a modest raise, a player just behind him calls, and you elect to call with your Q♠J♠. (We'll ignore for now the question of whether or not this was a prudent move.) In each case, the flop leaves you with a pair of queens.

1.   Flop A: Q♥8♠2♣

2.   Flop B: Q♦T♦9♥

3.   Flop C: A♣K♦Q♥

When analyzing the texture of a flop, keep the following facts in mind.

1.   People tend to play aces (especially in online play).

2.   People like to play suited cards. (In online tournaments, especially in the early rounds, you'll be up against plenty of opponents playing *any* two suited cards.)

3.   People like to play two high cards.

Given these tendencies, *what should we think about our three flops?*

Answer: Flop A clearly has great texture. There are no flushes on board, the cards are widely scattered so no open-ended straight draws are possible, and there are no high cards except our queen. You should like this flop a lot; you very likely have the best hand here, and you should plan on betting aggressively.

Flop B isn't so nice. You have a pair of queens and an open-ended straight draw. But someone holding king-jack may have already made a straight. Plus, there are two flush cards on board, so someone may be drawing at a diamond flush. You'll need to play this hand very carefully.

Flop C is even worse. Now you have a pair of queens and an inside straight draw (a ten gives you a straight). But you're a big underdog to anyone holding an ace or a king, which is very likely. In addition, someone playing jack-ten has already made his straight. Unless the betting is weak, this is a hand you'll have to throw away.

You can use the texture of the flop to generate some good stealing opportunities.

Example No. 2. You called before the flop with

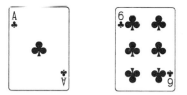

Another player stayed for the flop, and he has position on you. The flop comes

What should you do?
Answer: This is a good situation for you, and you should bet about half the pot. Yes, the flop missed you completely. But it probably missed your opponent as well. There are no flushes or straights on board, and none of the other cards that people like to play. In a situation like this, the first player who bets usually gets the money, so make sure you are that player. In my experience, you'll win this pot about half the time when you bet here (and you might win it later, even if you're called), and by betting half the pot, you're getting 2-to-1 odds on your bet.

Example No. 3. Once again, you call before the flop with

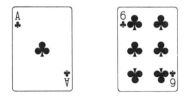

This time there are four other players staying for the flop, and again you're second to act. The flop comes

The first player checks. *What should you do here?*

    Answer: You shouldn't get involved in this pot, even though the texture is good. There are too many players to act behind you, and by virtue of the sheer number of players in the pot, they can't all have high cards. Somebody has probably caught a piece of this random flop, and they're likely to go through the same reasoning you have, and know they're in good position. Just check and fold when someone bets.

Analyzing Flops
for Typical Hands

Individual hands have different flops that fit them particularly well. Let's look at some typical hands and see what we think about different flops.

Starting Hand No. 1: A♦A♣. You raised four times the big blind in third position, and got called by one player in sixth position. This is the best possible starting hand, of course, but do you know what you'd really like to flop with this hand? The answer might surprise you!

Flop No. 1. 3♠3♦3♥. This (and a few hands like it) is your best possible flop. You've made the nut full house, but more importantly, your opponent may have made a weaker full house! (Notice how much better this is than A♠3♦3♥, where you have an even better full house, but most likely your opponent doesn't have more than two pair, and he's going to be afraid of the ace showing.) Note that you don't need to slow play this hand. Just take the lead in the betting and wait for him to come after you.

Flop No. 2. J♠5♦5♥. You're not going to see Flop No. 1 too often, but here's a flop that you will see frequently which is also excellent for you. This flop could give your opponent two pair, which in turn will be losing to your two pair. With this hand you want to check and trap a loose player, but bet against a tight player who might be afraid to bet. Make sure you don't give a free card to a player who you put on a pair and won't give action.

Flop No. 3. A♠K♦Q♥. This is a good flop for you but may not yield a lot of profit. You wish he was holding kings or queens, but since he didn't reraise you before the flop, that's unlikely. Here you may as well simply bet into the pot. If he's holding a lower pair like T♦T♣, he knows he's dead, and a check won't fool him into betting. Just lead out and see if you can make any money.

Flop No. 4. Q♠J♦T♥. This is a flop you definitely don't like. The cards are high enough that they're likely to have hit many of the hands that would have stayed in against you. There are also likely to be straight draws out against you. Check to start, but be prepared to call two moderate bets with your aces.

Flop No. 5. 9♠8♠7♠. This is reasonably good if you hold the ace of the suit, but otherwise it's very bad, with all the straight and flush draws floating around. Still, the fact that the cards are lower than in Flop No. 4 means it's less likely that they hit your opponent. Lead out with a bet and try to find out where you stand.

Flop No. 6. Q♠9♦4♥. This is a good flop. Your aces are still almost certainly good. Just lead out and hope the flop hit him somehow.

Starting Hand No. 2. K♦K♣. You raised in third position. This time you were called by two players behind you.
A pair of kings is obviously a great hand, but it's not invincible. Your alarm bells need to go off when an ace flops. This is especially true in online poker, where players religiously call with ace-small.

Flop No. 1. A♠K♦7♥. This is an excellent flop. It's very likely someone at the table made aces, and is ready to lose all his money. Either checking or leading out with a small bet is the recommended play.

Flop No. 2: A♠Q♦T♥. A dangerous flop, although it does give you an inside straight draw. It's essential here to define your hand in one stroke. Lead out with a good-sized bet, perhaps two-thirds of the pot. Checking here is out of the question, because it will leave you with no idea where you stand if the pot eventually gets bet.

Flop No. 3. A♠5♦3♥. Not as bad as Flop No. 2, but still dangerous because of the ace. Once again you need to lead out. If you encounter action, you're done with the hand.

Flop No. 4. 9♠7♦6♠ (but you don't have the K♠). You're probably winning now, but the potential drawing hands are too dangerous. Bet somewhere between three-quarters of the pot and the entire pot. You need to squelch resistance immediately and cut off the drawing hands.

Starting Hand No. 3. 9♦9♣. There was a raise in fifth position of twice the big blind. The player in sixth position called, and you called on the button.

A pair of nines is not a great hand, but so far neither of your opponents has shown much strength.

Flop No. 1: A♠9♦4♥. Your ideal flop. Hopefully one of your opponents is in there with ace-medium or ace-small. Your problem will be figuring out whether to bet out or trap if they check to you and whether to raise or slowplay if they bet.

Flop No. 2: A♠Q♦5♥. A bad flop. You're very likely to be beaten, with little chance of improvement. Fold your hand when someone bets at you.

Flop No. 3: 7♠4♦2♥. A good flop, since you have an overpair to the board. If there are two checks to you, definitely bet about two-thirds of the pot.

Flop No. 4: J♠J♦6♥. This is also a good flop. If no one has a jack, you are likely best at this point. If both players check to you, bet two-thirds of the pot. If there is a bet and a fold in front of you, just call. You are still all right with the hand until someone shows real strength, at which point you'll have a tough decision.

Flop No. 5: 8♠8♦6♥. Another good flop, since your pair is now higher than the board. If there is a check and a bet to you, you can call. If there is a bet followed by a call in front of you, the caller almost certainly has a pair. Again you can call.

Hand No. 4: J♠T♠. There are two limpers in front of you, and you call. Another limper comes in behind you. You're third to act after the flop.

Flop No. 1: A♠K♦Q♥. A great flop, obviously. Let the other players take the lead in the betting.

Flop No. 2: 9♠8♠3♥. Another great flop. Even though your hand isn't made yet, you have 15 outs with two cards to come, so you're the favorite. (Don't make the mistake of double-counting. There are nine spades that help you, plus four sevens and four queens. But the 7♠ and the Q♠ are in both groups, so only 15 different cards help you. The other jacks and tens might give you a winning hand, but you can't be sure.) You should lead out, and not mind a call.

Flop No. 3: 8♦5♥2♣. A good flop for texture, although it missed you completely, since at least you have two overcards to the board and it probably didn't hit anyone. If the action in front of you is check, check, try to steal the pot.

Flop No. 4. 8♦7♥4♣. This is a little better than the last one since you also have the inside straight draw. With jacks, tens, and nines all good for you, this hand plays well as a semi-bluff. You should take the lead in the betting.

Flop No. 5: Q♦9♠3♣. A good flop, with an open-ended straight draw and a backdoor flush draw (needing two running spades to complete it.) An open-ended straight draw is eight outs; the backdoor flush contributes the equivalent of about 1½ outs. If the first two players check, you can either bet the hand as a semi-bluff or check and probably see a free card.

Starting Hand No. 5: 6♦6♣. You call in fifth position, and the button and the small blind both call. The big blind checks.
With a low pair, the number of great flops shrinks. Unless you flop trips, you need to proceed carefully.

Flop No. 1: A♣J♦9♥. A bad flop, but it least it won't cost you any money. When someone bets, you fold.

Flop No. 2: J♣J♦5♥. This one is moderately good. If no one has a jack, your two pair is likely best. But you have to be careful, and any strong betting will probably chase you out.

Flop No. 3: 5♠4♦3♥. A good flop for a bet.

Flop No. 4: 7♠5♦4♥. Another good flop to bet.

Flop No. 5: A♣Q♦6♥. A great flop. Let someone else take the lead in the betting.

Flop No. 6: Q♠7♦2♥. A bettable flop. Be aware that if you meet resistance, the only likely hand you can beat is ace-high.

Value Bets

There's nothing mysterious or deceptive about a value bet. It is what it appears to be. You started out with two good cards before the flop. The flop helped you in some way, and now you have a hand which appears to be best, such as top pair. How should you proceed?

There's no need to be particularly clever here. Unless you've flopped a monster, you don't generally want to slowplay. Just load out with a hand like top pair and hope that someone with the second-best hand comes along for the ride and pays you for the privilege. I like to vary my bets in this situation between half the pot and the whole pot. If I've assessed the situation accurately, I'd make more money with the larger bet. But, as I've emphasized before, you need to pursue a balanced strategy so your opponents can't read you easily. Betting just half the pot blends in with the continuation bets and the probe bets (discussed below) and serves as a good way to disguise strength while still getting money in the pot.

How strong a hand do I need to slowplay? Trips can be slowplayed, but I wouldn't slowplay any weaker hand except in unusual circumstances. You hate giving someone a free card that beats you, so I believe in just betting top pair or two pair.

If you watch a lot of final-table action on television, you may get the impression that players *always* check a good hand after the flop. This isn't really the case. On television you're seeing people at the final table, where the field is small, the blinds are large, and many of the players are desperate to keep accumulating chips to stay in the game. Under these circumstances, it's very rare for a hand to be checked around after the flop. If you're the first to act, and you have a good hand, and you check, the second player will almost always bet to win the pot that's out there. He's aware that you may be checking a good hand, but he probably doesn't have time to wait around for a better situation. So in these circumstances, checking top pair with the idea of raising later is a high-percentage move. But early in the tournament, your opponents won't be so desperate to go after the pot, so betting out for value is generally more profitable.

Continuation Bets

A continuation bet is a bet made after the flop by the player who took the lead in betting before the flop. Its name derives from the fact that it continues the action begun on the previous round. It's a very important bet, which you'll find yourself both using and combating throughout a tournament.

For a bet to qualify as a continuation bet, the following conditions must hold:

1. The player making the bet was the betting leader before the flop.

2. After the flop, no other bets have yet been made.

3. The player making the bet missed the flop.

Under these circumstances, the pre-flop betting leader can consider making a continuation bet, even though the flop didn't help him.

When you make a continuation bet, you're obviously hoping to pick up the pot right there. Although the flop missed you, your opponent doesn't know that yet. The flop may have missed him as well. Since you indicated strength before the flop, your opponent probably assumed you had a better hand than he did, and if he missed the flop and you now bet, it would be natural for him to lay down his hand.

Example No. 1. You pick up

in early position. The blinds are $50/$100, and you raise to $300. One player in late position calls. The pot is now $750. The flop comes

(with one card in your suit). *Should you bet, and if so, how much?*

Answer: A continuation bet of $350 to $400 would be a good move here. It's possible that the king hit your opponent's hand, but more likely it didn't. If your opponent called with a hand like a pair of sevens, he may see the two overcards on the board, realize that his chance of improving on the next two cards is very slim, and throw away the best hand.

A continuation bet is a kind of semi-bluff. It's a move which can work in several ways. You may have the best hand, and the bet builds the pot. You may have the worst hand, but the bet chases your opponent away. Even if you have the worst hand and your opponent correctly calls, the bet may cause him to check on a later round, giving you a free card.

For a continuation bet to be a profitable move, the amount of the bet has to be carefully chosen in comparison to the pot. In essence, you are hoping to buy the pot right now. *If you overpay, you'll lose too much money when your opponent calls with a hand better than yours. If you underpay, you'll be offering your opponent correct pot odds to stick around with a drawing hand.* Neither situation is good, so the exact amount of the bet is very important.

I like my continuation bets to be about half the size of the pot, a small enough amount so that I don't lose too much when I'm called, while still being large enough to chase out a lot of drawing hands. When you bet half the pot, you need to win only one-third of your bets to break even. At the same time, you're not giving great drawing odds to your opponent. Suppose you bet $100 at a pot of $200. From your opponent's point of view, he would now have to put in $100 to call a pot of $300, so he's getting only 3-to-1 on his call. Most drawing situations need better odds than that.

Why not bet a little less to get even better odds? If you made a continuation bet of, let's say, one-third of the pot, you'd need to win only one time in four to break even. But now you're offering better calling odds to your opponent (4-to-1 on their call), so many players will now call your bet. On the other hand, if you bet more money to chase people out, you'll lose too much money when you actually are called. Betting about half the pot is a balanced play which gives you the best risk-reward ratio in most situations.

Remember, however, that as with all other bets, you must conceal what you're doing from your opponents. Although a half-pot bet is an ideal size, your actual bets should vary randomly around that number, say from about 40 percent of the pot on the low side to 70 percent on the high side. On average you'll be betting the amount you want, but the range is large enough to prevent your opponents from getting a clear read.

A flop doesn't need to consist of just low cards to be a good flop for a continuation bet.

Example No. 2. In fourth position you raised before the flop with

The player in sixth position calls, and everyone else folds. More often than not, calls from players in late position indicate low to medium pairs. A player with a high pair or ace-king would tend to raise, while many other high card hands would fold.

The flop comes

This is a favorable texture for you, and you should lead out with a continuation bet. In the most likely case that your opponent has a low to medium pair, he has to assume that the flop helped you, and his hand is now no good.

In the same situation, even though a flop of

would be very scary, you would still usually make a continuation bet, since your opponent can still have a hand that he would fold.

Example 3. You raised in sixth position with

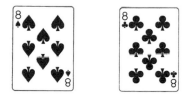

and were called by the button. The flop came

This is a very poor flop for you, which may have hit your opponent's hand in various ways. Don't try a continuation bet here. Just check and hope to get a free card. Fold if he bets.

Probe Bets

A probe bet is similar to a continuation bet, but it is made when you were not the leader before the flop, but the leader has declined to make a move after the flop. A probe bet gives you a chance to win the pot immediately, but also helps define your hand by forcing the leader to make a play, either folding, calling or raising. Depending on his response, you'll have a clearer idea of how to play the hand.

Example No. 1: You pick up

in late position. The blinds are $50/$100. Player A, in middle position, opens with a raise to $200. You call. The pot is now $550. The flop comes

Player A checks. *What should you do?*
    Answer: Now a probing bet is appropriate. You may have the best hand right now, since the board shows only one overcard to your pair. If you don't have the best hand, you need to define your hand sooner rather than later. If you

check, you won't have any information about your situation. So make a bet of about $200. You'll either win the pot or get a much clearer idea where you stand.

I like my probing bets to be a little smaller than my continuation bets, since I'm starting from a weaker position. (It was my opponent, rather than I, who took the lead in the hand.) Anywhere from 30 percent to 50 percent of the pot is a good range.

You can make probe bets on other streets as well. You might, for example, take the lead before the flop, check on the flop, and make a probing bet on fourth street. Approaches like this allow you to see (if your opponent cooperates) more of the hand before committing chips.

More Complex Scenarios

After the flop and the first bet, the number of possible situations gets too large to easily categorize. The best approach is to carefully study the problems for this chapter, which will show you how to reason your way through the maze. In all the problems, pay careful attention to relating your opponent's bet after the flop to his actions before the flop. When the two don't match, be careful. He's probably either making a move or running a bluff.

Playing Well
Before the Flop Versus
Playing Well After the Flop

If you hang around tournaments enough, you'll hear some players described as being "a great player before the flop," while others will be described as "a great player after the flop." What's being talked about here? Why wouldn't a great player be able to play well both before and after the flop?

All top players play at least acceptably well in both situations, of course. But playing well before the flop and playing well after the flop require somewhat different sets of skills, so there are players that are particularly adept at one phase of the game rather than the other.

Before the flop you have relatively little hard information on which to base your decisions. You know your own hand, of course, and you have some information on your opponent's position and betting patterns. But you probably haven't even seen the result of a complete round of betting, and you're forced to operate largely in the dark. Good pre-flop play requires keen alertness, a finely-honed intuition, and considerable courage.

After the flop you have much more information to work with. You've seen an entire round of betting, as well as the flop and your opponent's reaction to it. You can now begin to bet in a way that creates a story about the hand and your place in it. Good post-flop play is more analytical. The key qualities are now logic, planning, and cunning.

As you work on developing your no-limit game, you'll be trying to play both phases of the game well. But if you're like most people, you'll feel that one phase or the other is your natural hunting ground.

The Problems

Problems 6-1 and 6-2 show the danger in flopping a small to medium pair. You must be somewhat cautious after the flop, and be willing to let the hand go when danger surfaces.

Problems 6-3 through 6-8 cover continuation bets. As you move through the problems, note that a continuation bet is most effective against a single opponent, less effective against two opponents, and dangerous against three or more.

Problems 6-9 through 6-11 discuss the closely related probe bet. Pay particular attention to Problem 6-9, which shows the necessity for clear, logical thinking at the table. Problem 6-11 shows the power of treating most hands in an obvious fashion.

Some examples of analyzing the texture of the flop are given in Problems 6-12 through 6-14. Pay attention to the danger you can get in by not considering how the flop might have helped other players.

Trapping after the flop with a very strong hand is another key skill. Problems 6-15 and 6-16 give some insights into these plays.

The remaining two problems cover two miscellaneous topics. Problem 6-17 shows the danger of giving free cards. Problem 6-18 illustrates the value of playing in a way that leaves your opponent, rather than you, with the tough decisions.

Hand 6-1

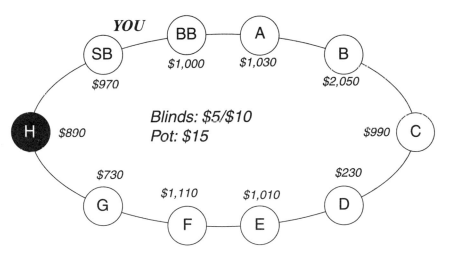

Situation: Early hand of a one-table satellite.

Your hand: A♦7♦

Action to you: Players A, B, and C all call. D and E fold. Player F calls. Players G and H fold. Pot is $55.

Question: *Do you stick around?*

> **Answer:** Yes, although you're not thrilled with your hand. Since you were the small blind, it costs you only $5 to call this $55 pot, which are irresistible odds. You have a chance of flopping the nut flush, or more likely a draw to the nut flush, and you could always catch some aces and sevens. But remain aware that you're calling with a fundamentally weak hand in early position, and you'll have to be careful after the flop comes.

Action: You call and the big blind checks. The pot is now $60.

Flop: 7♥3♣2♣

Question: You're first to act. *What's the play?*

Answer: The first rule here is: Don't get too excited. Sure, you flopped the top pair. But you're in the worst possible position, against five (!) opponents, and you've missed both your flush draw and your ace draw. Some players see that they have top pair and immediately think they've got a great hand, but in fact there's a lot that can go wrong here, starting with the club flush draw on the board.

Remember too, that in online and satellite play, the action is fast and loose, and people love to stick around with two suited cards. (In fact, all your opponents here might have two suited cards!) So you could easily be up against a couple of live flush draws.

I've given you the bad news, but now you still have to make a play. You do have top pair with top kicker, so you're entitled to bet for value. There's no sense in checking, because with five other players in the pot, every fourth street card becomes dangerous. I would stick a bet out there, perhaps two-thirds to three-quarters of the pot. ($40 to $45). You just might win the pot right now, and at least you'll cut down on the opposition, and see who's serious.

Action: You actually bet $55, the big blind, Player A, and Player B all fold. Player C calls. Player F folds. Pot now $170.

Fourth Street: T♦

Question: *What now?*

Answer: That's a great sequence for your hand. You eliminated four of your five opponents, and a non-flush card came on the flop. The ten might have paired your opponent, but that's a chance you'll just have to take.

You should bet about $100 here. If he's on a flush draw, which is the most likely danger, you're not giving him the correct odds to call. (He'd have to call $100 with a pot of $270. That's way short of the 4-to-1 odds of his filling a club flush.) You don't want to bet too much, because you don't want so much money tied up in the pot that you're committed to it.

Action: You actually bet $160, and Player C calls. Pot is now $490.

That was too big a bet, in my view, as was the first bet. Notice what's happening. You're building a bigger and bigger pot, but you can't be certain where you stand, or even if you're a favorite. When you think you're a favorite but can't be sure, try to accomplish your goals with smaller bets.

Fifth Street: 9♣

Question: *What now?*
    Answer: You must check. He called your $55 and $160 bets, and it doesn't make sense to think he did that unless he had a hand already or he had a draw. If he had a draw, he just caught his flush. If he had a hand, it's probably better than your pair of sevens. So there's no reason to bet.

Action: You check, and he goes all-in. *Do you call?*
    Answer: No. He says you're beaten, and you have absolutely no reason to doubt him. Fold your hand.

Hand 6-2

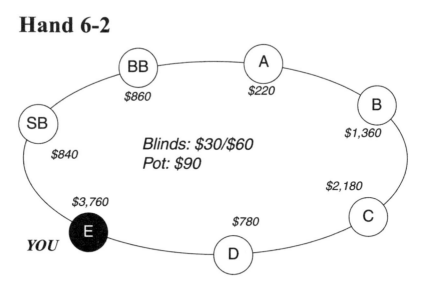

Situation: In the middle of a single-table online tournament. The big blind and Player C have been very aggressive, contesting most pots. The big blind has made several check-raises throughout the tournament.

Your hand: 8♦4♦

Action to you: Players A through D all fold.

Question: *Do you fold, call, or raise?*
    Answer: You should fold here because your hand is too weak to play, but in the actual event from which this hand is taken, the button tried to steal.

Action: You actually raise $120. The small blind calls, putting in another $90, and the big blind puts in $120, making it $60 to you. The pot is now $420. *What do you do now?*
    Answer: Your steal attempt was a mistake for two reasons. The main reason is that the big blind was known to be an aggressive player, who had contested many pots. Players like

that tend to fight when you try to steal their blinds, so if you're going to make a move on them, you need at least a semi-decent hand to attempt it. Your 8♦4♦ suited certainly didn't fit this category.

The second problem was that the size of your stealing bet, twice the big blind, was too small. Imagine for a moment that the small blind had folded instead of calling. The big blind would then have needed to put in only $60 to call a pot of $210. Those are inviting odds, and since you were on the button, in the most likely stealing position, he probably had a technical call with almost any hand. For your steal to have had any chance of success, you needed to put in more chips, perhaps $180 to $200. Then at least the big blind would have had a tough decision to make.

After the call and the small reraise, it costs you $60 to see a pot of $420. Those 7-to-1 odds are huge, so call and see what happens.

Action: You call. The pot is now $480.

Flop: A♠8♣3♥

Action: The small blind and the big blind check. *What should you do?*

Answer: There are no diamonds out there, but you do have middle pair. However, the presence of the ace is very bothersome. Either of the blinds might have stuck around with an ace-x and now be trapping. Given what you know about the big blind, a small bet will just be viewed as red meat. You should check and take a free card.

If you had no knowledge that the big blind was a trapper, then you'd make a normal value bet here of about half the pot. The bet would tell you where you stood in the hand, and prevent other hands from drawing out and beating you.

Action: You actually bet $60. The small blind folds but the big blind reraises to $250. *What do you do?*

Your misguided stealing attempt has now cost you $240. Time to cut your losses and let this one go.

Action: You fold, and the big blind takes the pot.

Hand 6-3

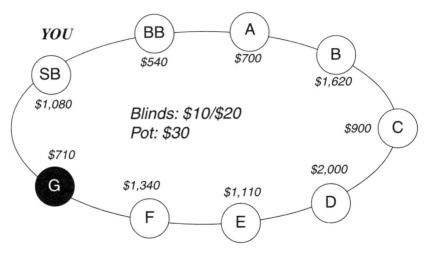

Situation: Early in a single-table online tournament.

Your hand: A♣J♥

Action to you: Players A, B, C, and D all fold. Player E calls. Player F calls. Player G folds. The pot is now $70.

Question: *Do you fold, call, or raise?*

Answer: Here you're holding a reasonable hand, although your position after the flop will be poor. But you're up against two limpers, and while in a brick and mortar tournament that might mean they had some strength, in an online tournament players will limp in with almost nothing. Here you're completely justified in making a move for the pot. You should put in a substantial raise, about $100. A large chunk of the time, that raise will take the pot outright. If it doesn't, you still have a hand to play, and it may well be the best hand.

Action: You raise $100. The big blind folds. Player E calls. Player F folds. The pot is now $260.

Flop: 9♦7♣3♦

Question: *What do you do?*

    Answer: That should be a safe flop for you. It's possible your opponent limped in with something like a ten-nine or a jack-nine and now has a pair, but in general that's a flop you're happy to see, given that it missed your hand.

    Now you have to bet to find out where you stand. You're against a single opponent, so make a standard continuation bet of about half the pot, say about $150, and see what happens. By betting half the pot, you have very favorable odds. If over three such bets, your opponents fold once and call twice and win after calling, you've broken even, even if you never win when called. If they fold more than one-third of the time, you're showing a profit for sure.

Action: You actually bet $100, and your opponent calls. The pot is now $460.

Fourth Street: 6♣

Question: *What do you do now?*

    Answer: Your previous bet was a little too small, and might have encouraged a weaker hand to hang around in the hope that you had nothing either. In any event, you should now check. You made a play at the pot, it didn't work, and now you're stuck in bad position with just an ace-high hand. At this point, you're finished; just see if you can check the pot down.

Action: You check and he checks.

Fifth Street: Q♥

Question: *Now what?*
  Answer: That was a bad card for you, since it fits a lot of hands that could have been calling up to this point. Check, and hope that he checks as well.

Action: You check, and he bets $100. The pot is now $560.

Question: *What do you do?*
  Answer: You're probably beaten, but the pot is offering you 5.5-to-1 odds, which is just too much. Call. Your ace-high just might be best, and you're being well-paid to find out.

Resolution: You call, and he shows K♦Q♦ and wins the hand with his pair of Queens.

  You were a bit unlucky, since he shouldn't have called your bet after the flop — there were just too many ways he could have been beaten. But your bet was a little on the small size, and he was too tempted by the pot odds to throw the hand away.

Hand 6-4

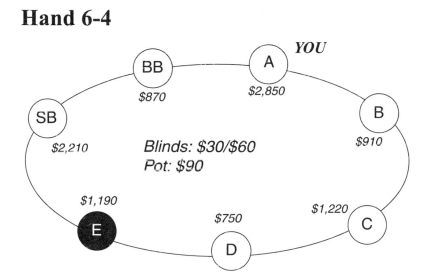

Situation: In the middle of a single-table satellite tournament. The small blind and Player C are very aggressive players.

Your hand: A♠7♠

Action to you: You are first to act.

Question: *Do you fold, call, or raise?*
   Answer: At a full table, this hand is clearly too weak to open in first position. Even at a seven-handed table, it's a little less than you should want for an opening bet. I'd open here with ace-jack or ace-ten suited. Fold.

Action: Actually, you raise to $120. Player C calls and everyone else folds. Pot is now $330.

Flop: T♦4♥3♥

Question: *What's your play now?*

Answer: As always, your first job is to assess the texture of the flop. It missed you, of course, but it's a relatively harmless flop that probably missed your opponent as well. The cards are all low, with the highest card being a ten. The two hearts could give Player C a heart flush draw, but straights are very unlikely. If Player C was also playing an ace-x, or two face cards, the flop probably missed him.

As in the last problem, you should make a continuation bet here of half the pot, about $160, and see what happens.

Action: You check and Player C checks.

Your failure to bet your hand was a minor error (you don't, after all, have anything yet) but Player C's failure to bet was in most cases a major error regardless of his hand. All the reasons that indicated you should bet also indicate that Player C should bet. In addition, Player C has a piece of information that you didn't have, namely the knowledge that you have already checked.

Fourth Street: A♦

Question: *Now what?*

Answer: You've hit your hand, and your opponent hasn't given you any reason to think you're beaten. With the pot at $330, it's time to bet somewhere between one-half and three-fourths of the pot. You don't want to overbet the pot, because you'd like some action from a loose player. But you don't want to bet too little, in case your opponent is on a draw at a heart or diamond flush. A bet of $200 would be a good amount.

Action: You actually bet $60, and Player C calls.

Fifth Street: J♣

Question: *Should you bet on the end?*

    Answer: You bet much too little on fourth street. Player C had to put in only $60 to call a $390 pot, so if he had a flush draw, he was getting the odds he needed, and then some.

    Should you bet now? Usually yes. There are no flushes or straights out there, and Player C hasn't been acting like someone with an ace and a high kicker, so you probably still have the best hand. Bet half the pot and see what happens.

Action: You check and he checks. His hand is 5♥5♣, and your pair of aces takes the pot.

Hand 6-5

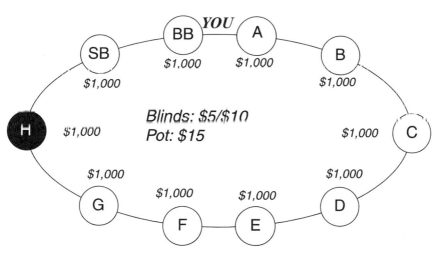

Situation: First hand of a single-table online tournament. You know nothing about the other players.

Your hand: J♥J♣

Action to you: Players A, B, C, D, and E all call. Players F, G, and H fold. The small blind calls. The pot is now $70.

Question: *Do you raise, and if so, how much?*

    Answer: In online player it's not uncommon to see five or six limpers in early pots. Most of these players are playing two suited cards, but some are calling with nothing, just to see a flop.

    Your jacks are probably the best hand now, but with six other players in the pot against you, they're unlikely to be the best hand after the flop comes. It's critical to raise and chase out some of the drawing hands. The real question is how much to raise. In online events, a raise to $50 or $60 won't chase away many hands. Players who will call for $10 with not much of a hand will just as easily call for $50 with the same hand, once they have a little money in the pot. A better play in my opinion is to raise about $200. This is triple the current pot, and it's enough so that only legitimate hands will stay. Ideally, you want to win the pot here, or go heads-up against a single opponent.

    You don't want to bet more than you have to, and objectively a bet of $150 ought to be enough to accomplish your goal. But online players aren't all that objective, and psychologically a bet of $200 seems much bigger than a bet of $150 or $180.

Action: You actually bet only $150, and are called by Players C and E. The pot is now $520.

Flop: A♦7♣2♣

Question: *What's your play at this point?*

    Answer: You don't like that an ace showed up, but you have to play. You showed strength before the flop, so you have to make a continuation bet, even though you now have two opponents. A continuation bet isn't as profitable against two opponents as against one, since you're hoping that both will fold, and that's less likely than the chance that a single opponent will give up. But it's still a good play in most cases. As against a single opponent, the right amount is about half the pot. If the pot is large in relation to the stacks, as here, a little less than half is perfectly all right.

Here you should bet about $200. It's a way of letting your opponents know that the flop helped you, or at least you're all right with it. Of course you really want to win the pot right here. If someone raises you, you have to fold.

Action: In fact, you check rather than bet. Player C bets $20 and Player E raises to $250. The pot now has $790 in it.

This shows why you want to bet rather than wait. Did player E raise because he paired his ace, or did he raise because no one else had shown strength, and it was time to steal the pot? You don't know.

Remember that poker is a game of information, and the more you don't know, the worse off you are. Here you've got to make a reasonable guess. There's an ace on the board, the card that would most have induced someone to call your pre-flop raise. One of your opponents says he has a pair of aces. Your position is bad. I'd cut my losses and get out now.

Action: You fold. Player C calls. Fourth street is an 8♠, and there's another $250 bet by E and a call by C. The river is a 7♦, followed by check-check. Player E shows A♣6♣, and loses to Player C's A♠9♠.

E called initially with A♣6♣ (a dubious call) and then raised aggressively with a pair of aces plus a draw to the nut flush (reasonable). In the end, his low kicker cost him the hand and most of his chips.

Hand 6-6

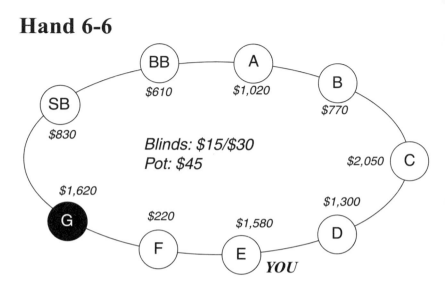

Situation: Early in a one-table online tournament.

Your hand: A♠Q♠

Action to you: Player A folds. Player B calls. Players C and D fold. The pot is now $75.

Question: *Do you call or raise, and if you raise, how much?*
  Answer: Ace-queen suited is a good hand, worth playing in any position. Here you're in middle position, behind a single caller. So a raise is appropriate. You should raise three to four times the big blind, which would be $90 to $120. Besides getting more money in the pot when you have a good hand, a raise here accomplishes three other key goals.

1. By discouraging players behind you from acting, it helps you get heads-up against Player B.

2. It helps you have good position after the flop.

3.   It helps to define your hand. Any player that enters after you will be entering a pot that has been raised in front of him. He'll probably have a very strong hand.

Action: You raise to $100. Players F and G and the two blinds fold. Player B calls for an additional $70. The pot is now $245.

Flop: 8♠7♠6♣

Action: Player B checks. *What do you do?*
   Answer: You need to bet here. There's a good chance you have the best hand. But if you don't currently have the best hand, you could still easily be a favorite to win the pot. (You have a nut flush draw and two overcards to the board, so you have plenty of outs if your opponent stays with you.) Also, your bet may make your opponent fold, which is desirable. I'd recommend a bet of about $160.

Action: You actually bet $200, and Player B calls. The pot is now $645.

Fourth Street: J♦

Action: Player B checks. *Do you check or raise again?*
   Answer: Your bet was a little higher than I'd like to see. Players do this because they're eager to steal the pot, and they think that a bigger bet is more likely to close the deal. That's perhaps marginally true. But a player who's willing to fold to a $200 bet will almost always fold to a $160 bet. And the player who calls the $200 bet almost certainly has you beaten at this point. (Remember, right now your hand is just ace-high.)
       Although I think Player B is ahead at this point, he did check, so you should check too and see a free card.

Action: Actually you bet another $200. Player B calls.

Bad decision. If you make plays like this, you need to stop and think about what you're doing. Here you're just throwing money away.

You bet on the flop because there was a significant chance that Player B had nothing and would throw the hand away. Instead he called a bet of $200. Therefore, he has something, at least more than you do. The J♦ came, which didn't help you but which might have helped him. Can you possibly believe that he'll fold this $200 bet when he called the last one? All you're doing is building a pot in which you're sure you're second-best with one card to come. That's not smart poker. (The bet might be okay if you were first to act and were trying to see the river more cheaply than if you checked and called. But in last position there is no such rationale.)

Fifth Street: 7♦

Action: Player B checks. *What's your move?*
Answer: You check. You still have nothing, and you're almost certainly beaten. If he bet, you'd lay down your hand, so be grateful you're getting a free peek.

Action: You check. He shows 9♥6♥. His one pair wins the pot.

A weaker hand than we expected, but still good enough to beat nothing. He had no business calling before the flop with this hand, but afterwards he had a pair plus an open-ended straight draw, so his later calls were reasonable.

Hand 6-7

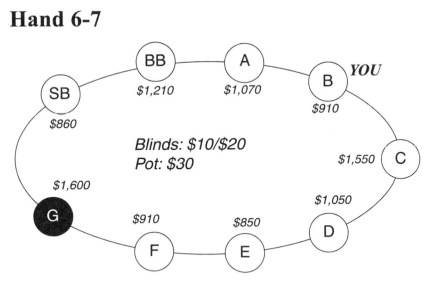

Situation: Early in a single-table online tournament. Players A and C have been very aggressive so far.

Your hand: A♦7♣

Action to you: Player A calls.

Question: *Do you fold, call, or raise?*

    Answer: A conservative player would simply fold in this spot. Ace-seven offsuit isn't strong enough to play in early position, and here you're coming in behind a player who has called, indicating some strength. Since he's known to be aggressive, you have to discount his strength somewhat, but you can't just ignore it.

    Aggressive and super-aggressive players like to steal pots, but even those players like to see a rationale for stealing, like good position after the flop, or the knowledge that several players have already folded their hands. There's none of that here, so just fold your hand.

Action: In fact you elect to raise to $40. Everyone folds around to the big blind, who calls, and Player A, who also calls. The pot now has $130.

Flop: J♥5♣2♠

Action: The big blind and Player A both check. *What should you do now?*

> **Answer:** This was a series of great results for you. No raisers, only two callers, and you ended with position on both of them. (Note, by the way, that both the big blind and Player A made the mistake of not betting to define their hands.) The texture of the flop was also excellent — two low cards plus a low high card, three suits, and the cards spread well apart. A flop like this has the minimum chance of filling your opponent's hands. Finally, both players check.
>
> As the aggressor in the hand, you have to take a shot at the pot here. Against two opponents, you want to bet a bit more than the standard continuation bet; something like two-thirds to three-quarters of the pot. It's big enough to win the pot if neither player likes his hand, but it's not too expensive in case you get check-raised.

Action: You bet $100, and the other two players fold.

"That's poker."
Players say this when they've suffered what seems to be some horrible beat — their opponent fills an inside straight on the river, or some such thing. But here's a key insight about poker. *Only your bad luck is visible — your good luck often slips by unnoticed.* You were actually exceptionally lucky this hand. A bad raise triggered a series of folds, no reraises happened, you got good position on the only two callers, the flop missed them both, and you picked up the pot. Most players would smugly gather the pot, congratulate themselves on their great skill, and go on to the next

hand. Avoid this pitfall. Stay aware of both your good luck as well as your bad, and you'll find it easier to keep an even keel when things go wrong (as they inevitably will).

Hand 6-8

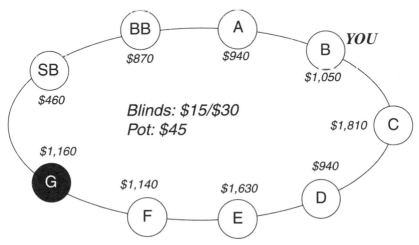

Blinds: $15/$30
Pot: $45

Situation: Early in an online tournament,

Your hand: A♣K♥

Action to you: Player A folds.

Question: *How much do you raise?*
    Answer: You should put in a good-sized raise with ace-king in early position. You don't want your opponents to be able to limp in cheaply. A raise to $120 or $150, four or five times the big blind, looks good here.

Action: You actually raise to just $60. Players C and D call. Players E and F fold. Player G calls. The blinds both fold. The pot is now $285.

Flop: 8♥7♣4♦

Question: You are first to act, with three callers behind you. *What do you do?*

> **Answer:** Three players behind you is too many to make a continuation bet. There's too great a chance that you won't be able to take the pot, in which case you've just put in some money with the worst hand. The flop certainly didn't help you, but it may have helped at least one of the other three players. You need to let this hand go quietly. Check.

Action: You check. Players C and D also check, but Player G bets $230.

Question: *What do you do?*

> **Answer:** Fold. You have nothing, and Player G, with position on you, says he has something. You have no reason to doubt him, so save your chips.

Action: You fold, as do Players C and D. Player G takes the pot.

Hand 6-9

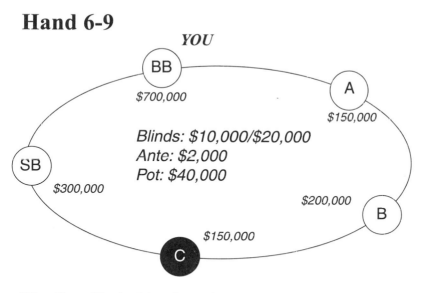

YOU

BB
$700,000

A
$150,000

Blinds: $10,000/$20,000
Ante: $2,000
Pot: $40,000

SB
$300,000

$200,000
B

C
$150,000

Situation: Final table of a major tournament. You are the chip leader. The small blind is a very tough, cool competitor, well-versed in no-limit hold 'em.

Your hand: Q♣J♠

Action to you: Players A, B, and C all fold. The small blind puts in $35,000, raising $25,000. The pot is now $75,000. It costs you $25,000 to call.

Question: *Do you fold, call, or raise?*

    Answer: Queen-jack is certainly not a great hand at a full table, but here you're at a short table and three players have already folded, so you have to evaluate the hand in the context of a heads-up situation. Heads-up against a random hand, queen-jack is a solid favorite.

    The small blind, however, has already bet, representing a better-than-average hand. But the bet was curiously small, offering you 3-to-1 odds to enter the pot. When you know your opponent to be a strong player, which is the case here, stay alert. Such a bet may indicate a very strong hand.

Still, you have position, and the pot is offering you 3-to-1 odds, so you can't simply throw away Q♣J♠; it's plenty good enough to call here.

Action: You call. The pot is now $100,000.

Flop: 9♦7♣4♥

Action: The small blind checks. *Should you check, bet $20,000, bet $50,000, bet $60,000, or bet $100,000?*

Answer: The bad news is that the flop missed you. The good news is that, since players mostly play high cards, there's a good chance that it missed your opponent as well. His check was a clue that the flop may have missed him. To find out for sure, you need to make a probing bet. But how big should that bet be?

You want to bet enough so that your opponent will give up the pot if he doesn't have anything, but no more than that. If you bet more than you need to chase him away, and he actually has a hand, you've just wasted money. A bet of half the pot or slightly less is the right size for this purpose. When you bet half the pot to win the whole pot, you're getting 2-to-1 odds on your money. That's excellent, considering that you'll probably take the pot about 50 percent of the time in this situation. Half the pot is a very good size for most probe bets.

If both players were playing high cards, the flop wouldn't have hit either one. Therefore, if this flop hit your opponent, he's very likely to have the best hand. What's more, *if he's a good player he knows this.* So when you bet, one of the following two situations will arise:

1. Your opponent didn't get a piece of the flop, and now you're betting at him. He's not going to chase you here. Instead, he'll just lay down and get on to the next hand.

2. Your opponent did get a piece of the flop. Now he's going to call or raise your bet, and that call or raise will indicate that you're done with the hand, barring some remarkable cards on the turn or the river.

Isn't poker wonderfully logical?

The difference between a probe bet and a continuation bet is the identity of the pre-flop raises. If you took the lead before the flop and then bet when the flop misses you, the bet is a continuation bet. (It's a continuation of your previous action.) If your opponent took the lead pre-flop and now checks, your bet is called a probe. (You're probing to see if he thinks the hand is worth playing.) Both bets are ways of gaining information and defining your hand. Continuation bets need to be slightly larger than probe bets because you are representing more strength with a continuation bet.

Action: You actually bet $60,000, and the small blind calls.

Fourth Street: 3♣

Action: The small blind checks. *What do you do?*
   Answer: Your $60,000 bet after the flop was a bit too large. You gave yourself only 3-to-2 odds on your money, rather than 2-to-1. Your opponent called, indicating that he caught some piece of the flop. But he didn't bet this time, so he's probably holding a seven or a four in his hand. You still don't have much, so you should check again.

Action: You check.

Fifth Street: 7♦

Action: The small blind checks again. *Should you check, or try to steal the pot with a $100,000 bet?*

> **Answer:** Don't bluff here. His check was a setup, and you'll be picked off.
>
> Your opponent doesn't think you have anything, for the reason I explained earlier. But if you did have something, you would have bet on fourth street, to prevent him from getting a free card on the river. Since you checked, he was sure you didn't have anything at that point. If you didn't have anything on fourth street, the river card, another seven, surely didn't help you. So now he knows he has the best hand, and he's giving you a chance to lose some more money on the hand by trying to steal.

Resolution: You actually bet $100,000, and your opponent calls, turning over K♠4♣. His two pair win the pot.

This hand repays careful study, so go over what happened here and make sure you understand it. This is a hand where a top player would have lost about $110,000 less than the player sitting in the big blind, simply by drawing the right conclusions after the flop[7] and sticking to those conclusions throughout the hand. Remember that the difference between strong and weak players doesn't lie in how much money they make with their good hands. Anyone can win a big pot when dealt pocket aces, or after flopping a set. *A good player loses less money with his marginal hands*, and in the course of a long tournament that edge turns the tide.

---

[7] Of course it could be argued that even the flop probe bet was wrong because it made no sense that your strong opponent did not make the routine continuation bet on the flop as he would if he had nothing.

Hand 6-10

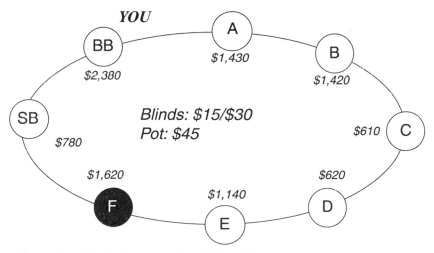

Situation: Early in a single-table online tournament. Players B and F are extremely aggressive.

Your hand: 7♥7♣

Action to you: Players A, B, and C all call. Player D folds. Player E raises to $60. Player F and the small blind fold. The pot is now $195.

Question: *Do you fold, call, or raise?*

    Answer: You're the big blind, so it costs you only $30 more to call with $195 in the pot. You should call because of the combination of the expressed and implied pot odds. The expressed pot odds are 6.5-to-1. The odds against your improving to trips on the flop are about 7-to-1 against. (You don't have to worry about odds after that, because if you don't improve on the flop with your low pair, you'll be out of the hand.) The expressed odds aren't quite enough to justify a call, but if you hit your trips, you'll likely win a substantial pot, so your implied odds are excellent.

If you're alert, you should have one additional concern about the hand. There are three live players who are still to act behind you. If one of them decides to raise, you may not be getting the odds you need when the betting comes around to you again.

While I agree you should be a little concerned, the fact is that you rarely see this move (the limp followed by the reraise) in online play. For that matter, you rarely see it in live tournaments either, although it used to be a fairly common move. I've made that play a few times myself. You should always be alert to live players behind you, but here you should just go ahead and call anyway.

Action: You call for $30. Players A, B, and C also call. The pot is now $315.

Flop: T♦6♣2♥

Question: You're first to act. *What should you do?*

Answer: Your first impression should be that this is a good flop for your sevens. Three low cards, three different suits, and three cards spread well apart. If you were facing just one or two players, you could lead out with a probe bet of about half the pot, and have some confidence that you would either win the pot immediately, or have the best hand if you were called.

The problem with this hand is that you're facing four players, and it's just too likely that someone at the table has you beaten. Against that number of opponents, you really needed to hit your trips to continue playing. Just check and fold when the pot gets bet. Probe-type bets aren't useful against several opponents because the chance of winning the pot without resistance is too low.

Action: You check. The pot is eventually won by Player E with a pair of kings in the hole.

As an aside, the player with the kings played badly by letting so many people into the pot cheaply.

Hand 6-11

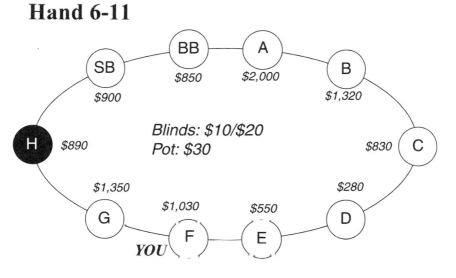

Situation: Early round of an online tournament. Table seems conservative, with little action and few players in each pot.

Your hand: T♠T♥

Action to you: Players A through E all fold.

Question: *What's your play?*
    Answer: You should bet between $60 and $80. You certainly don't want to fold, and a call is a poor play as well. You almost certainly have the best hand now, but you don't want to let a bunch of drawing hands in cheaply. Ideally, you'd like to win the pot now, or play it against no more than one

opponent. A bet of $60 seems like a good number to chase out the riffraff.

Action: You bet $60, players G, H, and the small blind fold, and the big blind calls, putting in another $40. The pot is now $130.

Flop: 7♦6♦5♠

Action: Big blind bets $70.

Question: *What's your play?*

    Answer: Your first job is to figure out just what your opponent's bet meant. Don't fool yourself into thinking that you can be precise about this. It's good enough to come up with a couple of the most likely possibilities. That's all the top players can do, despite what they may tell you.

    Obviously, he could be betting a pair you have beaten. Alternatively, he could be making a simple probing bet. If he didn't bet, you certainly would have, so he could be making his only play to win the pot. Now you need to figure out a defense against a probe.

    Note that the texture of the flop was good for you — no cards higher than your pair. It could be better, if three different suits were represented or there was no possible straight draw, but those are small risks. You shouldn't be worried that your opponent stayed with nine-eight or four-trey. It's more likely that he has one of the following five hands.

1.   He paired the board.

2.   He made a straight.

3.   He made a flush draw.

4. He's bluffing because three low cards came.

5. He has a big pair or trips.

You've got two choices. You can just call, or make a pot-sized raise, something like $200 or $250. If that bet gets reraised, though, you're up against a big pair or trips, and you're throwing the hand away. The low-risk approach to this pot is just to call, and if your opponent doesn't have anything, you'll find out after fourth street.

Action: You call. Pot now $270. Fourth street is A♥. Big blind now checks.

Question: *What's your play?*
Answer: The big blind might be setting an elaborate trap, but you should like to go with the simple explanation. He's got a couple of high cards, the flop missed him, and now the ace didn't help him. He's made one play at the pot, but he's unwilling to make a second play for it. So you should bet out, and expect him to fold.

Beginners are prone to fall into the trap of assuming that their opponents are totally inscrutable, and every play is part of some convoluted snare. In fact, *most bets mean what they appear to mean*. Remember this, because it will help you make a lot of money. If the action around the table indicates you have the best hand, then you probably do, and you should bet it accordingly.

Resolution: You bet $250, and the big blind folds.

Hand 6-12

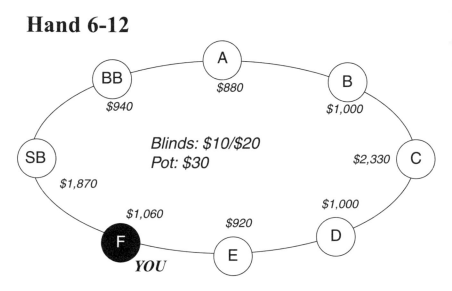

Situation: Early in a one-table satellite tournament.

Your hand: K♥J♠

Action to you: Player A raises to $40. Player B calls. Players C, D, and E all fold. The pot is now $110.

Question: *Do you fold, call, or raise?*

> **Answer:** Before you get too excited about your two face cards and your good position, review what just happened. The player under the gun opened with a raise, indicating a strong hand. The player behind him flat called. From the Gap Concept, you need a stronger hand to call a raise than you would to open the pot in the first place. Right now, there's no reason to believe your hand is other than third best. True, you have position, and that's nice, but it isn't enough to compensate for the fact that your hand doesn't belong in this pot in the first place. Throw it away.

Action: In fact, you elect to call. The small blind also calls, and the big blind folds. The pot now contains $170.

Flop: J♣T♥9♠

Question: *How excited are you about this flop?*
    Answer: Evaluating the texture of a flop is a crucial skill. Your quick impression might be that this is a fine flop for you. You now have top pair plus a king kicker, which sounds good. But now let's think about *how this flop would impact the other likely hands.*
    Presumably there are no high pairs at the table. (You'd better hope there aren't, otherwise you had no business in the pot in the first place.) But if not, then what were these three other people calling with? One of three hands actually — unpaired high cards, medium pairs, and low pairs. Someone who called with a low pair wasn't helped by this flop. That's good for you. Someone with a medium pair just made trips. That's real bad for you. But the high card draws are very dangerous as well — king-queen made a straight, jack-ten made two pair, and many of the others made at least a straight draw.
    Your sentiment right now should be "Proceed with Caution." You're not unhappy with top pair plus an overcard kicker, but one or two of your opponents are probably happy with this flop as well. You're actually very glad you act last here. You'll be able to see what they do, and proceed accordingly.

Action: The small blind bets $320. Player A raises to $650. Player B goes all-in for $960. The pot is now $2,100. *What do you do?*
    Answer: Presumably all questions have now been answered. Your jacks are worthless. Get out.

Action: You fold. The big blind calls the all-in bet. Player A goes all-in for his remaining chips. The hands were: Big Blind — 8♠7♥, Player A — A♥J♦, Player B — 9♦9♣. The big blind won all the money with a straight.

Recapping the hand shows us that Player A's initial raise under the gun with A♥J♦ was a little loose. Player B's call with a pair of nines was fine. The small blind's call with 8♠7♥ offsuit in bad position was a hopeless play which eventually won a huge pot. (That's poker, however.) After the flop and the small blind's bet of twice the pot, Player A should have realized that his pair of jacks weren't necessarily any good now.

Your fold on the flop saved you from a substantial loss. Be glad you got out cheaply.

Hand 6-13

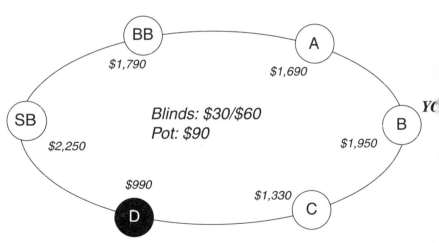

Situation: Late in a single-table online tournament. The small blind is aggressive.

Your hand: T♥T♦

Action to you: Player A folds.

Question: *Do you call or raise?*
    Answer: With a medium pair you can't let people in cheaply. You need to raise enough to hopefully chase out all but one opponent. Winning the pot right here is not a bad result either. You should raise three to four times the big blind.

Action: You raise to $200. Player C calls. The others all fold. The pot is now $490.

Flop: K♣T♠9♣

Question: You've hit a set. *What do you do with it?*
    Answer: Your first job is to look at the texture of the flop carefully. Many players, when they make a hand on the flop, forget to consider just what the flop might have meant to the other hands in the pot.
    This flop is actually quite dangerous. There are two clubs, plus three relatively high cards, and these three cards are not spread apart. Someone holding queen-jack, suited or not, already has you beaten, while many other potential holdings will be on flush or straight draws.
    Checking here is a little too clever. You haven't marked Player C as an aggressive player, so there's no assurance that he'll bet if you check, and you don't want to let him catch a free card to win.
    You should bet about $250. That way he'll be getting 3-to-1 pot odds for whatever it is he's trying to do, which might be enough to keep him around. It might also be interpreted as a standard continuation bet, not indicating any great strength. Under certain circumstances you might want to go a little higher, but $400 is definitely too much.

Action: Actually you go all-in, and he folds.

Comment: Going all-in is a pretty standard beginner's blunder. You see it all the time among players in their first or second tournament. Beginners, whose only real exposure to the game is TV poker, tend to see no-limit hold 'em as a battle of outrageous bluffs and all-in moves. When they finally catch a hand that they think they can legitimately bet all their chips, they practically fall out of their chairs getting the money in. (This is a very reliable tell, by the way.)

There are some rare circumstances where the all-in move with a huge hand is a good play. You need to be up against a very strong opponent, who also sees you as a strong opponent who would never stick all his chips in with a great hand. Then he might think you were trying to steal with a weak hand, and call you. It would also help if you were sitting on a moderately small stack, say four to six times the blinds and antes, so he would recognize the need for you to make a move soon.

Hand 6-14

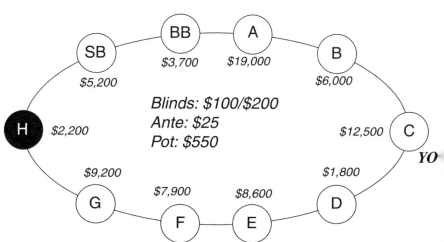

SB $5,200

BB $3,700

A $19,000

B $6,000

H $2,200

C $12,500

YO

G $9,200

F $7,900

E $8,600

D $1,800

Blinds: $100/$200
Ante: $25
Pot: $550

Situation: Several rounds into a major tournament. Your chip count is well above average but still trails the chip leaders. Players E and G seem solid, tight, and unimaginative.

Your hand: A♥Q♠

Action to you: Players A and B fold.

Question: *What do you do?*
  Answer: You've got a standard raising hand for your position, so just make a good-sized raise.

Action: You raise to $600. Player D folds. Player E calls. Player F folds. Player G calls. The button and the blinds fold. The pot is now $2,350.

  Quick — before the flop comes. What are the most likely hands that Players E and G are holding?
  You want to get in the habit of asking yourself this question before the flop. Once the flop comes, it's easy to get distracted by the cards that are showing and imagine all sorts of hands that fit neatly into the board. Instead, answer the question now, while your head is clear. Two relatively tight players called after a solid raise from third position. What are they most likely to be holding?
  The answer is — a couple of medium to low pairs. Neither should have a high pair, since they could (and should) have reraised. Hands like king-jack are too weak, and neither was getting the good, cheap odds needed to play suited connectors. It's a pretty safe bet that at least one of them has a pair, perhaps both.

Flop: 3♥3♦3♣

Question: *What do you do now?*
  Answer: Not a good flop for you. Since the most likely hands for your opponents are low to medium pairs, the odds are

right now that someone has already made his full house and has you beaten, and in that case you have only six outs.

But it's too soon to give up on the hand. It's certainly possible that you're facing some combination like a king-queen and a jack-ten suited, or even ace-jack coupled with ace-ten, or some other such pairing. It's also possible that one of your opponents has a pair of sixes but has the courage and discipline to lay it down in the face of what he thinks is your higher pair.

You have to take a shot at the pot. The trick is to give yourself good odds, so you don't need that many fold-fold combinations to break even on the bet. With the pot at $2,350, bet about $800, one-third of the pot. If you win the bet one time in four, you'll just about break even even if you never draw out. (One win = +$2,350, three losses = -$800 each = -$2,400.) Anyone who can call you will have a pair, and you'll be done with the hand unless you pull an ace or a queen on fourth street.

Action: You bet $800. Player E folds but Player G calls.

Fourth Street: 9♥

Question: *What now?*

Answer: You did your part and now you're finished. Don't invest any more money. Just check and fold if he bets.

Action: You check, he bets $2,000, and you fold.

Hand 6-15

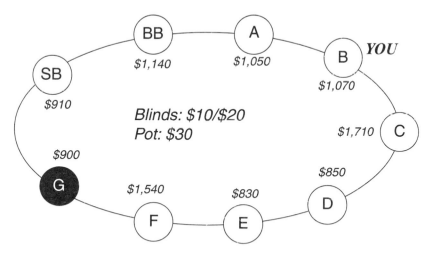

Situation: Early in a single-table online tournament. You don't know much about the other players, but the table seems fairly tight.

Your hand: A♣T♦

Action to you: Player A folds.

Question: *Do you play this hand?*
   Answer: No. A ten is a weak kicker and you're in early position. Don't waste your time. Just fold, and then observe the action around the table.

Action: Actually you decide to raise to $40. Players C and D fold. Player E calls the $40. Player F folds. Player G calls the $40. The small blind folds, and the big blind calls an additional $20. The pot is now $170.

Not a good result for you. You've managed to create a big pot with a weak hand. There are four players in, and you'll be acting second. Overall, you shouldn't be happy about this.

Flop: A♠T♥5♠

Action: The big blind checks. *What do you do?*
   Answer: After a dubious opening, you've hit a fantastic flop. The only downside are the two spades sitting out there. With three opponents, there's a reasonable chance that someone has a draw to a flush.

   You've got two goals here. You almost surely have the best hand right now, so you want to get more money into the pot. But you don't want to bet so little that any drawing hands are getting the right price to draw. A pot-sized bet usually accomplishes both goals. It's big enough to chase out the weak hands and the drawing hands, but not so large that someone with ace-x or a pair of tens can't think about calling you. You should bet between $170 and $200 here.

Action: You actually bet $300. Player E calls. Player G and the big blind fold. The pot is now $770.

You bet too much, but your decision worked because you did get a caller.

Player E, by the way, has almost certainly blundered. He should have either folded or gone all-in. By calling, he's left himself in a position where the pot is $770 and he has only $490 left. If he had a hand that was good enough to continue to play, almost any future betting will offer him such great pot odds that he will have to stay in the pot, and eventually all his chips will go in the center. If that's the case, he's better off betting them now, since that move has some chance of driving you out. (Remember, from his point of view you may be bluffing.)

You'll sometimes hear talk around the table about a player "making a decision for all his chips." Calling here is just that sort of decision. When you're contemplating a call in the middle of a hand, always compare your remaining chips to the pot. As your stack gets small relative to the pot, it's an indication that your real choice is not between folding and calling, but between folding and going all-in.

Fourth Street: 7♦

Question: *What do you do?*
    Answer: That's a good card for you. It's not a spade, and it's lower than your ten, so someone staying around with ace-seven is still losing to you. It would be crazy for someone with sevens to have called your last bet, so this card couldn't have helped your opponent — therefore it helped you by default.
    You have to bet here, and you have to bet a good amount to shut out a flush draw. You have $730 left, and Player E has $490. I'd say the minimum bet is about $300. You could also go all-in — nothing really wrong with that. You're committed to the hand in any case.

Action: You bet $320, and Player E goes all-in for an extra $170. The pot is now $1,580. *Do you call?*
    Answer: Of course. He may have a set, but he might have an ace that you can beat. At any rate, the odds are irresistible.

Action: You call. He shows A♦J♣. The river is a 6♥. You win.

Your only real mistake this hand was playing it in the first place, and a slightly over-enthusiastic bet after the flop. But a great flop gave you plenty of cover, and you made some good money.

Hand 6-16

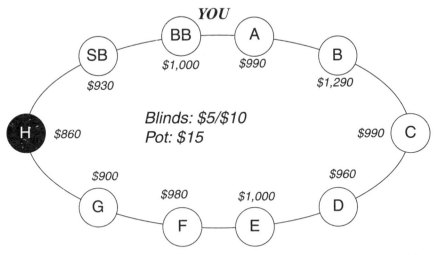

Situation: Early in a single-table online tournament. No solid information on the players yet.

Your hand: A♥T♦

Action to you: Player A raises to $20. Players B and C fold. Players D and E call $20. Player F folds. Player G calls $20. The button and small blind fold. Pot now $95. It costs you $10 to call.

Question: *Do you fold, call, raise, or raise all-in?*

Answer: Here's the same holding as the last problem, but the situation is quite a bit different. Ace-ten offsuit in poor position is not a strong hand. But here no one has shown great strength, and the pot is offering you fantastic odds of 9.5-to-1. So you call. Be aware that you will mostly be checking and folding this hand after the flop unless something very exciting happens.

Because you're up against four callers, and you're frequently throwing your hand away next round, don't make the mistake of putting in a small raise. This won't chase everybody out, and you'll mostly have to let the money go.

Raising all-in is also wrong, but a little more interesting. This play will mostly win the pot right now, but on the occasions when there's an ace-king or ace-queen or high pair sitting out there and slowplaying, you'll be a favorite to lose all your chips. That's just too expensive. There is a time for plays like this, but it comes later in a tournament, when your opponents are playing less and protecting their chips more.

Action: You call for another $10. Pot now $105.

Flop: A♦T♣6♠

Question: *What's your play?*

> **Answer:** Something very exciting just happened! You flopped top two pair. Now your job is to extract the most money from the hand. If there were just one player behind you, you'd have to put in a small bet, just to start building a pot. (If your opponent folds to that bet, you weren't going to make any money on the hand anyway.) But with four active players behind you, the right play is usually to check, intending a check-raise.

Action: You check. Player A bets $35. Players D and E fold. Player G calls $35. The pot is now $175.

Question: *What's your play?*

> **Answer:** Your plan has worked and you're certainly raising. The only question is — what's the right amount? In a live tournament or later in a tight online tournament, you should probably pick a number like $140 or $150 — somewhat less than the pot, but not too cheap. You want callers, but you want to bet enough to make some real money. That's often a

tough balancing act, but my feel is that $140 or $150 — about 80 percent of the pot — is the optimal amount.

Small online tournaments, however, tend to be quite loose, so there you should go with a bigger number here, and bet $200. You want to sell the pot for as much as you can. The only hand you should fear now is trip sixes.

Action: You raise $200. Players A and G both call. Pot now $775. Fourth street is 7♠.

Question: *Do you call, bet 250, go all-in?*

Answer: In an online tournament, you should be delighted with this result. You've snared a couple of doofuses, probably with a pair each, and you're going to clean their clocks. You don't want to go all-in for your last $780, because you might still lose to one or both of them. At this point player A has $735 left and player B has $645, and you still want as much of that money as possible. A $250 bet into a $775 pot should entice at least one of the players with the good pot odds.

But in a live tournament, and especially if you know that Player A is a good tough player, it's quite a different story. He made a modest bet after the flop, then he called your $200 raise, even with a third player still to act behind him. What kind of hand lets a player make that sequence of bets? Either trips, or two pair. With no flushes or straights on the board, there's not much else.

Should that change your play? No. You should still bet out. In tournaments, you're under severe time pressure to keep moving ahead and acquiring chips. You've got to fade the possibility that he's holding trip sixes, because you've got a good hand here with the possibility of doubling or tripling up. Those situations are rare enough so that you can't let them go.

Action: You in fact go all-in. Player A calls, and G folds. Player A shows 6♦6♣. The last card is the Q♥, and Player A wins with his trip sixes.

There were two players trapping in this pot! Player A played the hand perfectly. With trips in middle position, you just want to call and let the action come to you. Online, I'd make a note that Player A was a serious, tough player and play him accordingly in any future events.

Hand 6-17

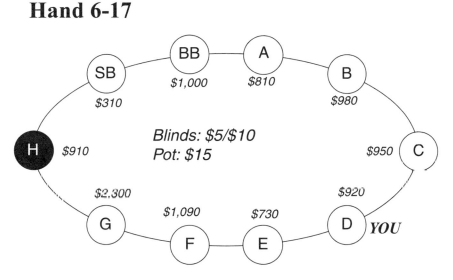

Situation: Early in an online tournament.

Your hand: A♦K♦

Action to you: Player A calls $10. Players B and C fold. Pot is $25.

Question: *What's your bet?*

Answer: Ace-king suited is the strongest of the unpaired high card hands, and can be played in various ways. With aggressive betting in the pot, you'll sometimes just call with it. If no one has shown strength, you can certainly raise, but you don't want to raise so much that you discourage action. In this situation, with one caller already, a bet of four to six times the big blind is a good amount, so put in about $50.

Action: You actually raise to $90, and Players E and F fold. Player G, the big stack, calls. The button and the blinds fold. Player A, the initial caller, puts in another $80 to call. The pot is now $285.

You bet too much, but got two callers anyway. Not really that unusual a result for online poker, where much of the betting is pretty random compared to live play. Player A, for instance, limped in first position for $10, then called a big raise. If his hand was strong enough to call on the end, it was certainly strong enough to open the pot aggressively in the first place.

Flop: J♣7♦2♥

Action: Player A checks. *What's your move?*
   Answer: A standard continuation bet of about half the pot is right here. You still have two overcards to the board plus two backdoor hands, and there's no guarantee that the jack paired anyone. Although your bet is more of a bluff than a semi-bluff (you only have ace high right now), betting half the pot gets you 2-to-1 odds on your bluff, which is pretty good given that one player has already checked.

Action: You in fact check, Player G bets $20, and Player A calls. Pot now $325. *What's your play?*
   Answer: The pot odds are now 16-to-1, and you have six outs twice, so it's a monster call. Once you forgo the initial continuation bet, there's no need to do more than call. You're

basically getting a free card here, which, since you don't have anything yet, is a fine result for you.

Action: You actually raise $50, and both players call. The pot is now $475.

The hand takes another bizarre twist. Check-raising usually indicates a strong hand, but here, you've check-raised so little that the pot odds compel both opponents to call almost regardless of the hands. With a pretty random sequence of bets, you've managed to build a big pot while learning almost nothing about the quality of the opposing hands.

In playing poker, your real goal is to do just the opposite of what's been done here. You want to bet enough to find out crucial information. Once you're pretty sure you know what they have, you're then entitled to make the big move.

Fourth Street: 4♦

Action: Player A checks. *What do you do?*

> **Answer:** You should just check here. You still have nothing although you have picked up a draw to the nuts, and it will be hard to chase anybody out without putting all your chips in jeopardy. Let's hope to get a free card.

Action: You check and Player G checks.

Fifth Street: K♣

Action: Player A checks. *What now?*

> **Answer:** Lightning strikes, and with no straights or flushes on board, you rate to have the best hand. Since no one has been betting, an all-in or other big bet is probably just going to chase people away. It's time to try to extract a little extra

money with a bet that's just small enough to be called. $100 looks about right.

Action: You bet $100, and Player G calls. He was playing with a J♥T♥, and his pair of jacks loses to your kings.

Sometimes even a random set of bets will produce a good result. Here our big pre-flop bet, coupled with the weird check-raise, probably prevented Player G from betting or raising at some point when his pair of jacks were good. Once again, look at the danger of giving your opponent a free card. Because Player G let you hang around cheaply, you were able to fill your hand on the end and win a nice pot.

Hand 6-18

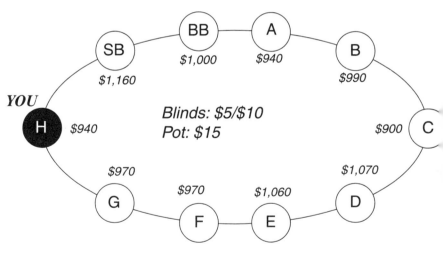

Situation: Early hand of an online satellite tournament.

Your hand: Q♦J♠

Action to you: Players A, B, C, D, and E all call. Players F and G fold. The pot is now $65.

Question: *Do you raise, call, or fold?*

Answer: The action so far has been just about perfect for your mediocre hand. The sensible play here is to put in $10 and try to see a flop. You almost certainly don't have the best hand at this point, but you're on the button with position, and your hand has some potential of developing into something good on the flop. So put in your $10, take a cheap flop, and see what happens.

The player we're watching here decides to bet $50 to steal the pot. What's wrong with this approach?

The first problem is a simple one: In online tournaments, this bet just isn't going to work. In a live tournament, where every bet is taken seriously, there's some chance that you could get away with this play (but not enough of a chance to make me try it). In online tournaments, most of the players who called for $10 will merrily call the $50 bet as well. So what's going to happen is that you'll build a big pot with a bad hand. If you really want to try and chase people out in online poker, a bet of $100 to $200 chips is necessary.

The second problem is even worse: One of the early callers, who almost certainly has a better hand than yours, may elect to raise, and then what do you do? (Hint: fold.) By raising instead of calling, you've given the early limpers a chance to act again.

What you've actually done with this bet is make a move that poker players call a *pot-sweetener*. It's a small raise that will fold no one, but which is designed to get more money in a pot when you believe that your position will give you an advantage after the flop. In online poker, a raise of this size isn't enough to chase anyone out, so it only functions as a sweetener.

Action: You raise $50. The blinds fold. Players A, B, C, D, and E all call for another $40 each. The pot is now $315.

Flop: J♣6♥5♦

Action: Players A and B check. Player C bets $300. Players D and E fold.

Question: *What do you do?*
    Answer: The flop was a very good one for you — it gave you top pair, and the three mixed suits means that the flush draws were stymied. (With five callers, there were likely to be two or three folks playing two suited cards.) But since your hand wasn't that good to begin with, you could still have problems, so you have to proceed cautiously.
    Player C's bet of $300 says he has something. Your problem is that many of the hands that would justify his bet have you beaten. He might have called before the flop with ace-jack, king-jack, sixes, or fives, all of which leave you crushed. But he also might have called with jack-ten, jack-nine suited, nines, or eights, all of which explain his bets and all of which you can beat. This is a close decision, but I would call here.

Action: You actually decide to go all-in with your last $890. Player C calls for his last $550. Players A and B fold. Player C shows J♥T♥.

Resolution: Fourth and fifth street are the 3♣ and the Q♥, and your jacks and queens beat his pair of jacks.

    Your all-in play was a mistake because you didn't take into account Players A and B, who were still in the pot. If you had just called, and both those players folded, you would probably have gotten all your money in the pot on fourth street or fifth street. But suppose one of those players had gone all-in after you called? In that case, you'd have an option to realize that you were probably beaten and lay down your hand. By going all-in, you denied yourself that option, a costly mistake. *Never forget that a player who checked is still alive in the pot, and must be reckoned with!* A beginner would be delighted that he won a big pot here, but a seasoned player would recognize that this was a very dangerous hand where he was lucky to get out alive. The pot-stealing move before the flop created a very tough decision after the flop, with a big bet in front of you and active players still to act behind you. One of the hallmarks of good poker is to play in such a way that you don't have to make tough decisions with all your chips riding on the result. Let your opponents struggle with those decisions. As much as possible, try to leave yourself with easy decisions and clear-cut plays, and avenues of escape.

Part Seven

Betting on
Fourth and Fifth Street

Betting on Fourth and Fifth Street

Introduction

By the time the hand gets to fourth and fifth street, your play will depend less on general principles and more on the specific tactics of the situation. You're going to be weighing the strength of your hand, the strength your opponent (or opponents) has represented, your position, their style and their perception of your style, the relative stack sizes, and so on. Nonetheless, there are a few ideas that apply specifically to fourth and fifth street play. Let's take a look at them.

Playing to Win
the Most Money Possible

Suppose I told you that there was a type of no-limit hold 'em problem that good players spent a lot of time contemplating, but beginners hardly ever think about it all. Would you be interested in knowing what that problem was? You would? All right, here it is.

It's fourth street, you're heads-up against one player, and you believe you have the better hand. You have two remaining opportunities to bet, on fourth street and, if your opponent is still around, on fifth street. You'd like to win two bets instead of just one, or one bet instead of zero bets. What's the best way to play so as to extract an extra bet from your opponent?

To most beginners and many intermediates, this question seems incredibly pedestrian. Their idea of good no-limit hold 'em is acting weak when they're strong, flopping the nuts, shoving all their chips in the pot, then getting called and doubling up. Who cares about winning a measly extra bet on some average-plus hand?

Well, you should care, because over the course of a long tournament, these extra bets here and there add up to a lot of chips, chips that can keep you alive while your profligate opponents are floundering. If I've succeeded in convincing you that these plays matter, let's see how they are done.

Example No. 1. You hold

You raise before the flop from middle position and get called by one player behind you. You both have large stacks. The flop comes

You again make a bet, and you again get a call. From your knowledge of this opponent, who is a relatively weak player, you think his likely holding at this point is queen-small. Fourth street comes a deuce. *How can you bet to extract the most money from the hand?*

Answer: Note first of all that if your opponent had been a strong player, he probably wouldn't have played the hand this way. Holding, say, a queen-ten, you don't want just to call on the flop because you won't know what to do if you then face another bet on fourth street. You have top pair, but is it good, or are you beaten? You won't know. A better play is to try to settle the hand with a raise on the flop. If that wins the pot, great. If it doesn't win the pot, you're almost certainly beaten. In any event, the question is settled, and you won't lose any more money on the hand.

But our opponent wasn't a good player, so he just called, and we find ourselves in the current situation. A good place to start is by asking "What's the most we could reasonably expect to make on this hand?" A good answer is — two moderate-sized bets. There's no reason to think your opponent is going to call a big bet with his hand, either now or on the river. You showed strength before the flop and strength after the flop, and all he has is top pair with a weak kicker. Unless he's very weak, he should not lose a lot of his chips with this hand.

The best way to proceed is just to make a modest bet on fourth street, one that you're pretty sure will be called. A good number is something like 30 percent to 40 percent of the pot. With the big pot odds you're giving, it should be hard for anyone with top pair to lay the hand down, regardless of the kicker. Then do the same thing on fifth street. Trying to trap with a check is too dangerous, because there's too great a chance that your opponent will check behind you to see another card.

Example No. 2. Another situation occurs when you believe he has a pair under your queens. Let's say that once again you hold A♦Q♣ and the flop is Q♥7♣3♠. You read your opponent for a pair of tens. You bet before the flop, and you bet on the flop, and both times you get a call. *What's the right play on fourth street?*

Answer: This is a more complicated situation than the first example. You have three plays.

1. **Make a big bet, between three-quarters of the pot and the whole pot.** This is the conservative play, and it's very reasonable. You knock out the free card, and give yourself the best shot at winning the pot right now, but the least chance at winning another bet on the end. I like this approach if the board is moderately dangerous.

2. **Check**. This is a good play if the board is either very dangerous or very weak (as in the example). If the board is dangerous you don't necessarily want to commit any more money to the pot. If the board is weak you can afford to trap. Checking shows weakness, and is best used when you think that a bet on fourth street will prompt a fold, but a check, showing weakness or uncertainty, will prompt a call on fifth street when your bet gets interpreted as a steal attempt. This strategy is also best used when you have position on your opponent. The sequence of his check and your check behind him, passing on your only chance to bet, signifies real weakness. If you act first and check, he may check and feel that he avoided a check-raise attempt! In this case he's much less likely to conclude you're weak.

3. **Bet just half the pot**. This usually isn't an optimal play, since if you have any kind of clear idea about your opponent's hand, you usually want to make a big bet or check. But as part of a balanced strategy, it's essential to make this play sometimes. Remember that preventing your opponents from reading your betting patterns is as important as making good bets.

The Fourth
Street Continuation Bet

Many times you will find yourself in the same position on fourth street that you had on the flop. You have a hand, and it might be the best one, but it might not. You took the lead in the betting either before or after the flop, or both. Your opponent might fold if you bet, but you can't know for sure. You can try a continuation bet on fourth street. Just lead out with a bet of about half the pot. As before, you're not risking much money and you're getting very favorable odds. If the bet wins the pot one time in three, you've at least broken even. And no matter how your opponent responds, you'll have learned something about the strength of his hand.

It's important to have alternate approaches to the same end, as a way of varying your play and making yourself hard to read. Let's suppose you led out before the flop, and after the flop you find yourself with a pair and a relatively weak kicker. Your normal move would be to lead out with a continuation bet to define your hand. Once in a while, however, you should just check. If the hand is checked behind you, lead out with a continuation bet on fourth street instead. This approach will still give you some information, while at the same time representing that the fourth street card helped your hand in some way.

Always be on the lookout for creative ways to gain information while remaining inscrutable.

Playing Drawing Hands

Here's a very common situation on fourth street. You have a real hand, and you think it's probably the best hand right now. You think your opponent is on a drawing hand. If he makes the hand he's drawing to, he'll beat you. What should you do? What should he do?

The first point to notice is a simple one: If you suspect that you're up against a drawing hand, you must bet on fourth street, not on fifth street. Checking on fourth street and betting on fifth street is a huge error. By checking, you've given your opponent a free card to beat you, which is one of the worst blunders you can make in poker. But almost as important is the fact that if you wait until fifth street to act, your opponent will know if he made his hand or not. If he didn't make it, he won't call your bet. So you can make money *only* on fourth street.

Suppose, however, that you are the one with the drawing hand. On fourth street, your opponent bets at you. What pot odds do you need to call?

Let's take the simplest case: You're drawing at a club flush, with two clubs in your hand and two on the board. So far you've seen 6 cards from the deck, with four clubs and two non-clubs. The remaining 46 cards contain the last nine clubs and 37 non-clubs. So the odds against filling your flush on fifth street are 37-to-9 against, or just over 4-to-1.

If you're pretty sure that hitting the flush will win for you (which is usually the case), then as long as you're getting 4-to-1 odds you can call the bet on fourth street. Actually, 4-to-1 are more odds than you really need, for two reasons.

1. After you hit the flush, you may win another large bet on fifth street. They are the implied odds that we discussed in Part Four. They can't be estimated precisely, because you don't

344

know if a bet will be called, or how big a bet might be called. But the possibility is clearly worth something.

2. You may not need to hit the flush to win. Simply pairing another card in your hand might be enough to win, or your opponent may be on a complete bluff (that he abandons on the river) and you may be winning already.

These are imponderables, but they both have some effect on reducing the odds you really need. Obviously 4-to-1 odds are sufficient. In practice, I tend to call these bets with a little over 3-to-1 odds. But that can change depending on my assessment of how much I can make my opponent call if I bet.

For the odds of hitting other common drawing hands, refer back to our table of outs in Part Four.

Playing
Against Drawing Hands

If I have the solid values, and my opponent is on a flush draw, then I have the opposite side of the problem from the previous discussion. My basic problem here is to figure out how much to bet. From Sklansky's Fundamental Theorem of Poker, I want to bet enough so that, if he's on a flush draw and he calls, he's making a mistake. As long as I force him to make a mistake, I've done my job, whether he then draws out on me or not.

By adjusting my bet to the pot size, I can control the odds that I'm offering. Here's a little chart that shows how my bet affects his odds

.

If I Bet	Odds I Give My Opponent
Twice the pot	3-to-2
The pot	2-to-1
Three-quarters of the pot	7-to-3
Two-thirds of the pot	5-to-2
Half the pot	3-to-1
One-third of the pot	4-to-1
One-fourth of the pot	5-to-1

I like to bet between two-thirds and three-quarters of the pot in these situations. From the previous section, we know that his call to the flush is reasonable if he's getting about 3-to-1 pot odds, so betting half the pot is a little light. On the other hand, I don't want to overbet the pot. Remember, if I bet too much and he folds, *he hasn't made a mistake*, and my real goal here is to induce an

346

error. In practice, bets of two-thirds to three-quarters of the pot frequently get called in these situations, which is what I want.

If I put him on a straight draw rather than a flush draw, my problem is only slightly different. Let's say a player has

in his hand and the board is

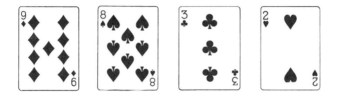

He can fill his straight with any seven or any queen, a total of eight cards. So of the 46 cards remaining in the deck that he hasn't seen, eight fill his straight and 38 miss. His odds are 38-to-8 against, or somewhat over 4.5-to-1. In this case I don't need to bet quite as much. A bet of just half the pot gives him 3-to-1 calling odds, less than he needs even taking his future implied odds into account.

When the Bad Card Hits

You're playing a solid hand, and you believe your opponent is on a draw. On fifth street, a card hits which either puts three flush cards on the board, or seems to help a hand drawing at a straight. Your opponent bets. What do you do?

There are no easy answers to questions like this, but here are a few guidelines.

1. If he's betting at two or more people, fold. It's just too likely that one of you is going to call him, and he knows that, so his bet represents real strength.

2. If he is a known bluffer, call. Sometimes he'll have the hand he's representing, and you'll feel stupid. But you'll pick off enough bluffs to make the call a profitable play.

3. If he's not a known bluffer, be sure to check the pot odds. With odds of 1-to-1 or 1.5-to-1, you should tend to fold. With odds better than 2-to-1, you should tend to call.

Don't Make a Bet
that Can't Make You Money

A common beginner's error is making a bet on the end that can't show a profit, because it will be called only by a hand that can beat you. You need to be alert to the difference between making a value bet on the end, which has a good chance of showing a profit, and making a bet which has no upside but a huge downside.

Study these two examples carefully.

Example No. 1:

1. You hold Q♠J♠ before the flop and make a raise from late position. The button calls you.

2. The flop comes Q♦7♣2♥, and you make another bet. Again you get called.

3. Fourth street is the 6♠. Again you bet, and again you get called.

4. Fifth street is the K♦. *Should you bet?*

   Answer: The answer is yes. There are no straight or flush possibilities, but your opponent has been calling throughout the hand. He has some sort of hand, but you don't know exactly what. The king almost certainly didn't help him. If he had two kings or king-queen in his hand you were beaten anyway, and if he had K-x his calls didn't make sense because he had too few outs. He's probably been calling with a worse queen or lower pair that you have beaten, so give him a chance to put in a little more money on the end.

Example No. 2.

1. You hold Q♦J♣ before the flop and make a raise from late position. As before, the button calls you.

2. The flop comes Q♠7♣6♥, and you make another bet. Again you get called.

3. Fourth street is the 8♥. Again you bet, and again you get called.

4. Fifth street is the 9♥. *Should you bet?*

Answer: Now the answer is clearly no (except in rare cases as a possible bluff). From the way the hand has developed, there's a very large possibility that your opponent has been drawing to a straight or a flush, or both, and may now have hit his hand. If he has been drawing and he actually missed his hand, he'll fold your bet. If he hit, he will raise you. It's very unlikely that he will call and then show down a hand you can beat, so you must check. If he bets, you'll have to fold unless the pot odds are just too tempting.

All-in on
Fourth and Fifth Street

Among good players, all-in moves are a rare occurrence until they start getting short-stacked. The reason is pretty simple. When you go all-in, you're putting your whole tournament life at risk. Good players don't like to do this. They're confident of their ability to keep outplaying their opponents and accumulating chips, so they see time as being on their side.

A certain segment of newcomers and weak players, however, like shoving all their chips in the pot. These players see no-limit hold 'em as a game of big bluffs and big moves, and they're thrilled to catch a hand and bet all their chips. On the first day of a major tournament, a significant portion of the field will be playing this way, and when a bunch of these folks butt heads at the same table, watch out! Not only will several players get knocked out, but whoever survives the melee will have a really big stack. These phantom chip leaders, however, usually don't hold up well as the tournament goes on. In the last 20 years, the opening-day chip leader at the World Series of Poker has never won the tournament![8]

Compare the merits of an all-in bet to the merits of betting just the size of the pot. If you have a strong hand and your opponent has a weak hand, either play will chase him away and claim the pot. If you have a strong hand, and your opponent has a weaker hand, but one which he still wants to play, a pot-sized bet is more likely to win some extra money than an all-in move. And if you have a good hand, but your opponent has a well-concealed

---

[8] For a more detailed discussion of this issue see *Tournament Poker for Advanced Players* by David Sklansky.

monster, a pot-sized bet will give you at least one more chance to reconsider before you lose all your chips.

Having said all that, there are a few circumstances where I'll make an all-in play. Usually three conditions have to apply:

1. I'm a little short on chips, but not yet desperate.

2. I have a good, but not great hand, which still rates to be the best at the table right now. A typical example might be

in my hand, and a board of

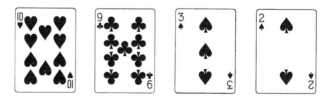

(with no obvious flush draw.)

3. I'm not looking for more action; I'm happy just to win the pot.

In these circumstances, an all-in move isn't a bad play.

The Problems

Betting on the end causes problems for all sorts of players. Beware of making bets which will be called only if you are beaten. For some examples of this tricky topic, see Problems 7-1 and 7-2.

Problem 7-3 shows how to decide between a fourth street raise and a fifth street raise.

Problem 7-4 shows the danger of slowplaying a big hand.

Problems 7-5 through 7-7 are examples of interpreting the betting you see around the table.

Hand 7-1

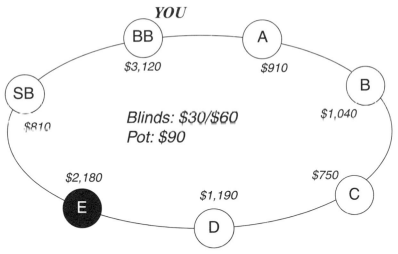

Situation: Early in a single-table satellite. Player D is a solid player who has made continuation bets.

Your hand: K♣J♥

Action to you: Players A, B, and C all fold. Player D raises to $120. Player E and the small blind fold. The pot is now $210.

Question: *Do you fold, call, or raise?*

    Answer: A call is reasonable here. Your hand is not that strong, and you're out of position, but the pot odds (3.5-to-1) are quite good, and you're certain that no one can enter the pot behind you.

Action: You call for $60. The pot is now $270.

Flop: J♣5♠2♠

Question: You're first to act. *What should you do?*

    Answer: You now have top pair on board with a good kicker. That's certainly a strong hand, and you want to get more money in the pot. What's the best way to do it?

    If you knew nothing about your opponent, you'd want to lead out here with a good solid bet. But here you have a little more information. You've observed that Player D likes to make continuation bets after he's taken the lead in the pot on the previous round. With that knowledge, you should play the percentages and lay back, hoping he'll take the lead himself and you can then toss in a raise. So just check.

Action: You check. He bets $120. The pot is now $390. *What should you do?*

    Answer: Your plan worked. Now you want to raise, and it should be a big raise, about the size of the pot. In case he's on a spade flush draw, you don't want to give him the right odds to call you.

Action: You raise, but only to $240, and he calls. The pot is now $750.

Too small. From his point of view, the pot was $630, and it cost him $120 to call. He was getting a little better than 5-to-1 odds, which means he was perfectly correct to call with a spade draw, even if he knew your hand.

Fourth Street: 4♦

Question: *What do you do now?*
   Answer: The four probably didn't help him, and you still have top pair with a good kicker. I would lead out again, for about $350. If you're beat, you're beat.

Action: Actually you check, he bets $110, and you call. The pot is now $970. You have $2,650 chips left, and he has $720.

Fifth Street: 7♠

Question: *Should you bet on the end?*
   Answer: The third spade came, so if he was drawing to his flush, he just hit it. However, he hasn't been betting as though he had a drawing hand. (He led out after the flop, and again on fourth street, when he could have checked and gotten free cards.) If you have a feeling that he's been bluffing, you should check to induce one last bluff. (If he's been bluffing, that will be his last chance to win the pot.) If you don't think he's been bluffing, you should check and make your final decision after he bets. In either case, a check is probably the correct action.
   This is a situation which allows top players to make a lot of money that lesser players can't make. All the top players have a good feel for these situations. That feel typically takes

many years of practice to develop, although a few whiz kids arrive on the scene with their instincts fully matured.[9]

Action: You check, and he bets $190. You call. He shows K♥9♠, and you take the pot with your pair of jacks.

Your Rope-a-Dope strategy worked perfectly, inducing a final bluff on the end. Your checks convinced him you had made a check-raise bluff, and he kept trying to steal the pot from you. But his stealing bets were so small that you could never seriously consider folding.

Hand 7-2

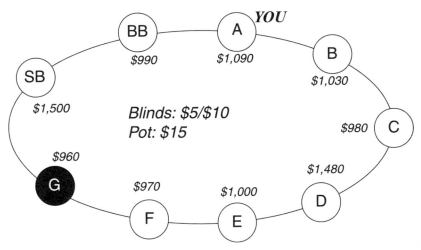

Situation: Fourth hand of a single-table satellite tournament. One wild player has already busted out. No hard information on the remaining players.

---

[9] Some of this can be logically deduced. See the "Heads Up On the End" chapter in *The Theory of Poker* by David Sklansky.

Your hand: J♣J♦

Action to you: You are first to act.

Question: *Do you call or raise, and, if you raise, how much?*
   Answer: Calling is almost out of the question. Your hand is probably the best hand at the table right now, but won't look good if several players stay and a couple of overcards appear on the board. Your job is to narrow the field, and go up against hopefully just one, but certainly no more than two players. At the same time, there's no need to overbet the pot. You should raise three to four times the big blind.

Action: You raise to $30. Players B, C, D, E, and F all fold. The button and the small blind call, and the big blind folds. The pot is now $100, and you're in the middle between two opponents.

Flop: 7♠6♥4♥

Action: The small blind now checks.

Question: *What's your play?*
   Answer: This is a great flop for you. It's unlikely anyone called your bet with eight-five or five-trey, and no one has shown strength, so you should still have the best hand. A pot-sized bet should be big enough to chase out the drawing hands, so I'd bet $100.

Action: You bet $100. The button folds, but the small blind calls. The pot is now $300. Fourth street comes the 5♦. The small blind checks.

Question: *Check or bet?*
   Answer: Most players would check here, because the 5♦ looks like a very scary card, since it puts an open-ended

straight on the board. But remember this: If your opponent has been playing for a straight, *he's supposed to have the five in his hand already.* He surely hasn't been calling hoping to hit an inside straight — that's too much of a long shot even for most beginners. There are only two hands that the five really helped. The first is a nine-eight, suited or offsuit, and it's a real longshot that's he's called two bets with that holding. The other, and more likely, is an eight-seven, where he might have made a loose call before the flop, then called after the flop with top pair and an inside straight draw.

Are there other hands that he might hold? Sure. Two high hearts would make sense. In that case his call before the flop is okay, and after the flop, he's drawing to a flush. Another holding would be something like ace-seven, with top pair and top kicker. Less likely, but still possible, are six-five or five-four.

So what's the play? You shouldn't like checking. You're passing an opportunity to win the pot right now (after all, he may be thinking that you just hit your straight), and, if he's in fact drawing for a flush, you're giving him a free card, which is a huge blunder. So you have to bet. But you don't want to overbet the pot. You want to be able to throw your hand away if a big reraise comes back at you. Betting just half the pot is a little light if he has a heart flush draw. He's then being offered 3-to-1 pot odds, which, combined with the implied odds if he hits the flush and can get some action on the end, make for a reasonable call. Betting two-thirds of the pot, which cuts down on his odds somewhat, looks better. Also remember that you don't want to bet so much that you're just walking into a trap if you're reraised. Two-thirds of the pot looks like just enough to get the job done.

Action: In fact, you just check. Pot still $300. The river comes 2♦. Small blind goes all-in for your last $960.

Question: *Call or fold?*

Answer: When your opponent makes a bet that's out of character with how the hand has developed, you want to take a deep breath and survey the situation carefully. This could be a major turning point in your tournament, so make sure you don't do anything hasty. Resist your first impulse to throw away your measly pair of jacks in the face of his obvious straight, and let's see what's happening.

When you have a monster hand, the idea is to use it to make some money, not to chase everybody out of the pot. A rank beginner bets all-in when he hits his straight because he's excited and doesn't know any better. "I've got a big hand! I can bet all my chips! Yee-haw!" Then he's crestfallen when everybody folds. A normal player with some sophistication would think "I've got the nuts, I need to make something more on this hand. I'll bet $150, maybe the 3-to-1 odds will induce a call. Better than nothing."

But if this guy is just a beginner, why did he check on fourth street? After all, the deuce didn't make his straight (unless he had ace-trey, in which case his first two calls don't make much sense) If he has a straight, he had it on fourth street, where he checked. Was he planning to check-raise? That's not the mark of an excitable beginner who can't control himself. I'm thinking this betting pattern doesn't add up. Looks to me like there's a good chance this bet is just a pot-stealing bluff. You should seriously consider calling.

One last thought. A world-class player is quite capable of shoving all his chips in the pot with a straight in a situation like this, hoping that his opponent will go through the same reasoning I just did and call. When you're up against someone really good, watch out, and take nothing for granted!

Resolution: You call, and the small blind shows down A♥7♥. Your jacks win a $2,220 pot.

Let's make a couple of notes about our opponent's play.

His bet on the end was a big mistake — a standard example of a no-win bet on the end. He had only top pair, and almost no one would call this bet in the face of the straight possibilities on the board unless they could at least beat top pair. But since he had top pair, there was no need to throw in all his chips to force you out. Top pair might be good enough to beat whatever you had, so he should have been happy to show the hand down.

His hand was also good enough to make a play on the flop. At that point he had top pair (sevens) plus an ace plus four cards to a flush. He could reasonably think he had 14 outs twice (9 hearts, 3 aces, 2 sevens), which meant he was a slight favorite, plus a bet might win the pot right there. Checking was a mistake.

Hand 7-3

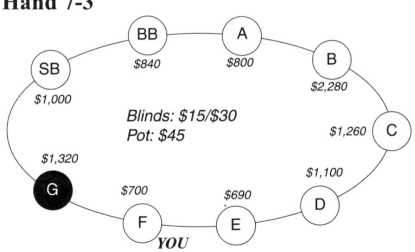

Situation: Early in a one-table satellite. The table is generally tight.

Your hand: A♠Q♣

Action to you: Player A raises to $60. Players B, C, D, and E all fold. Pot now $105.

Question: *Do you call or raise?*
    Answer: Call. At a tight table with a full complement of players, you need to assume that bets mean pretty much what they're supposed to mean. The guy in first position put in a raise under the gun, so he's supposed to have a good hand — a pair, or maybe ace-king or ace-queen. According to the Gap Concept, you need a hand at least as good as that to play. You've got it, but just barely, so you should play, but you shouldn't get that excited about your hand yet. It's a nice hand, but not a great one. In limit poker, you would frequently fold ace-queen in this position. At no-limit, position is far more important than at limit, since it carries the possibility of winning someone's entire stack, rather than just a couple of bets. Your good position lets you call here.

Action: You call. The button and the small blind fold, and the big blind calls $30. The pot is now $195.

Flop: T♠T♥9♣

Action: The big blind checks, and Player A bets $100. *What's your play?*
    Answer: Fold. Here's an example of the sandwich effect in action. You've missed the flop, but his bet of half the pot could be a standard continuation bet. If you were the only two players in the pot, a call could be justified. But now there's still another player to act behind you, and that's too much.
    Don't be seduced by the fact that the big blind only checked. Sure, he might be weak, but players who flop a set usually check as well. You can't assume a player is out of the pot until he's really out of it.

Action: You actually call, and the big blind folds. The pot is now $395.

Fourth Street: J♣

Action: Player A checks. You have an open-ended straight draw, and think you might be able to steal the pot. *Should you try to steal, and if you say "yes," should you bet $200 or go all-in for $540?*

> **Answer:** You shouldn't try to steal here, but it's not a hopeless play. A better approach would be just to take a free card, and see if you can make a hand. So far you've committed only $160, and if you can get out of the hand without investing any more, you still have a shot (albeit not a great one) at the tournament. A steal attempt could end up in your being knocked out right here.
>
> If you really wanted to steal, you should probably put in $200 instead of $540. If your opponent has nothing, either bet should chase him away. If he raises you all-in after you bet $200, you can decide then what you want to do. Going all-in simply robs you of some flexibility with no real upside.

Action: You in fact go all-in, and Player A calls. He turns over J♦J♠, and you're dead to his full house. His check on fourth street was just a trap.

There's one more technical point to note about this hand. If you had bet $200, your opponent would have had a choice with his lock hand — put you all-in right away, or call and hope to get the last $340 out of you on fifth street.

The latter play looks more clever and sophisticated, but it's actually just an elementary blunder. With the board showing jack-ten-nine and two clubs, he should assume that you have a draw at something, either a straight or a flush. If he goes all-in now, the draw possibility will force you to call. If he waits until fifth street, and you miss your draw (likely), you'll fold his bet. So with a lock hand and a draw showing, bet on fourth street to get all the chips.

Hand 7-4

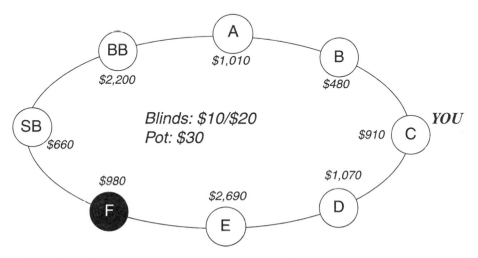

Situation: Early in an online tournament. The big blind is a wild and aggressive player who likes to get in a pot and raise with anything. Player F seems solid and tight.

Your hand: T♥T♣

Action to you: Players A and B fold.

Question: *Do you call or raise?*

> **Answer:** You can't just call, because your hand is likely to be the best right now, but may well not be best if several players get in the pot, and the flop comes with a card or two higher than your tens. So you have to raise to cut down on the callers.
>
> I like to have a range of possible raises for a hand like this, so my opponents can't read the meaning of my bets easily. For this kind of situation, my range is three to five

times the big blind. Within that range, I might vary my bets randomly, or I might let the situation govern my choice.

Here you see that the player in the big blind is a wild and crazy guy who likes to play a lot of pots and raise aggressively. You shouldn't be afraid of driving him out with a good-sized bet, and you want as much of his money in the pot as you can get, so go to the high end of the range and raise to $100 here.

Action: You actually raise to $60. Players D and E fold, but the button (Player F) calls. The small blind folds and the big blind calls for another $40. The pot is now $190.

Flop: 8♣7♠6♣

Action: The big blind checks. *What do you do?*

   Answer: That's a good but not great flop for you — three cards all lower than your pair, but with possible straight and flush draws out there. You should now bet something like three-fourths of the pot. If you get raised, be prepared to go all the way. Since you have two tens, it's unlikely you're facing someone with the high end of the straight, and it's very unlikely that anyone called before the flop with a five-four.

Action: You bet $160. Player F calls, and the big blind folds. The pot is now $510.

Fourth Street: T♦

Question: *What do you do?*

   Answer: You should bet a goodly amount here. If Player F has a nine, you're beaten, but he is unlikely to have one. He is a solid, tight player who probably would not call a raise with ace-nine or king-nine. In these small satellites and online tournaments, you have very little time to pile up chips, worry much about the freak holdings that contain a nine. If you get raised, plan on calling.

Action: You actually bet $200, and Player F calls. The pot is now $910.

Fifth Street: 4♦

Question: *What do you do?*

    Answer: Now a straight draw on the other end! Yes, it's possible he's been calling all along and now you're dead. But you only have $490 left, and if you lose the tournament with your set of tens, so be it. This could be the best hand you see for quite awhile, and you should be prepared to go all the way with it. It's unlikely he's holding a four or a nine from the way the hand developed.

Action: You go all-in for $490, and he calls, showing down a pair of aces. You win the pot.

    Mystery revealed — he was slowplaying aces all the way, and lost the hand on fourth street. It was a dangerous play, but worth doing very occasionally to keep your opponents guessing.

Hand 7-5

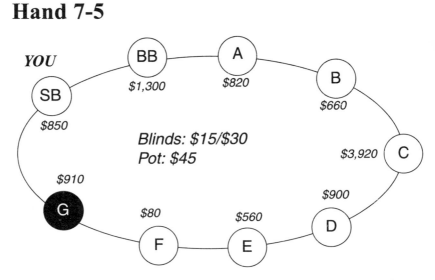

Situation: Early in a one-table satellite tournament. Player C is a wild man who plays most pots and likes to raise aggressively. Player G and the big blind seem solid.

Your hand: J♠T♠

Action to you: Players A and B fold. Player C calls. Players D, E, and F fold. Player G calls. Pot is now $105.

Question: *What do you do?*

    Answer: Since you're in the small blind, it costs you only $15 to call this bet. Despite your bad position on subsequent rounds, the 7-to-1 pot odds make this a trivially easy call. Remember that your goal with suited connectors is to see a cheap flop. Here the flop is as cheap as it gets.

    One concern you should have is the presence of a really active player with a huge pile of chips. If he were still to act behind you, this is the sort of hand you might let go rather than play. But here he's already called, so you're free to act.

Action: You call for $15 and the big blind checks. The pot is now $120.

Flop: J♣3♠2♠

Question: You're first to act. *What do you do?*

Answer: Short of flopping a straight or a flush, this is about as good as the flop can get for you. You've flopped top pair and a four-flush, and the two low cards help your flush while almost certainly missing the other players.

The question now is not whether to bet, but how much. You need to bet enough to make some money, but not so much as to drive people out. This is a hand where you don't mind callers, because of the flush possibility. I'd recommend a bet of about three-fourths of the pot, $80 to $90. Your only fears here are that you're up against a hand like queen-jack, or a very low pair that flopped trips. But right now those are long shots.

Checking (with the idea of check-raising) is not a terrible play. Remember, however, that you need to bet your good hands frequently as part of a balanced strategy. You will be making bluffs and continuation bets, and these bets can't work unless balanced with legitimate bets.

Action: You actually bet the pot, $130. The big blind calls, but the other two players fold. The pot is now $380.

Fourth Street: K♥

Question: *What now?*

Answer: The king didn't help you, but it may not have hurt you. Here's the problem, however, with bad position. You still have to lead here, and you're stepping into darkness. If you check, you'll still have to call a bet, and betting first gives you a chance to win the pot. I'd recommend a fourth-street continuation bet here, betting a little more than half the pot, something in the range of $150 to $220. With just a pair of jacks, you're not strong enough for a check-raise, so just make a straight value bet and see what happens.

Action: You actually bet $50, and the big blind calls. The pot is now $480.

Not a good choice of bet size. Remember that poker is first and foremost a game of information. Sometimes a larger bet is actually a defensive move, a way of protecting your whole stack, by sacrificing a few extra chips to get more information about the hand.

Fifth Street: 5♣

Question: *What's your play now?*
    Answer: All you have now is second pair, and you've represented that from the beginning. So if you make a large bet, he'll call only if he can at least beat the second pair. On the other hand, if you make a small probing bet, you might head him off from making a bigger bet which you will be compelled to call. So your choices are checking or making a smallish bet. I like checking, but wouldn't argue with someone who wanted to lead out with a little bet.

Action: You check, and he bets $200. *Do you call or fold?*
    Answer: You must call. The pot now has $680, and it costs you $200 to call, so you're getting 3.5-to-1 on your money. If you were sure you were beaten, you could fold. But here you can't be sure, since he hasn't shown any strength until this last bet.

Action: You call, and he shows A♠4♠, taking the pot with his low straight.

So he was drawing to the nut flush, an inside straight, and an ace throughout. After the flop, he had 15 outs (9 spades, 3 fives — don't count the fives twice — and three aces), and he still had 15 outs on the last card. Both his calls were proper, as was his $200 bet on the end. It was just the right amount to get you to put some more money in because of the pot odds, and not so much as to chase you away. That's good poker.

Be glad you didn't hit your flush, or you would have lost all your money!

Hand 7-6

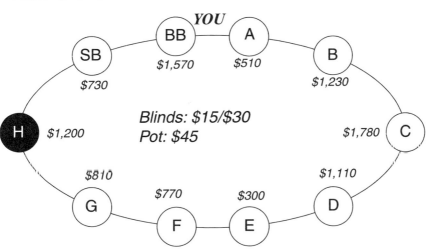

Situation: Early in a single-table online tournament.

Your hand: 4♠3♠

Action to you: Player A calls. Player B folds. Player C calls. Players D, E, and F all fold. Player G calls. Player H folds. The small blind folds. The pot is now $135.

Question: *Do you check or raise?*

Answer: This is a hand you would normally throw away, but you're delighted to see a free flop. Perhaps you'll get very lucky and flop a straight or a flush. You simply check.

Action: You check. Pot remains $135.

Flop: A♣2♣5♣

Question: You're first to act. *What do you do?*
    Answer: You've flopped a straight, but there are three flush cards on board. Some players are afraid to act in this situation, but you mustn't be. Remember, you've flopped a very strong hand. It's possible that you're already beaten. But it's much more likely that there are drawing hands out there that will beat you if you let them. If you don't bet, they'll bet at you and you'll have no idea where they stand.
    If someone has four clubs at this point, they're a 4-to-1 underdog to make their flush on the turn. You need to make a big bet now to make sure they don't get those odds.

Action: You are afraid to bet, and just check. Players A and C check also. Now Player G bets $170. *What do you do?*
    Answer: You can call, of course, because you have a straight. Unfortunately, because you didn't lead out, you won't really know anything about Player G's hand. He might have a made flush. He might have a high club, and be trying to buy the pot now, with a fallback draw if anyone calls. He might have an ace. He might be stealing the pot when no one else bet. Now you have to learn something from the rest of the hand.
    A better play is to raise $350. If Player C, the big stack, goes all-in, you can throw your hand away. Otherwise, you'll do at least as well as by calling. If someone has two clubs, you will lose either way. If someone has one club, you will

win instead of losing. And if no one has any clubs, you will make more money.

Action: You call. Players A and C fold. The pot is now $475.

Fourth Street: Q♥

Question: *What do you do?*
Answer: You have to lead out. If he's still drawing to his flush, he's going to check behind you (if you check) and get a free draw. That's a disaster for you. If he hasn't made his flush yet, he's a 4-to-1 underdog to get it on the last card, so bet enough to make a call by him incorrect. $200 is plenty.

Action: You don't bet, but check instead. He bets $200. *What do you do?*
Answer: Raise him all-in. He's not acting like a guy who had the nuts on the flop. Instead of sucking money into the pot, he's trying to chase people out with big bets. Think about it. Is this how you would play a lock hand? Also remember that a straight is a very strong hand. You're still probably best here, so make him pay.

Action: You fold. He scoops up the pot without showing his hand.

You made three big blunders. You didn't lead out with a very strong hand, so you didn't know where you stood when he bet. Then you repeated that mistake. Then you folded what was probably the winning hand. All of this might well have been avoided with a bet on the flop.

Remember that leading out with a bet buys you information and cuts down on your volatility by forcing your opponents to reveal their strength. Check-raising, on the other hand, buys you more information at a higher price and increases your volatility.

Hand 7-7

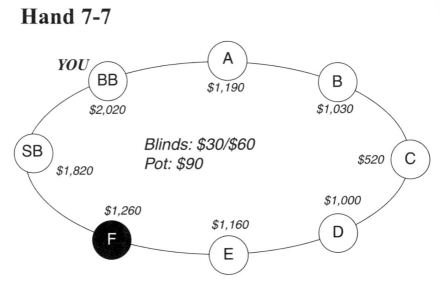

Situation: Middle of an online tournament

Your hand: Q♠T♣

Action to you: Players A and B fold. Player C calls for $60. Player D folds. Player E calls. Player F calls. The small blind calls for an additional $30. The pot is now $300.

Question: *Do you check or raise?*
   Answer: You're quite happy to check. You're in bad position, and you don't have that much of a hand. So seeing a free flop is great.

Action: You check.

Flop: T♠9♣2♦

Action: The small blind bets $130. The pot is $430. *What do you do?*

Answer: You've caught top pair, with a decent kicker. If the small blind had checked, you should have led out for about two-thirds of the pot, say about $200.

The small blind's bet puts you in a much tougher position. You're caught in a sandwich, and there's no good way out. You don't want to let the players behind you in so cheaply, since they're easily getting the odds to call with a drawing hand. But you don't really want to raise a lot here — you don't know where you stand, and there are a lot of active players. While it's not a happy play, here the best risk-reward ratio might just be a passive call.

Action: You call for $130. Player C calls. Player E folds. Player F calls. The pot is now $820.

Fourth Street: T♦

Action: The small blind checks. *What do you do?*

Answer: You have trip tens. The board now shows two spades and two diamonds, so there are plenty of draws available. You probably have the best hand now, but deciding how much to bet is a problem. You've got two competing goals: betting a small enough amount to get people to call, but a large enough amount to get the drawers to fold.

Right now the pot is big enough so that getting lots of new money in is not as high a priority as winning the money that's already out there. You should bet about three-fourths of the pot, about $600. Anyone drawing to a flush won't be getting the right odds to call. (They'll need 4-to-1, and they'll be getting only a little over 2-to-1.) If anyone else wants to call that bet, well that's fine.

Note that there's no need to go all-in, because such a bet is more likely to chase away the weaker hands that you want to stick around.

Action: You actually bet only $320. Player C folds. Player F calls. The small blind calls. The pot is now $1,780.

Fifth Street: A♠

Action: The small blind goes all-in for $1,310. *What do you do?*
 Answer: Cry because you bet too little last turn. Notice what happened. The pot was $820, you bet $320, then Player F put in $320, making the pot $1,460. The small blind now had to put in $320 for a shot at a pot of $1,460, meaning that he had better than the 4-to-1 odds he needed if he was drawing at a flush. And then the flush card hit.

 You have to fold here. He's been representing a flush draw all along, and the third spade came, and now his bet says he has it. More important, he's going all-in against two players, not just one, so it's unlikely he's running a bluff. If I had to guess, he's probably been playing something like K♠J♠, with the flush draw and two overcards to the board. It's tough to fold trips, but be glad you've at least kept some chips.

Resolution: You fold, and Player F folds.

Conclusion

We've covered a lot of ground in *Volume I*. Even if you've never played in a major event, you should now have a good idea of the kinds of things that good no-limit hold 'em players are thinking about as they work their way through a tournament.

There are three main ideas that you should take away from this book:

1. **No-limit hold 'em is a very complex game.** It's not all about running outrageous bluffs or interpreting your opponent's facial ticks (although both will happen from time to time). Instead it's a game of memory, position, calculation, alertness, and patience, where you need to constantly reorient yourself with respect to your position at the table, the changing stack and blind sizes, the demonstrated habits of your opponents, and the actual strength of your cards.

2. **Pot odds are paramount.** Like all gamblers and investors, a no-limit hold 'em player is constantly trying to make good bets at favorable odds. Without knowing the pot odds, you can't even make an educated guess as to the wisdom of shoving your chips into this particular pot. Calculating pot odds must be automatic and routine.

3. **There are different styles of playing no-limit hold 'em, but no "correct" style.** Any style can win in the hands of a skilled practitioner. You should adopt a style that suits your temperament and energy level. The advice in this book, especially hand selection before the flop, mostly reflects a conservative style of play, partly because that's how I play and partly because that's the easiest style to learn if you're a

newcomer. But remember that it's not the only way to play poker.

With the basics of no-limit hold 'em strategy now covered, I'll move on in *Volume II* to more advanced topics. Here's a quick preview.

Making moves. In *Volume I* I focused mostly on what are called value bets, where you bet either because you believe you have the best hand and want to get more money in the pot, or because you might have the best hand and think the pot odds justify playing. But there's another whole category of plays called moves, where you hope to win the pot (or a much bigger pot) by fundamentally misrepresenting the value of your hand. In this section we'll look at the types of moves available and the preconditions for making certain moves successful.

Inflection points. When your stack is large relative to the blinds and antes, you're free to play more or less as you wish. As the blinds and antes increase relative to your stack, your approach must change. I call the places where your strategy changes inflection points. An understanding of these points, and how to adjust your play accordingly, is the most important skill in tournament no-limit hold 'em poker.

Playing at short tables. As the number of players at your table shrinks, your strategy changes as well. I'll explain how to play at short tables (5-6 players), very short tables (3-4 players), and heads-up.

If you feel you learned a lot in *Volume I,* you're going to love *Volume 2.* Until then, good luck!

Index

NOTES

NOTES

NOTES

NOTES

NOTES